cs

Fear, Power, and Politics

The Recipe for War in Iraq after 9/11

Mary Cardaras

LEXINGTON BOOKS
Lanham • Boulder • New York • Toronto • Plymouth, UK

Published by Lexington Books
A wholly owned subsidiary of The Rowman & Littlefield Publishing Group, Inc.
4501 Forbes Boulevard, Suite 200, Lanham, Maryland 20706
www.rowman.com

10 Thornbury Road, Plymouth PL6 7PP, United Kingdom

British Library Cataloguing in Publication Information Available

Library of Congress Cataloging-in-Publication Data Available

ISBN: 978-0-7391-7994-9 (cloth : alk. paper)
ISBN: 978-0-7391-7995-6 (electronic)
ISBN: 978-1-4985-1539-9 (pbk : alk. paper)

∞™ The paper used in this publication meets the minimum requirements of American
National Standard for Information Sciences Permanence of Paper for Printed Library
Materials, ANSI/NISO Z39.48-1992.

Printed in the United States of America

For Francesca, Harrison, Nicholas
. . . and Sedona.

Iraq is going to go down in history as the greatest disaster in American foreign policy. Now, that's quite a statement, because it means I think it is worst than Vietnam. Not in the number of Americans who died, or Vietnamese versus Iraqis, but in terms of those unintended consequences.

—Madeleine Albright, Former United States Secretary of State, March 8, 2007

Contents

Prologue

We remember the terrorist attacks of September 11, 2001, the way some remember the attack on Pearl Harbor, December 7, 1941, the way others remember the assassination of President John F. Kennedy on November 22, 1963. We remember where we were and what we were doing. We remember how we heard the news and what we did after we heard the news. September 11, 2001, was another one of those days in history that will live in infamy.

I was a journalist for much of my professional life. My interest as a journalist was politics and policy, both international and domestic. When the attacks happened, I was teaching journalism and studying politics and policy in a PhD program. I do remember where I was and what I was doing when the country was attacked. I remember what I did after I heard the news. Like all of us, I was interested in what the country would do in retaliation because we all understood, to a certain degree, that the attacks on New York City and on Washington, DC, could not possibly go unanswered.

Retaliation in Afghanistan, where camps for aspiring terrorists were thriving and where Osama bin Laden was doing the training, seemed both right and just. The nation now looked to a president, who had come to office under a dark cloud of suspicion and doubt about his legitimacy as the rightful commander in chief. Could he, would he now rise to the emergency that was thrust upon the country? As is almost always the case, it is the times that make the president.

After 9/11, we were collectively swept into a patriotic stupor. We were fearful of the immediate future as we were advised to prepare for the possibility of more attacks and a protracted war on terrorism, wherever that might lead. We were unable or unwilling to do any measured or careful thinking about what was being proposed very soon after our military invaded Afghanistan. Something was not right.

Something was not right when the president began to introduce us to Iraq and Saddam Hussein in the same breath as the attacks of 9/11 and Osama bin Laden. This transformation began to occur just a few short months after our military began neutralizing the influence of the Taliban in Afghanistan and hunting for bin Laden. In a state of the union address the following January 2002, President George W. Bush introduced us to the concept of the Axis of Evil, which included Iraq and its president, Saddam Hussein. But this was only the beginning.

The weeks and months pressed on. Hussein came into clearer focus. Bin Laden and al Qaeda faded from prominence. The drumbeat against Iraq and Hussein intensified as the United States began to circle the wagons, itching for a fight, but now with Iraq. Weapons of mass destruction became a mantra. A war with Iraq became imminent. Something was not right.

Elisabetta Burba, friend, colleague, and accomplished Italian journalist, also felt in her gut that something was not right. This was affirmed when a source gave her some documents, which showed Saddam had purchased uranium from Niger. This uranium could be used in the production of nuclear weapons, providing more evidence that Iraq was armed and dangerous. She traveled to Niger to trace the documents, only to find that they were fraudulent. She reported back to her editor and reported her findings also to the U.S. Embassy in Rome. That was that.

But in January 2003, in yet another televised State of the Union address, President Bush cited those exact fraudulent documents as the final straw and undisputed evidence that Saddam was a threat to the world. To say the least, Elisabetta Burba was beside herself as she read the news in her morning paper and choked on a strong cup of Italian coffee. Something definitely was not right.

Elisabetta shared her story with me. We discussed her research and her findings about the Niger story. By this time, Iraq was a foregone conclusion. Hussein was on the run and would later be captured. People were dying. There were no weapons of mass destruction. Not anywhere to be found. Not to this day. And who forged those documents is another story entirely.

As a citizen of the United States, as a journalist and as a political scientist, I was both incredulous and mystified. How did we as a country go so wrong? How could we have invaded a country that had absolutely nothing to do with the attacks of 9/11? How did we unwittingly force a change of power in one country and dangerously shift the balance of power in an entire, already volatile region of the world? How are we responsible for the deaths of thousands of American soldiers and tens of thousands of innocent Iraqis?

All this was not right. And it brought me to this book, which explains how this misguided tragedy was orchestrated. In turns out that the mess of Iraq was by design, thanks to the George W. Bush administration. And there were accomplices in Congress and in the news media. Hindsight is 20/20, to be sure, and this is a cautionary tale. I can only hope this book offers more perspective. Finally this: We must be diligent about drawing wisdom from decisions past and learn to apply them to the future. And also, we must find the courage and fortitude to hold to account those who make decisions that have enduring and sometimes devastating consequences at home, around the world, in politics, in policy, in reputation . . . and in human life.

Introduction

How did the Iraq war happen? While in the midst of an aggressive assault on Taliban targets in Afghanistan directly in response to the 9/11 attacks, the Bush administration spearheaded another military offensive. This one was on Iraq. The following offers a new perspective on the run-up to the war and will explain how the confluence of several key factors led the United States to attack the sovereign nation of Iraq on March 19, 2003.

Those factors include the following:

1. Fear. There was a prevailing climate of fear and uncertainty for most Americans after the terrorist attacks on September 11, 2001. A special emphasis on the media must be highlighted because it reflected those sentiments and the overall mood of the country in their news coverage.
2. The power of the executive branch. Out of necessity, the president and his administration built consent for a new foreign policy going forward after 9/11. However, they also promoted the war based on information they understood to be questionable and, in some cases, patently false.
3. Political factors, which influenced members of Congress. The reaction and decisions of Congress in response to the administration's plans after the invasion of Afghanistan appeared more acquiescent than serving its role to balance and check the power of the executive branch. Congress gave its consent for an impending war with Iraq, but why? The political mood of the country and the electability of individual members of Congress may have affected behavior.
4. Politics certainly influenced how the news media covered the unfolding story of the Iraq war. The result was that accurate, honest news coverage was lacking. Rather than serve as another check on power, the news media was frightened away from the story, covered it with little objectivity and covered it tethered to the government as primary source.

From the terrorist attacks on America in 2001 to the invasion of Iraq in 2003, fear, power and politics converged. The president of the United States, the United States Congress, and the American news media all were responsible in varying degree for taking the nation to war.

Public policy scholar John Kingdon has written about the confluence of policy "streams" born of political problems, policies, and politics. When those streams converge, Kingdon argued, they can create a window of opportunity or a "policy window" that, if capitalized on, affect policy change.[1] He contended that those policy windows emerge suddenly and occur only when political constellations are in near perfect alignment. The 9/11 attacks provided the George W. Bush administration with a political window of opportunity through which was catapulted a sea change in foreign policy. Strategically, this ultimately launched the Iraq war.

The following were examined and from which logical conclusions were drawn: primary source interviews, transcripts of interviews, official testimony of administration officials, official transcripts from press conferences and other public communication by the president and members of his administration, Congressional documents and transcripts, newspaper articles, magazine stories, television and radio transcripts, public opinion polls, scholarly and contemporary books written on the subject, and other various publications.

The goal here is not necessarily to make judgments, although they are unavoidable and will emerge naturally as the course of events unfold. Also, judgments have been plentiful, made by scholars, political pundits, politicians, legislators, the press and the people. The focus here is rather to demonstrate *how* the great linchpins of our democracy—two branches of government and the news media—behaved during this fixed period of time at a defining moment in our country's history—that is, from the attacks on September 11, 2001, to the start of the war in Iraq on March 19, 2003.

The progression of that official storyline has been well documented, meaning how the United States government and the Bush administration decided to attack Iraq and target its president, Saddam Hussein. The decision to go to war was based on information the Bush administration claimed was both credible and compelling, gathered by U.S. intelligence, other agencies around the world, and our allies.

The administration touted the war in Iraq as a necessity and an expansion of the so-called "war on terror," which began directly in response to 9/11, on October 7, 2001, when the United States launched an offensive against Taliban targets in Afghanistan. The mission was called "Operation Enduring Freedom." Afghanistan is the country where Osama bin Laden was presumed to be operating camps to train the next generation of terrorists. By then, bin Laden was known to the world as the self-proclaimed mastermind behind the 9/11 attacks.

Iraq was included with Iran and North Korea as global menaces, the "axis of evil," an expression President George W. Bush coined in an emotional State of the Union address. It was the president's first State of the Union address after 9/11, on January 29, 2002. He connected that triad of nations—Iraq, Iran, and North Korea—under one political umbrella. They were our enemies, he asserted, and were dangerous threats to the world because each was a state sponsor of terror.[2]

The president and his administration publicly began to build a case for war against Iraq within a year after 9/11, without having apprehended the man directly responsible for the attacks and who detested Saddam. In fact, there is evidence that a plan to invade Iraq was a war in waiting. It was waiting for the perfect set of circumstances, real or imagined, which would justify such action.

According to the White House, the justification for the invasion of Iraq, called "Operation Iraqi Freedom," was based on three, serious claims. They were the following:

1. Iraq's Saddam Hussein and Osama bin Laden had a political relationship, and Saddam had a hand in the 9/11 attacks.
2. Iraqi President Saddam Hussein was producing and stockpiling weapons of mass destruction (WMD) with which to attack the United States and/or our interests abroad.
3. Hussein was purchasing or had purchased uranium from the African nation of Niger from which a nuclear bomb could be created.

It had been perfectly clear to rational political actors around the world that Hussein for years had been a global menace and a brutal dictator. There is evidence that he mercilessly bullied his own people and jailed or killed those in opposition to his authoritarian regime. He engaged in a bloody, brutal war with Iran, which lasted eight years, and he invaded a tiny neighboring country (Kuwait) without provocation, sparking another conflict in which the United States got involved. Nevertheless, the following facts are now indisputable.

Iraq was in no way responsible for the events of 9/11. There was no clear evidence that Iraqi President Saddam Hussein was creating and stockpiling weapons of mass destruction (WMD). Saddam Hussein had no positive or supportive relationship with Osama bin Laden and al Qaeda. In fact, Peter Eisner and Knut Royce wrote that "analysts believed any such ties to be highly improbable, given that bin Laden considered Hussein to be an apostate—a Muslim worthy of death—and the secular Hussein, in turn, was a staunch opponent of Islamic fundamentalism."[3] Saddam had not purchased uranium from the African nation of Niger, and, in fact, the document to justify such a claim was a fake.

Dozens of books have been written on the subject of the Iraq war. Hundreds of articles have been published. Thousands of minutes of airtime on radio and television have contributed to the discourse. Websites have attracted millions of people to report, discuss, challenge, and protest in cyberspace what ultimately may be regarded by many historians and politicians as among the worst foreign policy decisions in American history: the time between the attacks on America, September 11, 2001, and the launch of the Iraq war, March 19, 2003.

To date, for training purposes, a very small U.S. military presence in Iraq remains, despite the official withdrawal of troops in December 2011. The country is a fragile democracy. At times, at least on appearance, the country has tumbled in and out of a festering, particularly brutal civil war between religious factions. Divisions and differences based on ethnic and political allegiances have persisted in varying degree. A political solution to the problems and an Iraqi government that can stand on its own are months, if not years, away. President Bush compared our military presence in Iraq to our sustained military presence in South Korea. Translation: A lengthy military commitment of some form in Iraq is probable, no matter who occupies the White House.

It is fair to say at this point, and it will be noted in greater detail later, that when he was a candidate for president, George W. Bush believed that Hussein should be toppled. And after George W. Bush was elected, his administration contemplated military action in Iraq long before it became a reality. The Bush White House waited for a compelling reason to bring the possibility of an attack to the American consciousness.

On the CBS News magazine *60 Minutes*, Paul O'Neil, President Bush's first Secretary of the Treasury, said that as early as the first national security meeting, ten days after the inauguration of the president in January 2001 and eight months before 9/11, Iraq and Saddam Hussein topped the agenda. O'Neil said it was all about finding a way to take Saddam out. "From the beginning there was a conviction that Saddam Hussein was a bad person and that he needed to go. Saddam was 'topic A.'"[4]

The president's legacy and the effectiveness of his administration will be reflected in the decisions it made about Iraq. There is no doubt much will be written by historians in the years to come. In the case of this presidency and every one that will follow, the people are dependent on the news media for the lion's share of information they receive, especially in the sphere of foreign policy. Bernard Cohen explained that American reporters who cover foreign affairs *participate* in the formation of policy itself because they are the conduit between the policy and the American people, telling them not *what* to think, but what to think *about*.[5]

Inevitably, the people must rely on the information they receive through the news media about those who govern and how they govern. The onus is on our leaders to explain and, in some cases, justify matters in foreign policy. Those foreign policy decisions ultimately should result in what is in the best interests of the United States, or at least we hope that they would. That is what people expect. That is what they trust will happen. The way the people learn about the decisions of our leaders in foreign policy and the way they understand it in all its complexity is directly from our leaders and elected officials as filtered through the news media. There is no other way, and it has proven to be among the most transparent political and social systems in the world.

The allegory of the sword of Damocles applies to a real threat of terrorism and its use politically. It has been a key tool in motivating the people to support a new American foreign policy, whether or not intentional. With his closest and most influential advisors, President Bush advocated a new path forward known as the Bush Doctrine, whose essence is military, as described by Arthur M. Schlesinger.

Schlesinger writes that the Bush Doctrine subscribes to the notion of striking "a potential enemy unilaterally if necessary; before he has a chance to strike us. War, traditionally a matter of last resort, becomes a matter of presidential choice. This is a revolutionary change. Mr. Bush replaced a policy aimed at peace through prevention of war by a policy aimed at peace through preventive war."[6]

The notion of pre-emption was not new to America, but President Bush took the practice to a heightened level. According to a report by Army Lieutenant Colonel Steven D. Westphal about counterterrorism and a policy of "preemptive [military] action," noted were President Woodrow Wilson's occupation of Haiti in 1915, President Lyndon Johnson's dispatch of the Marines to the Dominican Republic in 1965, and President Ronald Reagan's invasion of Grenada in 1983. "Pre-emption has thus been used in many instances." But, he continued, "No president has explicitly raised, emphasized and moved the practice into a stated and used government policy."[7]

President Bush insisted this was justified. His decisions were made during a prevailing social climate of fear, which was fed, whether intentionally or not, by its monstrous genesis, the terrorist attacks of 9/11. This singular event and the decisions to follow would define his presidency and give the man himself an opportunity to prove he was up to the task of commander in chief.

George W. Bush came to office in January 2001, nine months before the attacks, after a bruising presidential campaign against Vice President Al Gore in which Gore had won a popular plurality of the vote. The U.S. Supreme Court awarded Bush the contested Florida votes, guaranteeing his Electoral College majority.[8]

There was a lingering suspicion over how this president came to office and created a climate of national political animosity. A succession of controversial foreign policy decisions emerged during a time of great vulnerability for the American public and its government, whose responsibility, in part, is to keep them safe. In illuminating a new perspective about the run-up to the Iraq war, a number of basic questions must be addressed. They are the following:

How did prevailing feelings of fear and vulnerability in the American people affect the political process? Did the president and his administration exploit that fear to promote a war they knew was not justified? Was it a timid Congress that trusted its president and offered only tepid requests for more verification of the claims made? Was it an insecure news media that failed to ask enough questions or the right questions? Were those news organizations not persistent because they were intimidated by an administration that perhaps subtly threatened their access to the news and newsmakers on which they rely for their very survival?

In essence, did we lose control of our government after 9/11, as political scientist E. E. Schattschneider might have asked? Did we surrender our voice and will in the face of an ambitious administration—perhaps an incompetent administration? Was the administration in over its head as it approached some very complex foreign policy decisions?

Schattschneider described "the contagion of conflict," which means the audience determines the outcome of the fight. "At the nub of politics," he writes, "are, first, the way in which the public participates in the spread of conflict and, second, the processes by which the unstable relation of the public to the conflict is controlled."[9] Did the administration unnecessarily promote the spread of conflict and refuse to admit that it was wrong as more information came to light?

The road to war in Iraq in a post-9/11 world may have presented a classic case, one in which the government, the news media, and the people have since better learned their roles in our democracy. In a perfect world, the news media depends on the transparency of the government to report to the people the business, politics, policies, and relationships it makes domestically and internationally. On the basis of that information, the people make decisions about their lives, including what leaders they choose to represent them. Honest and credible information is what provides the fuel to the engine of democracy. It gives confidence to those who participate in their communities, communicate with their leaders, and may ultimately provide incentive *to participate* for those who usually are not inclined to do so.

A broken relationship between our elected officials, the news media, and the people is troublesome at best and disastrous at its extreme as we experienced with the debacle that was the Iraq war. One of our founding fathers and one of our greatest presidents, who later was tested by a nation broken and split, understood the importance of this relationship and the repercussions that result when it falters.

Thomas Jefferson wrote, "The functionaries of every government have propensities to command at will the liberty and property of their constituents. There is no safe deposit for these but with the people themselves, nor can they be safe with them without information. Where the press is free, and every man able to read, all is safe."[10]

As a young lawyer, Abraham Lincoln warned about the results when a government effectively alienates its citizenry. He said in part, "The strongest bulwark of any government, and particularly of those constituted like ours, may effectively be broken down and destroyed—I mean the attachment of the people."[11]

NOTES

1. Kingdon, John. *Agendas, Alternatives, and Public Policies* (New York: HarperCollins, 1995), 87–88.

2. Official White House transcript, State of the Union Address, January 29, 2002.

3. Eisner, Peter, and Knut Royce. *The Italian Letter* (New York: Rodale, 2007), 5–7.

4. Official transcript, *60 Minutes* with Leslie Stahl, January 11, 2004.

5. Cohen, Bernard Cecil. *The Press and Foreign Policy* (Princeton: Princeton University Press, 1963), 13.

6. Schlesinger, Arthur M. *War and the American Presidency* (New York: W. W. Norton & Company, 2004), 21.

7. Westphal, Lt. Col. Steven D. "Counterterrorism: Policy of Preemptive Action." USAWC Strategy Research Project, April 4, 2003.

8. Graubard, Stephen. *Command of Office* (New York: Basic Books, 2004), 539.

9. Schattschneider, E. E. *The Semi-Sovereign People: A Realist's View of Democracy in America* (New York: Wadsworth, Thompson Learning, 1975), 3.

10. Jefferson, Thomas. *The Writings of Thomas Jefferson*, Andrew Lipscomb, ed. (Washington D.C.: Thomas Jefferson Memorial Association, 1901), 553.

11. Constitution Society. Official transcript, "Abraham Lincoln's Address Before the Young Men's Lyceum of Springfield, Illinois," January 27, 1838.

ONE

The Fear Factor

How It Shaped Political Decisions and Policy

Collective fear stimulates herd instinct, and tends to produce ferocity
toward those who are not regarded as members of the herd.[1]

—Bertrand Russell

Over the years, the United States has mostly watched as the people of
other countries suffered at the hands of terrorists, including in Europe,
the Middle East, and across parts of Asia. However, terrorism is not
completely new to Americans. Save for the attack on Pearl Harbor
decades ago, which brought World War II to American shores, there have
only been two other significant attacks in the United States.

In 1993, the World Trade Center was bombed, which damaged a relatively small part of one of the twin towers killing six people and injuring
hundreds. In 1995, in a so-called homegrown terrorist bombing in Oklahoma City at the Murrah Federal Building, 168 were killed, including 19
children.

It is safe to say Americans believed both were isolated incidents and
attributed them to the likes of common criminals, crazies, and religious
fanatics. The same can be said for the assassinations of four U.S. presidents, Abraham Lincoln, James A. Garfield, William McKinley, and John
F. Kennedy, all gunned down while in office.

There have been other attacks, which specifically targeted, killed, and
injured hundreds of Americans in the past twenty-five years, but they
have occurred far from America in troubled parts of the world. They
include the bombing of the Marine barracks in Beirut, Lebanon, in 1983
during the Reagan administration; the bombing of two U.S. embassies in
Nairobi, Kenya, and Dar es Salaam, Tanzania, in 1998; and the attack on
the USS *Cole* in 2000, which was docked in Yemen.

1

These incidents occurred during the second term of the Clinton administration. These were tragedies to be sure, but somehow were more easily digested by the American public, given the rather volatile regions of the world in which they occurred. Also, Americans found some solace and experienced a false sense of security in that those attacks did not happen on American soil.

By any measure, September 11, 2001, was different. It was the shear enormity of the attacks that made it different. Such an event was so totally incomprehensible to Americans. It was the shock of such a catastrophe. It was the calculated, cruel audacity of it all that made it different. It was the method of destruction that killed 2,996 people that made it so hideously unique.

The targets were both towers of the sleek, austere, imposing World Trade Center, which was reduced to twisted metal and ashes, and the Pentagon, a portion of the building where the Naval Command Center resided, where an enormous hole was blown through it. These buildings were considered indestructible and were iconic structures representative of America's might and prosperity. That is what made these attacks so brazen and symbolic.

What happened to America on that day changed the way Americans regarded themselves. Somehow it altered our identity as a people. The strength of the nation was challenged and so was our naïve notion that we are, for the most part, safe and protected. The terrorist attacks of 9/11 rendered America fragile, nervous, on edge, and frightened.

Jim A. Kuypers wrote, "Entire generations of Americans had never experienced a major war, much less an attack on U.S. soil; the attacks pushed Americans into new emotional territory. Graphic images were repeatedly seen on television and in print, searing them into the consciousness of Americans who were hour by hour increasingly wondering about their safety. This combined emotional physical setting forms the background of the rhetorical situation in which President Bush and the press were to act."[2]

The country was targeted and so were Americans in their own country by a mysterious and terrifying enemy that could strike at any moment, anywhere, at any time. The Bush administration would reinforce this repeatedly during the months to follow. A new era had dawned for the United States. The age of terrorism had arrived and with a vengeance.

President Bush declared in his State of the Union address on January 29, 2002, the second major address after the 9/11 attacks, "Our war against terror is only beginning. Thousands of dangerous killers, schooled in the methods of murder, often supported by outlaw regimes, are now spread throughout the world like ticking time bombs, set to go off without warning. A terrorist underworld, including groups like Hamas, Hezbollah, Islamic Jihad, Jaish-i-Mohammaed—operates in remote jungles and deserts, and hides in the centers of large cities."[3] The implication, of course, was that many of those large cities, which could, and likely would be future targets, are here in the United States.

We were encouraged to go about the business of our daily lives. We were also ominously cautioned to be on our guard, vigilant and wary of what might lurk in the shadows of our relatively open, trusting society. This was an enemy, we were told, which had infiltrated our country and established what we came to know as "sleeper cells." Over time we learned that this is a term used for small groups of people who conspire to orchestrate elaborate, violent schemes and are poised to attack predetermined targets when they deem the time is right.

These groups blend quietly into a society, a segment of which they will later turn on. We Americans began to regard our neighbors with some suspicion. We became more wary of those we interacted with, especially those who may have seemed different, who dressed differently, and who were not originally from this country. What began to emerge was a subtle, yet pervading anti-foreigner sentiment—a xenophobia—that in this case was a direct by-product of fear.

President Bush continued to tell us the country was strong, that our nation would prevail, that we would hunt down the enemy wherever it was hiding and bring that enemy to justice. We are the people of the United States of America, after all, the president reminded us on television and on radio. We are a beacon of light and the strongest nation on the face of the earth. We possess an unyielding will to protect our democracy, our freedoms, and our people.

What emerged in the United States was a public that became fervently patriotic again. The events of 9/11 brought the people of the United States together and brought many in the community of nations around the world to our defense, aid, and support. We experienced a renewed love of country and what it stands for. We assumed a collective, national posture of pride and purpose, perhaps not seen since World War II. Pride and patriotism in times of crisis are not unusual, and this, certainly, was no exception.

Arthur M. Schlesinger wrote in his final book, "Nothing in a democracy demands more searching discussion than the choice between peace and war. But voters rallied round the flag after September 11, 2001, because Americans felt, as never before, personal vulnerability to enemy attack."[4] People across the country, and not only in New York City and Washington, DC, were feeling vulnerable and that the safety of our cities had been compromised. The news media reflected this mood in their reporting of the attacks.

As the weeks and months passed, the press reinforced a stunned, vulnerable collective consciousness as it continued to cover the aftermath of the destruction of the towers and the Pentagon. In stories about the people killed, the cost of the destruction, diplomatic efforts in bringing other nations to our side, we assessed who the enemy was and speculated about the extent to which others might go to harm us. The behavior and attitude of the news media and their coverage was not unusual.

Thomas Patterson noted "abrupt shifts" in the press during other more recent crises in American history, including the Iranian hostage crisis in 1979, the bombing of the Marine barracks in Lebanon in 1983, the brief Gulf War in 1990, and war in the Balkans during the 1990s. The press covers a crisis with a lingering objective eye when diplomatic efforts precede an actual event. The press may focus on the president and his administration and Congressional involvement in resolving an issue. It may cover stories about the government of other nations and their leaders as a story builds to the level of an actual crisis or calamity, but when the country or its interests are blatantly attacked, the press becomes a more sympathetic entity. It assumes a different posture in covering the news. It stands with the people and tends to reflect "our" pain, "our" concerns, and "our" fear, and that is the manner in which the news copy is written.

The 9/11 attacks happened here at home, not on some distant shore, so the press was empathic in its approach to this story that quite literally hit home. The stakes were higher for America, and so "NBC outfitted its peacock logo with stars and stripes following the World Trade Center and Pentagon attacks, and computer generated flags festooned the other networks."[5] The television networks especially, but all the news media, demonstrated their patriotism as they covered the hundreds of stories associated with the attacks.

Did fear play a role to the extent that the press did not do its job as well as it could have? Had it been more vigilant and curious, could it have prevented an ill-fated invasion of a country that had nothing to do with the 9/11 attacks? What role did business interests play in terms of coverage and attitude? Did the Bush administration deliberately use the mood of the populace and the sympathetic tenor of press coverage to promote its political agenda?

Arthur Schlesinger blamed the press and television for the "lack of debate" about what was happening in the country. A new and dangerous foreign policy was taking shape and "editorial pages of our most distinguished newspapers," he wrote, "were shamefully and incredibly oblivious to the drastic significance of the shift to preventive war" as the basis of that new American foreign policy.[6]

This was not evident immediately following 9/11 because the administration was occupied, and rightly so, with hunting down bin Laden in Afghanistan and marginalizing or eliminating entirely the oppressive, dogmatic Taliban. As the weeks and months passed and as American forces came up empty for the most wanted man on the planet, the Bush administration broadened its net for those who threatened America and the security of the world. Bush identified the "axis of evil" for Americans within a year of 9/11. This will be discussed in more detail later.

The role of the press was an important factor in the story of 9/11 and how it covered the unfolding story leading to the Iraq war. Had they not made the mistakes they did in terms of their relationships with members of the Bush administration and Congress, the news media may have helped prevent the war from happening at all. Generally, tension between the news media and the government officials they cover is common. In many ways that tension is inherent in the relationship between the press and those who run the country and has been so since the beginning of the Republic.

This, however, was a unique event during an interesting political time. Both the press and those leaders in government helped foster a national climate of fear, the genesis of which was born by a very real event. The fear was sustained by the Bush administration as it justified our need for immediate retaliation and, later, as it made a compelling case for expanding the operation to include Iraq. It pointedly put the press on the defensive.

While the press complained about how it was treated by the administration and that access to information was difficult to get, the American people were concerned about basics, which were the safety and well-being of their families and the security of the homeland. They had little choice but to trust that their leaders were telling the truth and that those leaders could both protect the country and diplomatically manage the burgeoning, rancorous international crisis abroad. Americans wanted to be assured they were going to be safe from further harm, and they wanted those responsible for the attacks to be apprehended and brought to justice in the light of day for the entire world to witness.

In essence, there was a clash of interests. The press had a job to do, and it was different from those in government and in the Bush administration. But in this case, how did these opposing interests manifest themselves? What other factors were at play? Were the United States and the American people better served if the press mostly reflected America's mood in their reporting? Could it have been more probing, ferreting out better information for the American people?

THE ROLE OF THE PRESS

The concept of a free and unfettered press is a founding principle of our democracy. It was neither born nor instituted by any partisan ideology. It is neither more democratic nor republican in nature, but is rather an inherent *American* value that was built into the constitution of a united states, the First Amendment to the document, and is a part of our Bill of Rights.

Admittedly it is simple and even vague in description: "Congress shall make no law respecting an establishment of religion, or prohibiting the free exercise thereof; *or abridging the freedom of speech, or of the press*; or of the right of the people peaceably to assemble, and to petition the Government for a redress of grievances." These words, however lean and sparse, have spoken volumes for the most established, enduring, and influential democracy in history for more than 230 years. In part, it has been that way because of a press that was free to do its work. It gathered and reported information for the interest and benefit of the public.

The passivity of Congress, a renegade administration, and the timidity of the press between 9/11 and the Iraq war provided a classic case, a perfect storm, and one of the strongest arguments in our history for the importance and the necessity of a press that works primarily for the American people. Members of the press should be public servants, not collectively a "fifth column" of government, as journalist Bill Moyers suggested, but a "fourth estate" for the protection of the American people and the preservation of the democracy in which they are able to thrive, live freely, happily, and prosperously. These are our ideals. There have been many wise and influential men over hundreds of years since the country's creation, which have included founders, pundits, presidents, politicians, and journalists. All have written about the importance of information and a press that challenges those in power.

Consider these: James Madison to W. T. Barry in 1822, who wrote, "Nothing could be more irrational than to give the people power, and to withhold from them information without which power is abused. A people who mean to be their own governors must arm themselves with power which knowledge gives. A popular government without popular information or the means of acquiring it is but a prologue to a farce or a tragedy, or perhaps both." Thomas Jefferson in a letter to A. Corey in 1823 wrote, "The press is the best instrument for enlightening the mind of man, and improving him as a rational moral and social being." In 1831, from "Democracy in America" Alexis de Tocqueville wrote, "In order to enjoy the inestimable benefits that liberty of the press ensures, it is necessary to submit to the inevitable evils which it engenders." Abraham Lincoln in 1864 wrote, "Let the country know the facts, and the country will be safe." Mark Twain, an insightful cynic, circa 1882, in response to British critic Mathew Arnold wrote, "A discriminating irreverence is the creator and protector of human liberty." PBS journalist Bill Moyers when he spoke at the National Media Reform Conference in 2008 said, "Democracy without honest information creates the illusion of popular consent while enhancing the power of the state and the privileged interests protected by it."

All reflect idealism in their sentiments, but the point is that these are not new concepts in America. These ideas are as old, as treasured, and as true for the country today as the day they were born. But in practical terms, for the modern day, what do they mean and how can they be relevant? Should the press behave irrespective of any rules and without responsibility to any authority? Should it demean or intend to embarrass those in power? Should its mission tear down the overriding belief and trust in those who are elected to run our country and manage our affairs at home and abroad? Should it be "mad dog" instead of "watch dog"?

The press is in existence to protect and represent the public's interest. Today, theoretically, the news media does so by disseminating information via television, radio, print, and the web to educate, enlighten, inform, and sometimes even to entertain, so that people can make decisions about their lives and about who they elect to represent them in the White House, in Congress, in cities and town governments, and on school boards across the country. Ideally, those journalists in the news media operate as the eyes and ears of the people. Without them, the people could not know what those elected to represent them are doing. It would be impossible and impractical, for example, for a working person to sit in day after day at town council meetings, Congressional hearings, and presidential press conferences. Journalists and others who work in news must be proxy for the people and for them hold those in power to account.

There has been mounting criticism that the news media is too aggressive, abusive, partial, inflammatory, shrill and, by nature some say, unnecessarily invasive. All of those more scurrilous qualities exist in some form in some media. Those qualities represent the worst of the craft, but there are better ways to get news than others, and arguably the best of the craft exists today in organizations such as the *New York Times, Washington Post, Wall Street Journal*, PBS, CNN, ABC, NBC, CBS, and others. Even they are not perfect, but we must assume that most of the people who are employed by those organizations take their work to heart, are storytellers in the best sense, and take their responsibility as public servants seriously, believing the information they impart is information the American people may need, want, and do depend on.

The American people have a responsibility as well. They must be voting citizens and engaged. They must participate in our democracy and sift through the information, eliminate the "infojunk," and discern which information is reliable. We live in fascinating, fast, complicated times and, more than ever, the news media are vital to our interests, personal, local, national, and international. Those who work in the news media are public servants and must operate in the best interest of the people they serve. With regard to their relationship to power and the people who hold it in government, criticism should be leveled on points of policy not personality traits and behaviors that have little or nothing to do with governing.

Many say that the press was different in times gone by. It was more reticent to embarrass leaders on personal matters or tear them down without justifiable cause on policy, but it was not the press that was different. It was the leaders who were different. Presidents such as Washington, Jefferson, Lincoln, both Roosevelts, and Kennedy were extraordinary men who served in interesting times. All possessed human traits, personal failures and frailties, but they possessed a larger than life vision, courage, and conviction when there were issues and problems that concerned the country and her people. They led the nation through challenging times, certainly some would argue in darker and direr times than today.

The press seemed to have more respect for them, but the point is that *they* demonstrated respect and care for the citizens of the country, which was reflected in the press coverage about them. The founding of the country, the building of the country, a civil war, the Great Depression, a world war, and the Cuban missile crisis admittedly imposed great and real challenges to our leaders, but those problems were no less challenging than the attacks of 9/11. It was the arrogance of leadership and intoxication of power that shifted during Vietnam and later with President Richard M. Nixon and Watergate. The government somehow became tainted and toward, which manifested an enduring suspicion and cynicism in the people about their elected leaders. It also emboldened the attitude of the press and the way it went about its work.

We forgot the lessons learned during the time of the Pentagon papers case and Watergate, and we forgot them again during 9/11. Authority without checks and balances can result in unbridled power, power unto itself for its own self-interests and motivations. That is a strong argument for a so-called free press. It is one check on power, but it is an important check on power.

The lesson is that the news media and the government are not partners. They are, by design, and necessity, adversarial entities. One observes on behalf of the public what the other says and does and reports its findings back to the people. It asks those simple journalism textbook questions—who, what, where, when, why, and how—and it attempts to verify information without passion or prejudice. This is most especially critical in questions of war and peace, when people are at risk, and when taxpayer money is spent. It is also important when relationships that will either preserve or break the delicate balance of powers in an increasingly smaller world are at stake, when entire countries and their populations may be just as vulnerable as ours.

September 11, 2001, was that time, as America continued to write its history and when we needed to know the truth about Iraq. There should have been more intensive questioning by the press. Why was Iraq targeted? Where were those weapons of mass destruction? What was the relationship of Hussein to bin Laden? Was Iraq in any way responsible for 9/11? How could knowingly bad intelligence clear the way for war? In the absence of answers to these questions, the people did not hold the president to account because they could not hold the president to account. This was because the news media was largely complacent in their work. Information imparted to them by the Bush administration was largely accepted at face value and reported as such back to public.

As Justice Louis Brandeis wrote, "The function of the press is very high. It is almost holy. It ought to serve as a forum for the people, through which the people may know freely what is going on. To misstate or suppress the news is a breach of trust."[7] Trust from the people and the news media is what President George Bush had in abundance post 9/11. He squandered that trust and what could have been a golden, historic opportunity.

SETTING THE STAGE

By the summer of 2001, George Walker Bush had gotten mixed reviews as president. There was some "eroding confidence" in his environmental policies, but by the time he delivered his State of the Union address in February, 86 percent of Americans said the country was headed in the right direction.[8] Gallup polls showed the president's approval rating fluctuating between 65 and 53 percent between January and May 2001.

The *Washington Post* and ABC News conducted two polls that summer, one in June and one in August. According to those, the president's job approval rating was at 55 percent and in August it had climbed slightly to 60 percent.[9] According to three other polls, including Fox News/Opinion Dynamic, Gallup Poll/*USA Today*, and CBS News/*New York Times*, all taken within days of the 9/11 attacks, the approval rating for the president in each survey had dipped to around 50 percent.[10]

Meanwhile, the press portrayed the president as a man who did not seem much interested in his job. Some began writing about the president's penchant for down time, noting the number of days he took off work, the eight hours of sleep he required, and that his was a nine to five administration, short on substance, tall on expedience.

There was persistent chatter on the airwaves and in print that the president was an administrator who wanted information quickly and in simple terms. This president was a bottom line kind of guy, not enjoying much of the minutiae, the detail of governing. Comics on television and pundits in the papers mused frequently about the lack of patience the president had for reading lengthy documents and how he often tired of the often tedious, time-intensive process of decision-making, leadership, and governing.

The president himself jauntily told college students during commencement exercises at Yale, his alma mater, where he was the keynote speaker, "To those who have received honors, awards, and distinctions, I say well done, and to the C students I say . . . you, too, can be president of the United States."[11] In sum, the president gave the impression that he was confident, calm, undeterred by his critics, and that he could do the job well enough without breaking much of a sweat. Was this president just confident in his abilities or was he just a fool?

With September came the public's concern about the economy and other domestic challenges. *Newsweek* was on newsstands a day before the attack. The cover story was about Mormons. The magazine called it a "mysterious religion" as Salt Lake City, a city with a preponderance of Mormons, was preparing for the 2002 winter Olympic games. Wall Street was uneasy as stock prices were down. President Bush began to talk about immigration reform and what to do about social security as baby boomers in droves were coming of age and ready to tap the system to which they had contributed.[12] *Time* magazine's cover story was about Secretary of State Colin Powell. It was a reflective article questioning whether Powell was the secretary of state the president had bargained for. The magazine also covered the increasingly noisy stem cell debate and the president's opposition to stem cell research on moral grounds.[13]

On the morning of September 11, 2001, the *New York Times* had on its front page a story about stem cells and the struggling economy. There was violence in the Middle East, and a campaign was underway to elect Rudy Giuliani's successor as mayor of New York City. On the opposite coast, the front page of the *Los Angeles Times* reported stories about the GOP tax plan to fix the economy, stock markets around the world were taking a beating, and there was a salacious story about the "Wonderland Murders" in Los Angeles, which occurred in 1981.

On the day of the attacks, key members of the president's administration were scattered. Secretary of State Powell was traveling to Lima, Peru. Secretary of Defense Donald Rumsfeld was at the Pentagon meeting with a delegation from Capitol Hill. Vice President Richard Cheney and National Security Adviser Condoleezza Rice were in their respective offices in the West Wing. C.I.A. Director George Tenet was having breakfast with a friend near the White House. The new F.B.I. Director, Robert Mueller, was at his office at headquarters on Pennsylvania Avenue. Henry Shelton, Chairman of the Joint Chiefs, was on a plane to Europe.

The president was in Florida. He had taken an early morning jog. At 8:30 a.m., the time of the attack, a so-called "soft event" was on his schedule. The president would read to a group of second graders at the Emma E. Booker School in Sarasota, Florida. It was an ordinary day. Even after the president was told that a plane had hit the North Tower of the World Trade Center, it remained, if only for a few minutes more, an ordinary day. Early details were sketchy. White House Chief of Staff, Andrew Card said, "The President and I thought it was a horrible accident, a pilot heart attack or something."[14]

Very soon after, as the president attended to the class of youngsters, Card came quietly to the president and whispered in his right ear these eleven words: "A second plane hit the second tower. America is under attack."[15] An image of this exchange is preserved in photographs and on tape. The president slowly nodded in acknowledgment of the message. His face visibly changed expression, his lips slowly pursed, his body stiffened, but he sat with the children to hear the remainder of the story. Some members of the press began to criticize the president about his behavior and his immediate response to the attack, and animosity began to grow between the administration and the news media in response to this kind of reporting.

Left-leaning documentary filmmaker, Michael Moore, in his Cannes and Academy Award winning film "Fahrenheit 9/11," mocked the president and actually timed how long he sat listening to the children's story before he left the event (seven minutes). Moore charged that the behavior of the president was evidence he did not take command of the situation. At that point, the president knew the incident was not an accident, but a deliberate attack on the city of New York and on the Pentagon in Washington, DC.

The administration defended its decision to maintain an appearance of calm and control. *The 9/11 Commission Report* reflected the president's thoughts at the time saying, "his instinct was to project calm, not to have the country see an excited reaction at a moment of crisis" and "the President felt he should project strength and calm until he could better understand what was happening."[16] Even the principal of the Booker School, Gwendolyn Tose'-Rigell, said she thought the president handled the situation properly. "I don't think anyone could have handled it better. What would it have served if he had jumped out of his chair and run out of the room?"[17] Within days of the attack, Gallup asked a sample of Americans if they were confident about the president's ability to handle the crisis. Forty-five percent said they were "very confident" and 33 percent said they were "somewhat confident" in President Bush.[18]

An hour after the attack, while still at the school, the president made this statement: "Today we've had a national tragedy. Two airplanes have crashed into the World Trade Center in an apparent terrorist attack on our country. I have spoken to the Vice President, to the Governor of New York, to the Director of the FBI, and have ordered that the full resources of the federal government go to help the victims and their families, and to conduct a full-scale investigation to hunt down and to find these folks who committed these acts. Terrorism against our nation will not stand."[19]

The president, with staff and the White House press corps in tow, boarded Air Force One and flew to two secret locations as they monitored events on the ground. The press was told they were being diverted and would not immediately return to Washington. Some reporters wrote about the tension on Air Force One that day. They realized how serious the situation was when they saw fighter jets at the wings of the presidential plane.

First, they flew to Barksdale Air Force Base near Shreveport, Louisiana, where the president made a brief statement. He assured the nation that its government was taking appropriate security precautions. He explained that the military was on high alert at home and all over the world and said that the functions of the government would continue. "Make no mistake," he said, "the United States will hunt down and punish those responsible for these cowardly acts." [20]

Later, the president flew to U.S. Strategic Command at Offutt Air Base in Omaha, Nebraska. There was some early and speculative intelligence indicating that the White House may have been a target as well, which meant there was genuine concern for the president's safety. These were the reasons the White House gave for the president not returning directly to Washington, DC.

The president did finally return to Washington. It was the evening of September 11, 2001, when he made a nationally televised statement at 8:30 p.m., a full twelve hours after the attacks. He extolled the greatness of America and said we would defend our country against this evil, committed by the worst of humanity. He again assured the country their government and financial institutions would function as normal. "The search is underway for those who are behind these evil acts. I've directed the full resources of our intelligence and law enforcement communities to find those responsible and to bring them to justice. We will make no distinction between the terrorists who committed these acts and those who harbor them." [21]

The president began to "frame the facts surrounding 9/11" and the administration's response to it for the people through the press. Jim Kuypers wrote, "The 9/11 attacks gave the President and the press a unique opportunity to create a metanarrative and re-shape public knowledge concerning America's new role in the world." [22] While the press dutifully reported the news of the attacks and the administration's response to it, there was also criticism.

On September 14, 2001, Howard Rosenberg, media critic for the *Los Angeles Times*, wrote that President Bush "lacked size in front of the camera when he should have been commanding and filling the screen with a formidable presence." He described the president as "slinking" and "almost like a little boy." He received anonymous death threats and anti-Semitic slurs from the public via e-mail for not supporting the president in times of crisis. [23]

Dan Guthrie and Tom Gutting, both newspaper columnists at the *Texas City Sun* in Texas City, Texas, and the *Daily Courier* in Grants Pass, Oregon, respectively were fired for being critical of the president. [24] One wrote that the president "skedaddled" after the attacks rather than return immediately to Washington from Florida. The other wrote that the president "flew around like a scared child" after the attacks. [25]

Garry Trudeau, creator of the politically charged "Doonesberry" cartoon strip, voluntarily pulled his "Featherweight Bush" series from newspapers across the country in which it was syndicated. It had been routinely critical of the president for not being intellectually or emotionally up to the task of commander in chief.[26] In the case of Trudeau, there is no indication that his opinions of the president had changed, nor was there any indication he had been encouraged to pull the cartoon. Perhaps, he simply realized the inappropriateness of such a cartoon and that there was a place and a time for critical commentary. This was neither the time nor the place. While many may argue that none of what Rosenberg, Guthrie, Gutting, and Trudeau wrote was news per se, all were paid to write opinion pieces, which sell newspapers and generate public discourse.

But at the time, there was little tolerance or patience for criticism of the president and certainly not while 92 percent of Americans said they approved of the campaign against terrorism that the president was initiating.[27] The people had rallied around their leader and, in this particular case, where the enemy was unknown and unpredictable, the press was expected also to "rally round the flag" and the president. It was simply un-American not to do so.

Sidney Blumenthal wrote that after 9/11 there was a "scent of fear in the air" and an "atmosphere rife with intimidation."[28] As the government formulated its plan of attack based on the events of 9/11, members of the news media became testy, sniping at each other, and taking jabs at the Bush administration for encouraging them to be supportive rather than adversarial, as many journalists believe is their central role. The administration was preparing to launch a war. The press expected it would be fully briefed about both its architecture and execution; however, there was dissension in the ranks about how to handle the story of the president's plan for action in the aftermath of a genuine national crisis.

Should it follow the president's lead and report the news as issued by his administration as partner, joining a national, all-encompassing initiative? Should the press assume the role of watchdog checking, verifying, holding the president and his administration to account for the decisions it would make from 9/11 forward? Could the press balance both positions? And most importantly, should a genuine national calamity with such expansive consequences alter the behavior and mission of the press?

A CHANGING POLITICAL CLIMATE

Arthur Schlesinger suggested that Americans felt a particular kind of vulnerability after 9/11. He compared these feelings to those during World War II, when the threat was worse, the enemy more dangerous. He cited a study by the Pew Research Center, a full two years after 9/11, six months after we attacked Iraq.[29]

"Two years after the 9/11 attacks," reported the Pew Research Center, "fully three-quarters of Americans saw the world as a more dangerous place than a decade ago." Schlesinger added, "Terrorism, striking from the shadows, gives a new and frightening dimension to life—a dimension intensified by Washington's color-coded exploitation of the politics of fear."[30] An overriding sense of doom took hold in the country. This feeling was exploited and nurtured after the terrorist attacks on 9/11.

The "politics of fear" was perpetuated by a press corps, not complicit, but intimidated by the story unfolding before it. The press as a collection of individuals was perhaps as frightened as other ordinary Americans. Reporters largely "stood down," abandoning, to a degree, principle and purpose. In essence, they waived their responsibility as journalists in deference to what they perceived as the right thing to do, a higher calling, if you will. They either experienced some indirect pressure from a rather determined Bush administration or they self-censored out of obligation as citizens first. Members of the press were faced with a bona fide dilemma, balancing purpose as journalists and obligation as Americans as most of the population was seriously worried about the future and their safety. Also, there is evidence of a news media under pressure.

Former White House Press Secretary Scott McClellan in his book, *What Happened*, called the press "complicit enablers" as the Bush administration developed its strategy for war.[31] Journalist Katie Couric, who worked on NBC's *Today* show at the time of the attacks and was Dan Rather's successor on the CBS *Evening News*, said she felt pressure from "the corporations who own where we work, and from the government itself to really squash any kind of questioning it. It was one of the most embarrassing chapters in the history of journalism."[32] Journalist Jessica Yellin agreed. She worked for MSNBC at the time of the attacks and is now with CNN. She said journalists "were under enormous pressure from corporate executives, frankly, to make sure that this was a war presented in a way that was consistent with the patriotic fever in the nation."[33] Andrew Heyward, CBS news chief at the network during 9/11, said, "The trauma of the September 11 attacks and the ensuing sense of patriotism might have muted press skepticism about the war."[34] Bill Moyers of *Bill Moyers Journal* on Public Broadcasting, in his special program, "Buying the War," called the press "compliant," accusing journalists of "passing on" propaganda as news and "cheering them" (those in the Bush administration) on.[35]

The invasion of Iraq was indisputably on the way, even though this was completely unknown to the public or press at the time. The rising justification for the war would emerge in the public consciousness as thoughtful, responsible, careful, and inevitable. We now know that behind the scenes, the president was actively building a case against Saddam Hussein just months after the attacks on the United States, while a critical operation in Afghanistan, presumably to hunt down, capture, and bring to justice Osama bin Laden, was well underway.

The press was conflicted, engaged in a dialogue with itself and with the administration about freedom of information, civil liberties, and its proper place in a democracy. It accused the administration of marginalizing its effectiveness, while also succumbing to some pressure over the tone and tenor of coverage. Meanwhile, the administration proceeded confidently as it put into effect safeguards in the name of protecting the homeland. Ruth Rosen of the *San Francisco Chronicle* noted a "flurry of federal orders" in the aftermath of 9/11 to presumably "beef up the nation's security."[36]

On October 12, 2001, former Attorney General John Ashcroft issued a new statement of policy regarding the 1974 Freedom of Information Act, an important tool for the press. In a memorandum, Ashcroft wrote that any federal agency can resist requests for information and can withhold information where there is a "sound legal basis" for doing so.[37] While the memorandum acknowledged the importance of a "well-informed citizenry" and "maintaining an open and accountable government," it also expressed "the need to safeguard national security, to maintain law enforcement effectiveness, to respect business confidentiality, to protect agency deliberations, and to preserve personal privacy."[38] This may have been one way to keep the snooping press at bay for as long as possible.

Second, on November 1, 2001, President Bush issued an executive order regarding the records of presidents. The order stated that a president can veto requests to open presidential records of any administration and gave the commander in chief an unlimited amount of time to consider those requests at all. The American Civil Liberties Union (ACLU) said, "This Executive Order openly violates the Presidential Records Act passed by Congress in 1978."[39] In testimony at a Senate Judiciary hearing, "America after 9/11," the president of the ACLU and its Legislative Counsel noted in great detail that these restrictions "undermine checks and balances" in our system.[40] Again, many claimed these new policy stances from the Bush administration signaled a reluctance to inform the electorate though the channel of the press by making it difficult for reporters to collect information.

The attorney general seemingly was comfortable with these initiatives and regarded them as necessary, saying in an interview, "My job is to disrupt, curtail, destabilize, delay and prevent terrorism . . . and I am going to do everything I can think of that's within the limits of the charter of freedom we call our Constitution."[41] These directives from the Bush administration were a precursor to its escalating penchant for secrecy. As the "war on terror" gained momentum, many people, including those in academia, some from past presidential administrations, and the press quickly weighed in on these controversial decisions.

Laurence Tribe, professor of constitutional law at Harvard University commented, "If we get accustomed to a system of detention and surveillance, we may wake up and find to our dismay that we live in a state that has sold more of its liberty in exchange for its security than it would do willingly."[42] First Amendment attorney Floyd Abrams was also critical of Attorney General Ashcroft, saying, "Part of the problem with Ashcroft is that he is tone deaf to civil liberty issues, so he often makes the worst case for what he wants to do."[43] Arthur Schlesinger wrote that this Bush administration "is the most secretive since Nixon," and he quoted John W. Dean, who worked in the Nixon White House during Watergate as saying, "George W. Bush and Richard B. Cheney have created the most secretive presidency of my lifetime. Their secrecy is far worse than during Watergate." Schlesinger added, "Dean should have added Ashcroft to his list of secrecy addicts."[44]

In a May 2002 interview for the *New York Times* about the Bush administration's secretive ways, Roger Pilon of the Cato Institute, a libertarian research group, said, "Government grows each time there is a crisis, and this is an executive branch that thinks it's a law unto itself. Your guard has to be up." Ronald Chen, associate dean at Rutgers School of Law in Newark, New Jersey, who was also interviewed, said this administration "is using the continued latitude the public is willing to give it in order to push back the frontiers of what the government can keep secret."[45]

Meanwhile, in an interesting poll conducted by the Pew Research Center for the People and the Press, fifteen hundred people were surveyed over the telephone during the course of a week in November, just one month after 9/11. A resounding 80 percent said they believed censorship of the news from Afghanistan was "a good idea." They were also asked what is more important—the media's ability to report news that it believes is "in the national interest" or the government's ability to censor the news as it finds any of it a "threat to national security." The respondents supported the government 53 to 39 percent. When asked who should have the discretion to report certain things or not, the military or the media, the respondents sided with the military 50 to 40 percent.[46]

Historically, these kinds of percentages are not unusual in times of crisis. Similar numbers regarding similar questions appeared during the Gulf War in 1991. Columbia University historian Eric Foner said all the fuss about civil liberties is not a new phenomenon. "For most of our history," he said, "the Bill of Rights was pretty irrelevant. There were egregious violations well into the twentieth century."[47]

For example, after World War I, the director of the Bureau of Investigation, later known as the Federal Bureau of Investigation (F.B.I.), J. Edgar Hoover, rounded up hundreds of people suspected of being Communists or anarchists, held them without due process, and subsequently deported them. All were foreign born and considered "radicals," and the U.S. Supreme Court supported the action. Two hundred were deported on December 21, 1919, including the most notable among them, activists Emma Goldman and Alexander Berkman. During World War II, more than 120,000 people of Japanese descent were detained in concentration camp-like settings. Two-thirds of those incarcerated were natural born citizens of the United States. The Supreme Court approved their detention.[48]

Critical times often demand radical measures. President George W. Bush insisted that this was a political time in the world like no other and that this war, the "war on terror"—had to be waged differently from conflicts that preceded it. This was a war that found us, and we had no choice but to engage in it. Given the nature of a war on terrorism, the Bush administration enlisted unusual and what might seem like harsh measures to combat our enemies and protect the United States. The president encouraged the public to accept and understand these necessary restraints and safeguards imposed by the government, which translated, in some cases, to limitations on our civil liberties and restrictions on the press.

The public may have believed those initiatives were temporary and would be restored when the danger is past; however, the ACLU said, "The war on terrorism, unlike conventional wars, is not likely to come to a public and decisive end." Former and first Homeland Security Director Tom Ridge, for example, equated the "war on terrorism" to the nation's continuing war on drugs and crime.[49] This is a significant distinction. In a never-ending war or crisis, the rhythm of the country does not and cannot return to normal. It must be perpetually on its guard. In our shrinking global village because of a fringe element of religious fanaticism and radical ideological difference, this may be a fact of life for the foreseeable future.

The president challenged like-minded people here and in other countries around the world to join his "crusade," an ill-chosen word he used, reminiscent of colonial conquest and interference that has agitated regions of the Middle East for hundreds of years. The enemy we were about to engage was not fully understood, and the historic significance of the word "crusade" was careless and provocative. Forging ahead, perhaps to signify to the American people that it was in control, determined, and decisive, the administration swiftly, and with little time for closer examination, implemented new policies and issued directives, while it also worked to enlist the support of the public and press behind its efforts. The press was cajoled and encouraged to behave as a supporter of policy. There was no point to adversarial journalism when this was a time of genuine crisis. Many in the press squirmed and were vocal about the administration's disregard of its intended role as the "fourth estate," the great arbiter of information, standing between the government and the people, the conduit by which the people understood their world to a certain degree.

Howard Rosenberg of the *Los Angeles Times* said if Bush's my-country-right-or-wrong dictum is followed by the press, "the US media might as well pack away their megaphones and allow their First Amendment liberties to atrophy."[50] Walter Cronkite, the legendary CBS news anchorman, once regarded as "the most trusted man in America," urged the public to also support its free press against a president who was taking extreme measures in defense of liberty.

In an interview with the *Toronto Star*, a month after the 9/11 attacks, Cronkite pointed to what he had written in his book, about freedom of the press and Nazi Germany. He wrote, "When (the Germans) yielded up their free speech so easily (to Hitler) they became responsible for what the government did in their name."[51] He insisted that it is the role, obligation, and duty of the press to help make sense of the world for people, that it is the watchdog for an electorate that must make decisions about a government, which should operate in its best interests.

Tension between presidential administrations and the press is a built-in, some would say necessary, characteristic of the relationship. The United States Constitution itself and many of our founding fathers expressed the necessity of a free press, but how free can it be? How free should it be in times of crisis? How have presidents in our recent past managed their relationships with the press? Previous conflicts give special insight into today's presidential relationships, particularly when the country is at war or engaged in armed conflict.

THE VIETNAM WAR

Vietnam served as a cautionary tale for both press and future White House administrations. It was a complex situation in complicated times. The relationships of press to administration to military were intriguing. There is little question that the press coverage of the conflict half a world away in Southeast Asia via the medium of television helped change the perception of the war at home and the subsequent support for American policies in Vietnam. Some have said the gradual and then tumbling loss of support for the war may even have been responsible, in part, for President Lyndon Johnson's decision not to run for another term in office.

Daniel C. Hallin wrote that the media's role in Vietnam was part of a larger problem. "The collapse of America's will to fight in Vietnam resulted from a political process of which the media were only one part." While there is little doubt, Hallin said, "control of images and information is central to the exercise of power," what contributed to the loss of support for the war was *the combination* of increasing, damaging media reports and an administration fraught with political division and troubles of its own. As the country was managing a war in Vietnam, there were also racial tensions at home that were coming to a boil. This underscores the effect of forces working in concert or in confluence. The press, the president, and the public's reaction to both, can trigger a sea change in perception and subsequent lack of support or increase of support regarding an issue, problem or crisis. Often it is not one isolated factor or another that creates the turn of public support from one direction to another.[52]

It has been conventional wisdom that it was the Tet Offensive, which began in January 1968 and lasted for months, that alone shifted public perception of the Vietnam War and our involvement in it. Journalist Peter Braestrup wrote that this was not so, according to Pentagon papers. "Tet hit LBJ when he was already in trouble."[53]

In 1965, Johnson's approval rating held fairly steady between 71 percent (in February) to a low of 62 percent (in December). In 1966, while Johnson's approval ratings slipped, support for his policies in Vietnam were at 64 percent, but by the end of that same year in December, Johnson's approval rating fell to 48 percent and support for his policies in Vietnam dove to 43 percent. Those numbers held through 1967. In early 1968, during the time of the Tet offensive, the job approval rating for the President fell to 36 percent. For his war policies, there was a decline to 26 percent.[54] Another interesting point is that each year from 1963 to 1967 in Gallup polls, Lyndon Johnson had been voted the most admired world figure. In 1968, he was not.

Braestrup said, "It is plausible to argue that the media's 'disaster' image of events in Vietnam aggravated dissatisfactions with the Johnson war policy . . . but the media did not drive Johnson from office."[55] For example, it was as early as 1965 when CBS broadcast a story, with pictures, about Marines who used Zippo lighters to ignite thatch roofs in the village of Cam Ne.[56] That year Gallup Polls showed the president was experiencing a fairly healthy approval rating at 71 percent. It declined slightly that year, but never dipped below 62 percent.[57]

Vietnam provided the ingredients for the perfect political storm to occur. It came at a time of emerging technologies. Television certainly did not help Johnson's war effort. "Television is a powerful instrument," said a Chicago Tribune editorial. "Its advantages in speed and imagery create special problems for the military."[58] During Vietnam it also created special problems for politicians who needed the American people to support their policies. Politicians were perhaps saying one thing. Television and journalists, with an emphasis on the most dramatic images designed to attract viewers, were communicating something different to the people at home.

During the Vietnam era, images of the war, mostly on film, were flown back to the United States and developed before anything could be broadcast on television. The process of newsgathering took time. Compared to the instantaneous technologies of today, that seems like an eternity, but for the time, the technology was revolutionary. Americans no longer simply heard reports about battles or read about battles; they experienced the images of war nightly in their living room. The war was even dubbed "the living room war" by author Michael Arlen in his book of the same title.

The press really began to cover the war when President Johnson dispatched large numbers of troops to Vietnam beginning in 1965. "The US troop commitment grew from 75,000 in 1965 to almost 500,000 in late 1976. So did the US press contingent in Saigon." Two weeks before Tet there were 464 accredited members of the press in Saigon. The minority was from the United States press corps and included freelancers from smaller publications and stringers from broadcast media. However, the Saigon bureau became the third largest bureau behind New York and Washington for many organizations.[59] News coverage did not begin that way.

Braestrup said there was a "small band of newsmen" in Saigon when President Kennedy increased the number of military advisors to the area in 1962. Some journalists supported our mission there. Others criticized their colleagues for not reporting, but rather for supporting American policies. In the early 1960s there were about twenty American and foreign correspondents in Saigon. Some were inexperienced, having never covered a conflict in a foreign country. They did not know the language, and they ventured out infrequently to understand, perhaps as well as they could have, the culture and the underlying historic reasons for the conflict.

Then, as now, Americans were not as interested in foreign news. Braestrup wrote that international news ranked below the comics, sports, local news, and news from Washington. Then, as now, international news was more expensive to cover. News departments did not have the budgets. News divisions were not molded and utilized as the money-making enterprises they are today. This kind of coverage was not "part of the professional experience of American news executives."[60]

For the most part, news reports lacked government spin, but they also lacked perspective and context. Reporters were not equipped to adequately understand the complexities of the situation and "were overwhelmed" with the magnitude of the story before them. Combine this lack of understanding with the very nature of television itself. Television is radio with pictures, creating an enhanced experience. With *dramatic* pictures television is a sensory experience on steroids and can often skew reality. Television is like a spotlight that seeks out drama and conflict. Drama and conflict make good television.

A case in point in 1968 provided another indelible image of the war, this one on NBC showing Col. Nguyen Ngoc Loan shooting a captive in the head in Saigon on the street. There were pictures of our troops, bloodied, fighting, and dying, which were landing in the homes of viewers. Meanwhile, protests and unrest became a way of life on college campuses and in large cities around the country, which also made their way to television screens. Over there and here, these striking images produced some of the most memorable and disturbing television images in the history of the medium.

According to Braestrup, the kind of journalism that emerged during Vietnam, now with new technological tools, provided a glimpse into the future. "We saw at Tet the first show of the more volatile journalistic style—spurred by managerial exhortation or complaisance that has become so popular since the 1960s. With this style came the often mindless readiness to seek out conflict, to believe the worst of the government or of authority in general, and on that basis to divide up the actors on any issue into the good and the bad," he wrote.[61]

Put these events in context. They unfolded at the beginning of an election year for an incumbent president whose policies were coming under more scrutiny by an increasingly skeptical public about a simmering, little understood conflict in Vietnam, which was costing money and lives. The war had become an American war. Our purpose for being there became increasingly fuzzy as clear images of bloody battles over there and violent protests over here were influencing Americans. The political stars had fallen into alignment, but not in support of the president and his hope for victory. This constellation spelled failure.

Did the press effect some change? Yes, some, but not with intent to do so. The president and his administration, who previously had been selling the war, justifying the costs in both human and monetary terms, and declaring that progress was being made, were confronted with the reality of the situation, magnified by the press, especially television. The president's rhetoric simply did not match up with the images Americans were experiencing.

By the time newsman Walter Cronkite all but declared on the air that the war was spiraling into a hopeless cause, it was already so, a situation the president perhaps had not been able to admit to himself. Remember, only 35 percent of Americans supported the war effort at that point. Fifty percent were in opposition to it.[62] The Tet Offensive was arguably a turning point, but it was a turning point because the American people had been led to believe that we were making progress in Vietnam. In late 1967, General Westmoreland said in Washington, "We have reached an important point when the end begins to come into view."[63] The determination of the North Vietnamese during Tet showed a very different picture. When Cronkite saw the early bulletins about the sudden, surging advance of the North Vietnamese, he said, "What the hell is going on? I thought we were winning the war."[64]

On February 28, 1968, Cronkite conveyed his thoughts to a war-weary, angry nation, having worked as field reporter on the ground and credible news source from behind the anchor desk. He was the face of the news, reliable and trusting—someone the American people heard from every night and felt as though they knew. He reluctantly reported the following to a national audience: "With each escalation, the world comes closer to the brink of cosmic disaster. To say that we are closer to victory today is to believe, in the face of the evidence, the optimists who have been wrong in the past. To suggest we are on the edge of defeat is to yield to unreasonable pessimism. To say that we are mired in stalemate seems the only realistic, yet unsatisfactory, conclusion. On the off chance that military and political analysts are right, in the next few months we must test the enemy's intentions, in case this is indeed his last big gasp before negotiations. But it is increasingly clear to this reporter that the only rational way out then will be to negotiate, not as victors, but as an honorable people who lived up to their pledge to defend democracy and did the best they could." [65] Journalist David Halberstam said, "It was the first time in American history a war was declared over by an anchorman." [66]

Interestingly, there is dispute about whether President Johnson actually said anything like "If I've lost Cronkite, I've lost the American people." Johnson did not watch the broadcast, as is widely reported, and there is no hard evidence he uttered those words, not even in his own memoir, *The Vantage Point*. W. Joseph Campbell said that after the broadcast Johnson continued to make pro-war speeches, "demanding a 'total national effort' to win in Vietnam," an effort that was becoming more and more futile. [67]

According to Associated Press correspondent and Saigon bureau chief Richard Pyle, who covered the news in Vietnam for five years, President Johnson and some in his inner circle wanted to censor some reports from Vietnam. In fact, they discussed doing so three times in 1965, but together "rejected" the idea as both "impractical" and "counterproductive." [68] Further, not only was the United States press covering the war; hundreds of other journalists from many other countries were also covering it. Any reports Johnson may have wanted to squelch would eventually leak out anyway through other channels. Much did leak out about the war later, and in grand fashion, during a seminal case in 1971 with the press at the apex. The Pentagon Papers case shaped the people's perception of its leaders and how power can often breed secrecy and arrogance. It also pointed to what can happen without the transparency of government as it formulates foreign policy.

Daniel Ellsberg was an analyst in the Department of Defense under Secretary Robert McNamara in 1971. He went to the *New York Times* with a seven thousand-page document about America's long and deep history in Indochina leading to the Vietnam War. "Among other things, it revealed that President Lyndon Johnson had been committing infantry to Vietnam while telling the nation that he had no long range plans for the war. Most damning was the overall impression it gave that the United States government did not believe it was possible to win the war." Power can be intoxicating. A president on whom millions of people rely does not want to be proven wrong, especially when thousands of lives were being sacrificed. [69]

Under the guise of "national security" President Nixon tried to stop the publication of the Pentagon Papers, perhaps to halt the slide of credibility for the government by the American people. It would also hurt his efforts to further manage the war, but the U.S. Supreme Court held that "any attempt by the government to block news articles prior to publication bears a heavy burden of presumption against its constitutionality. The government has not met that burden." In sum, the Court found that publishing the Pentagon Papers would not harm national security.[70]

Presidential administrations since Vietnam have a long and deep memory of the failures and vulnerabilities during that time and have reflected about how conflict can be exacerbated when doubts are raised, whether well substantiated or not, in press coverage. Television was the new technology then. Now with the additional complicating factor of the ubiquitous Internet, there is increased pressure to manage the press and the tenor of press coverage, if possible.

President George H. W. Bush and his son, George W., both tried to "manage" the press during their respective tenures and crises. Those delicate balancing acts produced new questions about the role of the press in critical times. Both were successful at accomplishing their respective missions in managing their march to armed conflict; the father in Kuwait, the son in Iraq. They massaged the press, guided them to stories of importance to their administrations, explained the politics behind their directives, and generated positive press coverage resulting in resounding public support for both men and their policies. In the case of the son, the reluctance of the press to be more skeptical, to question more the evidence provided, produced disastrous consequences, but in the case of the father, the outcome of the mission outweighed any gripe the press may have had about access to news and how the war was managed. Everybody loves a winner, and a victorious president makes great television and also generates good feelings for the viewing audience at home.

THE GULF WAR

The year was 1990. President George Herbert Walker Bush was experiencing an unremarkable presidency and had been dogged by the so-called "wimp factor" in a *Newsweek* cover story in 1987 when Iraq's President Saddam Hussein invaded tiny Kuwait on the Persian Gulf, assuming control of the oil rich country. The BBC reported "Iraq had accused Kuwait of flooding the market with oil and had demanded compensation from a disputed oil field on the border of the two countries." Hussein presumably went in to settle the score.[71]

Even twenty years later, politicians had a vivid memory of the Vietnam era and the fallout from that conflict on many fronts. Factor in new and sophisticated technologies for both the military and the press. Consider a new political time. This war indeed would be a different story. The news media had evolved. So too, had politicians. This Bush administration would do its best to corral the news media and manage newsgathering when the U.S. military went into Kuwait to push Iraqi forces out during "Operation Desert Storm," which began in January 1991.

A word about managed news coverage. The management of newsgathering is not necessarily improper, nor should the terminology necessarily denote criticism of the practice. The Pentagon has to run a war while securing the safety of those on the front to provide press coverage. For news organizations, they require protection while doing their jobs with expensive equipment and high-priced reporters and producers rotating in and out of a war zone. The Pentagon provides some order to what can be a chaotic situation and the inevitable fog of war. News organizations expect they will be safe to cover the stories of war. They also expect to be given access to stories they deem newsworthy and want to cover. These two interests frequently collide.

News organizations work with the Pentagon and with each other to "pool" reports, which means that the networks rotate to be the "pool camera" for the entire group. For example, one network is designated to collect whatever information the government releases on a story. The news event could be a press conference, for example, complete with military spokesperson, maps, charts, and "video" from the front. The government, in effect, decides what is newsworthy information and that is what it releases to the press. Everyone shares the same information. It is pack journalism, also referred to by some as "scrum journalism," which means there is little competition for a story. Everyone is in it together. Each television and radio network, newspaper, and magazine gets what it needs, but all essentially receive the same information. The Pentagon is able to tell the story it wants to tell through the press. The press attempts to collect its own information as much as possible. Reporters want to be able to venture out on their own and determine what and who is newsworthy. They are also after a scoop, an exclusive, a story no one else will have, but this enterprising practice in a war zone can have dangerous repercussions.

One example is when correspondent Bob Simon of CBS News went into Iraq on a tip for a good story. He was captured by the enemy and spent forty harrowing days in an Iraqi prison. This incident was one the administration and military would cite as an example of why reporters could not wander off on their own in a time of violent conflict. It is dangerous, both the administration and military contended, but escorting the press around also serves its interest to control what Americans would see and could hear, whether or not intentional. This circumstance, for better or for worse, creates powerful gatekeepers in the administration and in the military.

The Bush administration and its supporters would herald the Gulf War as a great success, orchestrated news coverage and all. There was a well-defined mission, which was to push aggressor Saddam Hussein out of Kuwait and back across the border into his own country. There was also a clear exit strategy. When the job was done and Kuwait was secured, U.S. forces could leave the area, and they eventually did. However, there were errors during the war, which became public afterwards, including questions about the real success of particular bombing missions and the official number of civilian and enemy casualties. Not that these stories were eliminated from the public consciousness, but they were not featured as prominently. This was by design. The deliberate management of information by the Bush administration was methodical and strategic. The plan was to build public support for the conflict, and it worked. The "wimp factor" all but disappeared, and the president enjoyed a huge boost in his popularity.

When the Gulf War was launched in January 1991, President Bush's approval rating was at 82 percent and consistently held until the spring. Those approval ratings began to decline that summer as Americans turned their attention to an economy that was struggling. The war was over and, for all practical purposes, done with. By 1992, which was an election year, 93 percent of Americans said the economy was their top priority, and the president's approval rating *on* the economy was only at 24 percent. According to Gallup pollsters, Americans chose President Bush as the most admired man in the world; however, his approval rating was at 33 percent. Eighty percent of those polled said the president's greatest achievement in four years was the Gulf War.[72]

The Bush administration offered a window of narrow focus and limited access for photojournalists, radio, print, and television reporters. They had to submit their copy to military censors for "security review" and complained that, as a result, their stories were diminished and questionable in terms of journalistic integrity. Those stories could also become less newsworthy because of the time it took to review them. Time is of the essence as journalists work under deadline pressure to get stories on the air or filed for newspapers, first, which is a business consideration. Being first on a story in journalism implies that a news organization is better connected as compared to the competition. An audience will more likely turn to a news organization if it is perceived as being on top of the news and on top of a particular story. This perception is sold to the audience and can translate into ratings, which equals advertising revenues.

It was true that news was delivered instantaneously because of new technology, including satellite dishes as compact and as easy to use as umbrellas, video night scopes, satellite videophones, computers, etcetera, but interestingly, there was a lack of real pictures from the front. The press was not allowed in, and videos were released by the administration, after the fact. Successful bombing missions looked like monochromatic video games, giving the impression and perception that the war was clean, simple, and administered with absolute precision and confidence. The images were sanitary and palatable to sensitive American audiences whose soldiers were in harm's way. Many would say that since Vietnam, Americans no longer had the stomach for a war perceived as having ambiguous goals with no discernible mark indicating an American victory.

In fact, despite the fact that CNN correspondents Bernard Shaw, Peter Arnett, and John Holliman broadcast live the initial bombing of Iraq, the images from the audience's point of view were rather banal. While no doubt frightful for the reporters as they huddled under desks, donning gas masks, bombs whistling through the air, the raid looked quite measured. This was a perfectly executed war and would stay that way. It would be reported by journalists, who were guided, albeit gingerly, by the Pentagon. The Pentagon established the ground rules for access, and the media accepted them, largely without much protest. It made sense to some. For others, it was just plain wrong. The Washington bureau chiefs of the major television networks and newspapers complained to the administration and called it the "the most undercovered conflict in American history."[73]

The New Yorker's Seymour Hersh appeared on a panel with a number of other national journalists before an audience of First Amendment lawyers, sponsored by the Libel Defense Resource Center in November 2002. He said, "I don't think it's our job to have meetings with them (the Pentagon). We should have complete access, but we don't even begin to think about that. We're so beaten down. We're so cowardly in our profession."[74] Top tier national journalists such as Hersh do not want to be considered partners of any branch of government. The government and the press need each other, but the press regards itself as separate and adversarial by nature.

Bob Simon of CBS News, who appeared on the same panel with Hersh said, "The Washington press corps is complicit. The game that's played in Washington and it's always been played this way is the trade-off of access for patronage. If you agree to sing their song, you'll be invited back for an audience. This is happening to somebody I can think of at CBS. I can think of somebody at NBC, somebody at the *Washington Post*. They go easy on the president and his people, and they keep on getting invited back and getting more access."[75]

The relationship between the executive branch of government and the press had been established for the son (George W.) by the father (George H. W.). A working template was already in place, a successful playbook which President George W. would use to control information and, as well as he could, also the tone and tenor of news coverage. George W. had reminded Americans that Saddam Hussein tried to kill his dad during the time of the Gulf War. Many people who worked with George W. also worked for the senior Bush and, in fact, many of those officials believed Hussein should have been assassinated during the Gulf War when there existed a legitimate reason for doing so.

George Bush, the son, learned from George Bush, the father, and from the presidency of Bill Clinton, who was a master at creating consensus for a policy. The biggest difference, of course, was that George W. was confronted with 9/11. It was a politically altering experience that affirmed there was purpose in the policies. There appeared to be a clear quid pro quo that was unavoidable. People hiding in Afghanistan attacked America. We would go to Afghanistan to avenge those for 9/11. This plan of action seemed completely justifiable.

SEPTEMBER 11, 2001

The event of 9/11 and the "war on terror" put additional pressure and unique restraints on the press. Some pressure and restraint was inherent in the event itself. Some came from an administration seeking to control and gain support for the grand plan yet to come. In any case, there was a profound unease in the country. This unease was reflected in the press, charging it was becoming more difficult to do its work, in part, because of the bunker mentality of the Bush administration.

"Operation Enduring Freedom" was launched on October 7, 2001, in quick response to 9/11. The United States invaded Afghanistan to hunt down Osama bin Laden. Many journalists thought this conflict would be a difficult one to cover and that they would be marginalized. The mission for the United States in Afghanistan was dangerous and difficult. It would be an operation waged in a dangerous political hot spot and in one of the most challenging terrains on earth. It would be unfamiliar for the military, let alone the press.

Bill Delaney, former CNN Boston Bureau chief did two tours of duty in Afghanistan for the network. He claimed that when in the country reporters lived in a sealed, protected camp. Presumably for their own safety, reporters were escorted in and out and only when the army thought there was something interesting for them to report about. Delaney said it was difficult, and in some cases impossible, to set up an enterprising story without being monitored to some degree. He experienced "the awesome beauty of the country," but for the most part, was unable to do the independent work of a correspondent, which meant restrictive and monitored movement about the country, the lack of freedom to cultivate his own sources, and the inability to get to know the people of Afghanistan from whom he could gather cultural information to weave together other angles of an already complicated story.

Other reporters also weighed in as the "war on terror" took shape. Many claimed, in essence, that the press was being stonewalled by an administration that simply did not want to be criticized or scrutinized so that it could have license to operate as it saw fit. The administration claimed it had to protect America by managing what and how it could make information public. The BBC reported that because "special operations troops expected to take a lead role in the conflict, this might be a war fought mostly in secret." Therefore, "George W. Bush will keep tight control of information" as his father did during the Gulf War.[76]

Two days after 9/11 the president said, "Let me condition the press this way: Any sources and methods of intelligence will be guarded in secret. My administration will not talk about how we gather intelligence, if we gather intelligence, and what the intelligence says. That's for the protection of the American people."[77] Defense Secretary Donald Rumsfeld would not comment on anything that could endanger troops or threaten specific missions, but said there would be no organized campaign to throw the press off track. He also said he had not lied to the press in sixty-nine years and would not start. Still, the press was not satisfied. Many believed the Bush administration would sabotage the press's efforts to gather news independently. Many in the press and some in the world of entertainment began to publicly disagree with the way the president was attempting to shame those he thought displayed a lack of patriotism by not supporting administration initiatives. The press was often kept at arm's length with little and, in some cases, no resistance.[78]

Former CBS news anchorman Dan Rather said the news media self-censored out of fear of retribution and that he and his colleagues stopped short of asking both tough and necessary questions. Being a patriot, he claimed, is to take government to task. "It is unpatriotic not to stand up, look them in the eye and ask the questions they don't want to hear . . . they being those who have the responsibility in a society such as ours, of sending our sons and daughters, our husbands, wives, our blood, to face death, to take death."[79] Former talk show host and political activist, Phil Donohue, was more direct in a *New York Times* interview. He said, "We all support the President. I support the President. It doesn't mean I have to keep my mouth shut."[80] Donohue echoed what other public figures were also feeling. They can be supportive of the president and also publicly criticize his decisions about matters as sobering as war and peace.

Bill Maher, the host of the popular satirical television program *Politically Incorrect*, was one who did not keep his mouth shut, and he paid a price. On his popular and highly rated program, after the bombing raid of Afghanistan began, he said that "cowardly" was not the right word to use for suicide bombers, but that it was the right word to use for the United States, who was "lobbing cruise missiles from 2,000 miles away" into Afghanistan. Maher was one who did not agree with America's response to 9/11 in Afghanistan, seeing it as the indiscriminate bombing of a country, instead of targeting the people directly responsible by quietly and secretly using special forces to go in and ferret out the enemy with minimal destruction to property and innocent civilians.

Advertisers deserted the program. Subsequently, some stations across the country independently dropped the program. Later, ABC dropped it entirely from its line-up on network and affiliated stations across the country. But that particular program also received feedback from the White House through Press Secretary Ari Fleischer. His comments were swift and sharp. He scolded Maher saying, "The reminder to all Americans that they need to watch what they say, watch what they do, and that this is not a time for remarks like that."[81] In defense of Maher, *New York Times* op-ed columnist and acerbic critic of the George W. Bush administration, Maureen Dowd, fired back saying she did not need instructions from Ari Fleischer "on the conduct of a good American."[82]

In 2002, *The Boston Globe's* Mark Jurkowitz in an overarching cover story about the current state of dissent in America since 9/11 wrote this for the Sunday magazine: "Protest, contrary viewpoints, and anti-authoritarianism have been reduced to mere whispers in the political wilderness. Those who express unpopular thoughts do so at their own risk. And no one knows how long it will last."[83] Journalists became wary of reporting viewpoints counter to the administration. Pervasive across America seemed to be an eerie restlessness about what to do, what to feel, and how to express it.

Many journalists, however, were debating with each other publicly about the mood in the country and the role of the press. Arguably one of America's most respected journalists, Ted Koppel, of ABC's award-winning *Nightline*, was the moderator of that panel on November 13, 2002, before a group of first amendment attorneys. He told the group, "If I'm running a war and I've got representatives of ABC, NBC, CBS, MSNBC, Al Jazeera, and the BBC, and they're out there with my troops and they've got the technical capacity to feed back what is happening live, so that the folks who are sitting in Baghdad have only to turn on their set to CNN and they can see what's happening on the front lines from the American vantage point, I'm saying it would be criminal to permit that."[84]

The New Yorker's Hersh countered by saying "you have to be absolutely pure about it." Verify information for accuracy and fairness, but report what you learn when you learn it, without control from government. Hersh won a Pulitzer Prize for his coverage of the 1969 My Lai massacre and said, "If you learn about it, publish it." John Kifner of the *New York Times* said journalists should not publish material that could endanger lives, "but I don't think you should go beyond that." Interestingly, the public seems to defend the press in this.[85]

A Pew Survey supports the press in gathering information. It indicated the public does not want a lapdog in the press. Sixty percent said the press is defending democracy. About three-quarters of the respondents said they also want news of America's enemies and over half agreed that reporters should dig hard for information rather than depend on information doled out by the government.[86]

A month after the 9/11 attacks, National Security Advisor Condoleezza Rice requested of executives at CNN, Fox News, CBS, ABC, and NBC not to broadcast unedited tapes from Al Jazeera, the Arab television network that operates in Qatar. At the time, it was receiving videotaped messages from Osama bin Laden during a time when people were speculating about his whereabouts and whether or not he survived the torrent of bombs on Afghanistan. Rice said the tapes could contain "hidden messages" or could serve as propaganda to inflame the disciples of the enemy. News executives relented and agreed that the tapes would be prescreened before broadcast.[87]

There was no edict from the government, nor was there a court order. The news media complied voluntarily. Presumably, for them, it was the right thing to do. Others in the press and some pundits were loath to entertain such requests from the administration and believed the press should have told Rice she was being unreasonable, was overstepping her bounds, and was interfering in their work because government and the press are not partners, but should operate independently of one another.

What did it matter if the American press broadcast tapes from Al Jazeera, the most popular network in the Arab world? The rest of the world, including people in the Middle East, could see Al Jazeera, without the filter of any American news organization. Perhaps the administration was trying to reduce the exposure bin Laden and his disciples were given on television in the United States because it reinforced the reality that he had not been apprehended, and could perhaps translate to an indication of failure in Afghanistan.

Professor Ted Madger of New York University's Department of Culture and Communication was more circumspect, citing the administration's desire to maintain control of bin Laden's image and message to the world as best it could. "They see that reprehensible image, and they feel like they're losing the propaganda war. His image is akin to saying to the world, 'we've lost the battle because we don't have him yet.' It shows he's alive and kicking and they're sitting in the White House saying, 'Jesus Christ, there he is. We can't find him! And there he is!"[88]

The press was encouraged to support and advocate for the Bush administration in a dangerous and precarious global climate, but it may have relented too quickly in abdicating its important role as fourth estate. Immediately following 9/11, most broadcast news organizations, many owned by giant media conglomerates, began to slather superimposed American flags on the screen, which electronically fluttered in the telebreeze.

Anchormen and women donned patriotic colors. American flag lapel pins appeared on the men. Some women wore jeweled flag broaches.

Stand with us because we stand with America seemed to be the message. The tone was encouraged by the Bush administration. The media publicly complied, but there was some division in their ranks. Many journalists challenged their colleagues to take a stand against an administration that appeared to disregard their intended role. Many complained that as a pack they were merely reporting Bush administration spin, which was a business decision as much as it was a patriotic one. This will be discussed later.

As media organizations by and large bolstered the administration's policies by doing very little investigative journalism, CBS's Bob Simon said, "Much of what the administration gives reporters is spin masquerading as information."[89] Eric Alterman of *The Nation* was much more pointed. He had forcefully written that "President Bush is a liar" on many points of policy and chastised the mainstream media for not taking their president to task as he was beginning to introduce Saddam Hussein as an imminent danger, one who had weapons of mass destruction and connections to Osama bin Laden, which signaled some serious implications. Alterman provocatively dared liberal pundits and colleagues such as Michael Kinsley, Paul Krugman, and Richard Cohen to join him in his questioning and criticism of the president, to hold him accountable to the American people for the information he imparted.[90]

The *Washington Post*'s Dana Milbank wrote a story accusing President Bush of "distortions, exaggerations and rhetoric that has taken some flights of fancy." Many reporters said that Milbank was punished for his remarks and singled out, meaning he was refused interviews or not granted access to information he requested as a journalist for the *Post*. Milbank told an interviewer on *National Public Radio* that nothing had really changed, saying "I have exactly as much access as I had when I began, which is to say, not very much at all. This administration does not release information."

Journalists also claimed there was resistance from this Bush administration to release "real news." Ted Koppel said they have little use for analysis that would serve to benefit the public. "They don't want to come on *60 Minutes*. They don't want to come on *Nightline*. They really don't want our formula. They want to take small bite size chunks and put it on CNN and Fox and MSNBC."[91] The point is the Bush administration wanted control of the message, managing the political and military news it would dole out as it was strategically prepared to do so. The press accepted the terms of access and allowed the president and his administration to frame the message without requesting more verification about the quality of information.

If the president was going to "sell" an invasion of Iraq to the American people, it was important, as Bob Simon of CBS said, that the administration could successfully manipulate the public's perception of reality. It had to make the connection between the attacks on 9/11 and

Saddam Hussein and Iraq. Simon pointed to the polls in which 66 percent of Americans believed that Saddam Hussein was somehow linked to 9/11. There was absolutely no evidence that supported the claim, but the American people accepted the president's argument.[92] In fact, as late as 2006, in three separate polls, each conducted by different organizations, there were still a notable percentage of people who said they still believed it. The highest number was 46 percent.[93]

The information the president put forth was deliberate and calculated. He did not simply make a mistake in his assessment of the situation in Iraq. "Everybody makes mistakes when they open their mouths, and we forgive them," Brookings Institution scholar Stephen Hess said. "But what worries me about some of this is they appear to be with foresight. This is about public policy in its grandest sense, about political wars and who is our enemy, and a president has a special obligation to getting it right," said Hess, in the *Washington Post*.[94] The president knew he was not "getting it right" because he needed a compelling reason to finish the work his father stopped short of eleven years prior.

This "war on terror" would be a unique news event to cover. The military would enable the press to be part of the action. The press could cover the news, while the military could protect reporters and television crews and also, at the same time, shape coverage, maintaining both national security and security for the press. The press thought it was maybe getting a fair deal in order to work on the front lines. The embedded press corps was reborn. This was another trumped up level of managed newsgathering. Reporters wanted to be as close to the "news" as possible, so being an embedded journalist may have been perceived as necessary under the circumstances, but it bred dependence and more sympathetic and sometimes unsubstantiated news coverage.

The U.S. government, the Navy, and the Marine Corps administered a program for journalists who were assigned to cover live combat. For most journalists, such training was mandatory before being assigned by their employers to a combat situation. The Defense Department reported that hundreds had signed up for what amounted to boot camp training. This arrangement supposedly serves two purposes. It protects journalists and also the lives of soldiers. However, given this arrangement, a reporter might be less scrutinizing of a particular story about the U.S. military when that very military is protecting his/her life and limb.

Andrew Jacobs, a reporter for the Metro section of the *New York Times*, was one of the embedded journalists and said the Bush administration claimed that the press would be given more access to the war than ever. He wrote, "It would be naïve to think the military isn't expecting a little something in return. Pentagon officials are hoping that the omnipresent television camera crews will beam triumphal clips to living rooms across the country."[95] Another hope, they say, is that American press coverage will serve as a foil to Iraqi propaganda or distorted reportage from the less objective news outlets in the Middle East. "Truth is our best defense," said Jay DeFrank, the Pentagon's director of press operations. "If the war drags on, or civilian and American casualties reach stunning proportions, that spirit of openness could be seriously challenged."[96]

A Pentagon spokesman also said, "There are certain things we are going to be concerned with that will hinder the immediate broadcast of stories. If, during an interview, classified information comes out, we will ask the media not to run it. If they go ahead and run it, that would jeopardize their access in the future." Such a scenario is plausible. A reporter could be interviewing a soldier or a source that inadvertently gives his position away or a clue to some strategy a unit was preparing to employ. There might be a request for that interview to be scrubbed or reshot.[97] Nevertheless, there were concerns about access.

Different conflicts in difficult times call for unusual measures. This is what the administration argued. Because the "war on terror" had unique characteristics, the inclusion of the press on specific missions could be justified or not. At the same time, if it chose to, the administration could pick and choose what it wanted the public to know. In any case, the press needed to be near where the news was being made.

The ombudsman of the *Washington Post*, Michael Getler, said that while there has always been a natural tension between the press and the military in times of war, "the press is about to face the most severe and confounding test of its mission in a free society."[98] Enterprising reporters may have wanted to break news stories and maneuver their way in and out of different and dangerous places, but they ran the risk of jeopardizing any favored network status with the administration and military. They also ran the real risk of inadvertently releasing incorrect or sensitive information and of being killed or seriously injured. In fact, several reporters and photographers were.

Walter Lippmann said the function of *news* is to signal an event. The function of *truth* is to bring to light the hidden facts.[99] The revealing of any truth was simply difficult to accomplish as the first chapter of this tense new national climate, immediately post 9/11, was taking hold. What seemed to be developing was a fear in the collective consciousness of America. The press began to self-censor for fear of retribution from its audience, which ultimately translates later down the consumer food chain to viewers, which attracts advertisers, which brings advertising dollars to the coffers of news organizations and those who manage them. The press was conflicted. Was it a collection of citizens who shared in the grief of their fellow countrymen? Was it a group compelled to do its work on behalf of Americans to learn the truth about what was happening? Could it be both?

While the press was reflecting on its identity during a unique moment in American history, the Bush administration applied the pressure it needed to in order to gather support for its actions and policies. Whether or not the American people were aware, the Iraq war was indisputably on the way, and the Bush administration needed public and political support to effectively execute an impending invasion of the country. This was the moment before any war began when the press should have been more aggressive in its search for information that could have been directly attributed to the Bush administration. Congress should have done the same. Both largely failed in their duty.

In a CNN/*USA Today*/Gallup Poll just weeks before the invasion, 53 percent of those surveyed supported military actions against Iraq, and the president was enjoying a respectable approval rating. "Again and again in interviews last week, Americans told *Time* [magazine] that their faith in Bush is what ultimately overcomes their reservations about his policy in Iraq. They trust that the leader they saw after 9/11 will not mislead them about the dangers that Saddam poses," the cover story reported. Days before the United States invaded Iraq President Bush had a 58-percent approval rating, which steadily increased in the early weeks of the invasion to 71 percent when Americans thought the war was quickly going to end.[100] Americans wanted to believe their president. They needed to believe him, and they ultimately did believe him. The press was reticent to challenge the beliefs of the American people in a time of great vulnerability for the country. The president was creating support for his policies from many constituencies. One of the most important and influential was the press.

Janet Kolodzy, a former print and broadcast journalist, now associate professor of journalism at Emerson College in Boston, said, "A Bulgarian journalist explained to me once that when she worked as a journalist in the country under Communism, she never felt the direct hand of government censorship. She said the government did not intervene in the news because the journalists always knew never to question too much, never to broach certain subjects. Self-censorship was the more powerful force."

This may have been the case for our press after 9/11. The news media may have self-censored out of fear of retribution, out of obligation, and in the interest of business. The press became a supporter of American policy, a promoter of American policy, not so much in what precisely it reported or did not report, but in how stories were presented. There was little challenge to the information and far too little questioning of the people who imparted the information.

THE BUSINESS OF NEWS

Much of the problem seems to be journalists and journalism today. It is not the same business as it was twenty-five years ago or even ten years ago. As seasoned journalists are retiring or dying, they are being replaced, in many cases, by young, overly confident, inexperienced reporters and presenters who believe they are on their way to riches and media stardom. In simple economic terms, those people *initially* cost less to employ. Many, coming from journalism schools, understand well the tools and ethics of their craft, but are not well-versed in crucial academic areas, such as political science, history, civics, economics, and sociology, which provide a base of knowledge for young journalists, who must or should provide context to the issues and the people they cover. Many lack sufficient training or experience in research, digging for accurate information, developing sources, enterprising a story, or sifting through material.

Remember that famous scene in the 1976 feature film *All the President's Men* when the two protagonists Dustin Hoffman and Robert Redford, who portrayed *Washington Post* super reporters Carl Bernstein and Bob Woodward, respectively, were sifting through hundreds of tiny slips of paper at the Library of Congress, looking for a piece of evidence they needed to break the Watergate story? The audience is fixated on the two of them, as they work in silence side by side. The camera pulls back slowly to the very top of that magnificent library dome as the reporters get smaller and the expanse of the space overwhelms them, mirroring the tedious task at hand.

Such an exercise in research does not happen much anymore for several reasons. Consider the immediacy, speed, and ease of information that comes over the Internet. Reporters and researchers can sit at their desks clicking away for electronic materials that can be delivered to their desktops from all corners of the world in an instant. So much information is available with little effort or expense. Also, most journalists today are spoon-fed information and have become accustomed to a new process of accessing information and distributing it.

This is the Wikipedia generation of culling information. They do not have to go anywhere for it because it can instantaneously be found on the web, whether or not completely accurate. This seems to do for a medium that is fleeting in presentation, speed, and style. Newsgathering and fact checking the old-fashioned way seem much more complicated, labor intensive, and expensive.

Also, there is the problem of journalists often reporting what others are reporting, as if quoting them eliminates responsibility if the information passed on is less than perfect. Most depend on information cultivated by the respected standard bearers, the *New York Times*, *Washington Post*, *Wall Street Journal*, and *Associated Press*. On television and cable, some news networks are now inviting the public to participate by submitting stories and opinions of their own. CNN has devoted an entire web page to this practice. "Want to be an iReporter?" it asks. It is a *different* business. And it is a *business*, which has also affected the behavior and intended mission of the press.

Tom Patterson has explored this point. He mentions Walter Cronkite, the father of television news, who was the preeminent anchorman for years on CBS. "The networks now do news as entertainment. [It is] one of the greatest blots on the recent record of television news," Cronkite said. Retired NBC anchorman Tom Brokaw defended the practice, saying the news business had to adjust to "changing news habits" and an intense climate of competitiveness for viewers.[101] Brokaw is realistic in times of great change in communications. Cronkite reflects on the glory days of crusading journalists.

The point is that softer news sells, and with the convergence of print, broadcast television, cable, and now even radio to the Web, there are hundreds of places to turn to for news. Also, the lines that once separated news from entertainment are also converging. They meet. They intersect. They interact. The focus has turned away from hard news to news consumers can use, respond to, and even participate in.

In the case of 9/11, broadcast, cable, and print media could not afford to alienate the audience. This is key. It was too vulnerable a time. It was also a time when everyone was tuning in for information about our safety and our security. The networks told heroic, epic stories, day after day. The news was more than just the news; it was a soap opera in which, in a sense, we all played a role. It was real-life drama, and to reflect that, news programs had special dramatic music written and special titling created, which seemed to herald certain milestones in *our* drama. Many news programs opened with electronically flying graphics with titles such as "America Mourns" and "America Remembers" and "America Fights Back."

The event itself changed the nature of how we regarded the president himself. Days before 9/11 the Gallup Poll indicated an approval rating for President Bush at 51 percent. Just ten days after the attack his approval rating had climbed to 90 percent.[102] Television has a way of transforming political players to bigger than life characters in a drama. The American people could not turn away as the press capitalized on one of the biggest stories in our history. Was it appropriate for the press to challenge a president during a genuine national crisis?

As depicted in the film *All the President's Men*, when reporter Bob Woodward meets "Deep Throat," the informant and his most critical source in a deserted Washington, DC, parking garage in the middle of the night, he tells the eager journalist, "Follow the money" to determine the root of the information he is seeking. Indeed. The same is the case here. The money is what we must also follow to understand modern news coverage, particularly on a story of such magnitude, which was 9/11 as it led us to the Iraq war. The bottom line: Money drives coverage.

Robert McChesney wrote, "Historically, journalism is something that newspapers, magazines, broadcasters and journalism schools regarded as an activity directed toward noncommercial aims that are fundamental to a democracy, aims that could not be bought and sold by powerful interests. Professional journalism was predicated on the notion that its content could not be shaped by the dictates of owners and advertisers, or by the biases of the editors and the reporters, but by core public service values."[103]

Today, news divisions operated by television networks and owned by just a few media conglomerates are compelled to turn profits through advertising and ratings. It is a balancing act for news personnel. It is increasingly unclear as to what is most important: News to serve the public good or what stories will best sell? Economic realities have complicated the relationships between press, people, and those in power.

Media critics Robert McChesney and Ben Bagdikian both have explained the encroachment of corporate interests on journalism. McChesney says we have "bid farewell to journalism." Bagdikian explains that the walls once used to protect the profession of journalism have crumbled away. Both agree the changes have been mandated from the corporate level and are now "systemic" and have impacted journalism at the "institutional level," the very point at which they impact viewers and readers.

One reason is that seasoned journalists, people who have been around the block and around for years, are now elites in terms of salary and position at the networks and on the staffs of prestigious and influential magazines and newspapers. They socialize with those they also will cover. One high-profile professional couple was the late Katherine Graham and Ben Bradley, a celebrity publisher and editor, respectively, of the *Washington Post*. They dined with presidents and kings. Today these kinds of people in the media are more prevalent because corporations now own most of our news and media organizations. In a fast changing landscape where news and entertainment are often indistinguishable, they have become high-profit-margin businesses.

McChesney discussed James Fallows, the author of *Breaking the News*. Fallows, he says, "chronicles in depressing detail the superstars of journalism." They are "those who do fairly mindless TV shows, give lectures for exorbitant fees, and generally earn annual incomes approaching seven figures."[104] They are obliged to contribute to their companies in unconventional ways. An example is Wolf Blitzer of CNN. Today he hosts his own show, assorted special programming, presidential debates, and he writes a "blog," which is a kind of online diary about his work. He boasts that it is one of the most read blogs on the Internet. Blitzer promotes his blog on television where there are viewers and advertisers. When those viewers and advertisers go to the blog, there are more ads for all those readers. The cross promotion is a bonus. These high-priced journalists are reticent to bite the corporate hand that provides such a handsome, privileged way of life and so much exposure.

Journalist and academic Richard Reeves defined "real news" as what "you and I need to keep our freedom—accurate and timely information on laws and wars, police and politicians, taxes and toxics." Reeves said good journalism is often regarded as bad business by media moguls, who are responsible for making the businesses they own and operate profitable.[105]

Those who rule the media world are businesspeople at the top. They have rewarded and recruited loyal journalist foot soldiers in newsrooms, who were once middle managers, editors, and executive producers, at the precipice of making a decent living and having some real influence. Many were promoted, but at a price. Bagdikian says it best: "Because the country's top editors are being integrated into the managerial imperatives of the corporations, journalists through their editor become less responsible for the integrity of the news and more for the profitability of the whole enterprise. That is not journalism. It is advertising and marketing."[106]

Janet Kolodzy also agrees that the American news media has been marginalized. She expands on the point where business and power meet saying, "The irony of the last decade of globalization of economies and technologies is the isolationism of the American news media. In the international arena, the mainstream media in the United States has delegated its decision making to the government, allowing the Bush administration to determine the parts of the world outside U.S. borders the American public needs to know about."

For news about our foreign policy, we are dependent on the president. This has always been the case. However, precisely because of globalization, a shrinking planet, and the proverbial global village, media outlets should be expanding foreign news coverage and opening more bureaus in other countries, not shrinking coverage and closing down foreign news bureaus. Journalists should help define more of the world and America's role in it for the American people by being there for them, a proxy witness to events, history, and culture, but foreign news is expensive to cover. Journalists also must participate in providing solutions for the problems of shrinking circulation and audiences and falling revenue so that the coverage of important news stories will not be compromised.

The story of 9/11 and what the United States did about it was both a domestic and international news story, which addressed our evolving foreign policy. Bernard Cohen reinforced the point by saying what the president mandates in that arena can only be reported to the people through the lens and pen of the journalist. Cohen wrote that for the foreign policy audience, their operational map of the world is drawn by reporter and editor.[107] The American public knows about its foreign policy through the president and his proxies, who communicate through journalists. Journalists must rely on those in power for their stories about America's behavior abroad and its foreign policy. Government officials such as the president and his cabinet assign importance, gravitas, substance, and flavor to these stories for the benefit of the journalist, and the journalist must "behave appropriately" to be given access to information, particular interviews, and the pictures they need for television. They should also be reporting directly from the countries the president and our country do business with, although that is happening less and less for economic reasons. Foreign press coverage is just too expensive, so foreign bureaus have closed down or operate with skeleton crews. However, in any case, if a journalist has ascended to a certain status and has become an elite member of the press, he or she may question less the integrity of the information and source of information.

Many interests in journalism were colliding during the time of 9/11. There was a team of elites from the top networks, magazines, and newspapers covering the story. There was also a team of younger reporters, writers, and producers. All work in corporate environments, organizations that must turn profits in order to survive. They must serve a corporate master. They must serve a viewing public. They must also serve and satisfy the newsmaker in order to have access to the news, which is the product they all sell. Gone is any healthy, ethical distance between the press and those they cover because they need each other. The newsmaker needs to get their message out to the journalists who will make it news. They sell it to the public who "buys" the news by watching, listening, and clicking on their computers. The audience, in turn, is being exposed to the advertisers who pay for space to keep those media organizations in business. In short, this is commerce.

New York Times reporter Andrew Jacobs remembers the last Gulf War when reporters were confined to hotels and hand-fed breathless military updates. "If this Iraq war comes to pass," he said before the invasion, it "will provide correspondents with unprecedented access to the troops and the front line" as promised by the Defense Department. He called it old-fashioned public relations as he and others are "marching commiserating and drinking with the Marines." All of it, he said, had made "for warm and fuzzy feelings on both sides, joy rides and show-and-tell sessions" about the latest war toys.[108]

Kyra Phillips was CNN's correspondent at Fort Bragg, North Carolina, covering Special Forces training just before the Iraq war. She was conducting an interview that was being fed via satellite to Atlanta, but there was something about the interview that the viewer would never see. Routinely, satellite transmissions such as this one can linger for minutes afterwards. In other words, anyone that has the technology, in this case anyone with a "downlink," can see what is up on "the bird," which is what those who work in television call a satellite. According to a producer, at the conclusion of her interview with a military spokesman, Phillips embraced him, presumably in gratitude for his interview and information. The producer grimaced and called Phillips's behavior "shameful." It is inappropriate for a journalist to be embracing sources, in reality or figuratively. In order to be as objective as possible, journalists should keep a professional distance. Today professional distance may no longer be as much of an advantage as journalists clamor for a story and an audience. They want their audience to believe they are closer to their sources. It is a folksier way to present news. It is a way to demonstrate that they have stories their competition may not.

Soon after 9/11, former CNN international correspondent Amanda Kibel had been in Kandahar, Afghanistan, cultivating good relationships with some remote tribal leaders. After many months, her time with these important contacts paid off. They agreed to take her thirty miles outside of Kandahar to an abandoned house stashed with a cache of weapons and artillery covering every inch of the place, "from floor to ceiling," she described. This was the house, they told her, where Osama bin Laden had been hiding before the Americans started bombing the country and from where he fled and vanished deep in the difficult mountain terrain on the border of Pakistan and Afghanistan. She and her crew were then taken to a group of mountain caves with a connecting system of tunnels, all loaded with more weaponry.

Clearly, Kibel said, the Northern Alliance was preparing for war. She reported back to base at CNN headquarters that she would have a series of valuable stories for air, but as she was carefully preparing her reports, CNN ordered quick live shots from the area with a "marquee reporter," a reporter better known to the viewing audience, but who had not been on the scene as long as she.

These "live shots" serve the immediacy of television as they herald a single news event, but do not provide enough explanation, context, or depth of information. Also, the story itself could have been much better told. Instead, the story itself was diminished, and by a reporter who knew less about the detail and intricacies of an important development but was better known. In this case the reporter was Bill Hemmer, who was popular and a more familiar face at the time to CNN viewers.

By the time Kibel was ready for air, CNN had decided the live truck could be better used to transmit the holiday greetings of soldiers back home. Kibel's story would eventually air, but late and lacking stature, having yielded to the business decisions of the network. Holiday greetings from the troops, courtesy of CNN, were a good business and public relations decision. Not only would CNN bring you the news of the war, it would be a part of the war effort, and it would include one of CNN's rising stars. This dangerous mix of press and the people they cover makes for a less informed, blindsided electorate. No one is better served under these conditions.

CBS newsman Marvin Kalb commented in a *Washington Post* column, "Journalists perform the highest act of patriotism and operate on the highest levels of professionalism when they subject all government hand-

outs and pronouncements to the sunlight of honest and truthful inquiry
and then fearlessly report the results. That is their job in times of peace
and war."[109] In the time between 9/11 and the start of the Iraq War, this
did not happen. Two crucial variables complicated Kalb's ideal for the
way journalists should work.

One was the fear factor in the American people, which the press was
hesitant to confront. The invasion of Iraq became more of a certainty
because the press failed to ask some important questions between 9/11
and the beginning of the Iraq war, the time period in which President
Bush was justifying to the American people his case for an invasion. The
news media was being controlled and used to sustain a certain degree of
fear in the populace, which was an invaluable tool for the Bush administration. In turn, information the American public received was specifically and strategically doled out. The president's policies and politics depended on it.

This situation subsequently changed for the press as the war dragged
on. The president's popularity faded. No weapons of mass destruction
had turned up. The story about a purchase of uranium in Africa was
debunked. Osama bin Laden was still on the loose, and slowly people in
and out of the administration, those who previously might have been
reticent sources on stories, began to speak out. Eventually, the press became more ambitious in its reporting.

The second reality that journalists have had to confront is the new
reality of capitalism, which has impacted negatively the world of responsible journalism. Like never before, news divisions are pressured to generate profits. There is pressure to contribute to the bottom line. Why?

In this new information age with an audience that has a diminished
attention span and hundreds of channels to choose from, plus the Internet, which now incorporates traditional media into digital form available
whenever the consumer wants it, television, newspapers, magazines, and
radio stations can ill afford to lose readers and viewers. The pressure to
help generate profits has resulted in compromising the integrity of the
product. This impacts story choice, story construction, and presentation.

For television, it has resulted in more grand, bold set designs, graphic
images, and information that both crawls across the bottom of the screen
and flies across it simultaneously; electronic gadgets used by people on
the set and in the field and lively, attractive personalities on the air rather
than seasoned reporters. All this is designed to attract viewers, who are
accustomed to information that is delivered in bite-size pieces, in the least
amount of time, and packaged more as entertainment. The news is interactive, opinionated, engaging, and in times of crisis, it is compelled to
support the country and the political choices it makes. In times of real
news events, the media have an opportunity to win over audiences, who
they hope will become loyal, lasting viewers and readers.

President Bush devised a case for the invasion of Iraq under false pretense, consciously employing the unique political circumstances for the country after 9/11. It was a case built with a weakened press that had already been compromised by economic forces as it regards its product, the news, as commodity simply to be bought and sold. Under this umbrella and as we will see, the Bush administration transformed its foreign policy and constructed a believable argument for the ouster of Iraqi President Saddam Hussein.

President Bush took a page from journalist and political commentator Walter Lippmann and began the business of "manufacturing consent" for his plan. It is what linguist, media critic, and political activist Noam Chomsky calls "thought control." The notion of "thought control" seems sinister on its face, and akin to propaganda, but we now know there was deliberation in the president's efforts to bring forces that often operate at opposing poles to the same conclusion.

The following chapters will demonstrate how this convergence of interests was funneled toward a common goal and grand plan. They will also later reveal why the media began to attack the president and his war. The news media gradually began to realize they were duped into helping to sell a war to the American people.

NOTES

1. Russell, Bertrand. *Unpopular Essays* (New York: Routledge, 2009), 106. Printed with permission from The Bertrand Russell Peace Foundation Ltd. and the Publishers Taylor and Francis.

2. Kuypers, Jim A. *Bush's War* (Lanham, MD: Rowman & Littlefield Publishers, Inc., 2006), 18.

3. Official White House transcript, January 29, 2002.

4. Schlesinger, Arthur M. *War and the American Presidency* (New York: W. W. Norton & Company, 2004), 33.

5. Patterson, Thomas E. *The Vanishing Voter* (New York: Vintage Books, 2003), 65.

6. Schlesinger, Arthur M. *War and the American Presidency* (New York: W. W. Norton & Company, 2004), 33.

7. Official testimony, U.S. Supreme Court Justice Louis Brandeis before the U.S. Commission on Industrial Relations, 1915.

8. The Gallup Cumulative Index, Public Opinion, 2001, pg. 48.

9. President Bush Approval Rating, *The Washington Post*, February 2, 2006.

10. BBC News Special Reports, Bush Approval Rating Tracker, January 20, 2001–October 22, 2005.

11. Official White House transcript, President Bush to the Yale graduating class, May 21, 2001.

12. *Newsweek* cover story, September 10, 2001 issue.

13. *Time* cover story, September 10, 2001 issue.

14. "Ask the White House," Online Interactive Forum with White House Chief of Staff, Andrew Card, April 16, 2003.

15. Ibid.

16. *The 9/11 Commission Report*, manufacturing by RR Donnelly, Harrisburg VA/Crawforsdville IN, July 2004, pg. 55.

17. *The Associated Press*, June 23, 2004, Sarasota, FL.

18. The Gallup Poll (with CNN/*USA Today*), Public Opinion, 2001, pg. 216.

19. Official White House transcript, September 11, 2001.

20. Ibid.

21. Ibid.

22. Kuypers, Jim A. *Bush's War*. Lanham, MD (Rowman & Littlefield Publishers, Inc., 2006), 19.

23. Rosenberg, Howard. "A New Kind of War of Words," *The Los Angeles Times*, September 26, 2001.

24. *The Associated Press*, Grants Pass, Oregon, September 21, 2001.

25. Fluker, Krys. "Columnists Fired for Criticism." *Masthead*, National Conference of Editorial Writers, Winter 2001.

26. Dowd, Maureen. "Liberties: We Love the Liberties They Hate," *New York Times*, September 30, 2001.

27. The Gallup Poll (with CNN/*USA Today*), Public Opinion, 2001, pg. 226.

28. Blumenthal, Sydney. "Journalism and its Discontents," *Salon*, October 25, 2007.

29. Schlesinger, Arthur M. *War and the American Presidency* (New York: W. W. Norton & Company, 2004), 69.

30. Ibid.

31. McClellan, Scott. *What Happened* (New York: PublicAffairs, 2008), 125.

32. Stelter, Brian. "Was Press a War 'Enabler'?," *New York Times*, May 30, 2008.

33. Ibid.

34. Ibid.

35. *Bill Moyer's Journal*, "Buying the War," PBS, April 25, 2007.

36. Rosen, Ruth. "The Day Ashcroft Censored Freedom of Information," *San Francisco Chronicle*, January 7, 2002.

37. Ashcroft, John, Attorney General, Department of Justice, Freedom of Information Act, October 12, 2001.

38. Ibid.

39. Strossen, Nadine, ACLU President, Forum on National Security and the Constitution, January 24, 2002.

40. Testimony before the Senate Judiciary Committee, "America after 9/11: Freedom Preserved or Freedom Lost?" January 18, 2003.

41. Klein, Edward. "We're Not Destroying Rights, We're Protecting," *Parade Magazine*, May 19, 2002.

42. Ibid.

43. Ibid.

44. Schlesinger, Arthur M. *War and the American Presidency* (New York: W. W. Norton & Company, 2004), 69.

45. Greenhouse, Linda. "Ideas & Trends: Executive Decisions; A Penchant for Secrecy," *New York Times*, May 5, 2002.

46. Schlesinger, Arthur M. *War and the American Presidency* (New York: W. W. Norton & Company, 2004), 69.

47. Weinstein, Henry, Daren Briscoe, and Mitchell Landsberg. "Civil Liberties Take Back Seat to Safety," *The Los Angeles Times*, March 10, 2002.

48. The Emma Goldman Papers Project at University of California at Berkeley.

49. Weich, Ronald. "Insatiable Appetite: The Government's Demand for New & Unnecessary Powers After September 11," April 2002, The American Civil Liberties Union, Washington, DC, legislative office.

50. Rosenberg, Howard. "A New Kind of War of Words," *The Los Angeles Times*, September 26, 2001.

51. Cronkite, Walter. *A Reporter's Life* (New York: Alfred A. Knopf, 1996), 268.

52. Hallin, Daniel C. *The "Uncensored War": The Media and Vietnam* (New York: Oxford University Press, 1986), 213.

53. Braestrup, Peter. *The Big Story: How the American Press Covered and Interpreted the Crisis of Tet in Vietnam and Washington* (New Haven: Yale University Press, 1983), 506.

54. The Gallup Cumulative Index, Public Opinion, 1967 and 1968, pgs. 2074, 2099, 2105, 2114, 2115.

55. Braestrup, Peter. *The Big Story: How the American Press Covered and Interpreted the Crisis of Tet in Vietnam and Washington* (New Haven: Yale University Press, 1983), 506.

56. The Museum of Broadcast Communications Archives, Vietnam on Television, Chicago, Illinois.

57. The Gallup Cumulative Index, Public Opinion, 1935–1971, pg. 2105.

58. *Chicago Tribune* Editorial, February 11, 1991.

59. Braestrup, Peter. *The Big Story: How the American Press Covered and Interpreted the Crisis of Tet in Vietnam and Washington* (New Haven: Yale University Press, 1983), 9–10.

60. Ibid., 7–8.

61. Ibid., 524–25.

62. The Gallup Cumulative Index, Public Opinion, 1935–1971, pg. 2105.

63. Braestrup, Peter. *The Big Story: How the American Press Covered and Interpreted the Crisis of Tet in Vietnam and Washington* (New Haven: Yale University Press, 1983), 49.

64. Ibid.

65. Official transcript, the CBS *Evening News* with Walter Cronkite, February 28, 1968.

66. The Museum of Broadcast Communications Archives, Vietnam on Television, Chicago, Illinois.

67. Shafer, Jack. "The Master of Debunk," *Slate Magazine*, May 21, 2010.

68. Pyle, Richard. "From Tonkin Gulf to Persian Gulf," CNN, special reports archives.

69. Lindsay, Daryl. "My Only Regret," *Salon*, April 28, 2000.

70. *The New York Times*, June 30, 1971.

71. BBC News, May 16, 2002.

72. The Gallup Cumulative Index, Public Opinion, 1991, 1992, pgs. 6, 10, 207.

73. Libel Defense Resource Center Forum, official transcript, November 2002.

74. Ibid.

75. Ibid.

76. BBC News, May 16, 2002.

77. BBC News, September 26, 2001.

78. Ibid.

79. BBC News, May 16, 2002.

80. Wallis, David. "The Way We Live Now," *The New York Times*, April 14, 2002.

81. Tapper, Jake. "White House Whitewashers," *Salon*, September 27, 2001.

82. Dowd, Maureen. "Liberties: We Love the Liberties They Hate," *The New York Times*, September 30, 2001.

83. Jurkowitz, Mark. "The Big Chill," *Boston Globe*, Sunday Magazine, January 27, 2002, pg. 10.

84. Official transcript, Libel Resource Center, November 2002.

85. Ibid.

86. Schlesinger, Arthur M. *War and the American Presidency* (New York: W. W. Norton & Company), 69.

87. Rayner, Jay. "How Much Can We Believe in the News Campaign?" *The Observer*, October 14, 2001.

88. McDonald, Gayle. "Media Fear Censorship as Bush Requests Caution," *Toronto Globe & Mail*, October 11, 2001.

89. Official transcript, Libel Defense Resource Center, November 2002.

90. Alterman, Eric. "Bush Lies, Media Swallows," *The Nation*, November 2002 issue.

91. Libel Defense Resource Center Forum, official transcript, November 2002.

92. Ibid.

93. Angus-Reid Public Opinion Polls.

94. Leiby, Richard. "Fighting Words," *Washington Post*, October 21, 2002.

95. Jacobs, Andrew. "My Weekend at Embedded Boot Camp," *New York Times*, March 2, 2003.

96. Ibid.

97. Cotts, Cynthia. "Smoke Signals," *Village Voice*, November 19, 2002.

98. Getler, Michael. "The Pentagon and the Press Again," Organization of News Ombudsmen, September 23, 2001.

99. Lippmann, Walter. *Public Opinion* (New York: Macmillan, 1949), 226.

100. The Gallup Cumulative Index, Public Opinion, (with CNN and *USA Today*), 2001, pg. 139.

101. Patterson, Thomas E. *The Vanishing Voter* (New York: Vintage Books, 2003), 77.

102. The Gallup Cumulative Index, Public Opinion, (with CNN and *USA Today*), 2001, pg. 139.

103. McChesney, Robert W. *Rich Media, Poor Democracy: Communication in Dubious Times* (New York: New Press, 2003), 49.

104. Ibid.

105. Reeves, Richard. *What the People Know: Freedom and the Press* (Cambridge, MA: Harvard University Press, 1998), 118.

106. Bagdikian, Ben. *The New Media Monopoly* (Boston: Beacon Press, 2004), 233.

107. Cohen, Bernard Cecil. *The Press & Foreign Policy* (Princeton: Princeton University Press, 1963), 13.

108. Jacobs, Andrew. "My Week at Embedded Boot Camp," *New York Times*, March 2, 2003.

109. Kalb, Marvin. "Whose Side Are We On," *Washington Post*, October 11, 2001.

TWO

The George W. Bush Administration

The Case for War with Iraq

None of us begins to understand the consequences, but it is no daring prophecy to say that the knowledge of how to create consent will alter every political calculation and modify every political premise.

It has been demonstrated that we cannot rely upon intuition, conscience, or the accidents of public opinion if we are to deal with the world beyond our reach.

—Walter Lippmann

INTRODUCTION

The case for war with Iraq and its President Saddam Hussein was based on three assertions. They were mentioned earlier, but bear repeating: 1) Iraq was affiliated with Osama bin Laden, the chief architect of the 9/11 attacks, and his terrorist network, al Qaeda. Saddam, therefore, also bore some responsibility for the attacks; 2) Saddam Hussein was stockpiling weapons of mass destruction (WMD), nuclear, biological, and chemical weaponry or the materials to produce them, which he was plotting to someday use against the United States and/or its interests abroad; and 3) Iraq had purchased uranium from the African nation of Niger and was also procuring aluminum tubes from which could and likely would be constituted a nuclear weapon. These were the premises for war, charges on which President Bush made his case to other nations, the Congress, the American people, and the news media for the invasion of Iraq.

Not a single one of these claims was true. The president of the United States said he built a case for war on some compelling (select) intelligence reports. Even if those reports seemed credible immediately after 9/11, the fact is he learned over time, between October 2001 and March 2003 that a case for war against Iraq would not, ultimately, be prudent. Evidence was emerging, compelling enough, which not only challenged the intelligence he relied on, but instead supported a responsible, restrained change of course regarding Iraq. This was especially the case from November 2002 to March 2003 when weapons inspectors resumed their work in Iraq searching for weapons of mass destruction, ultimately finding no hard evidence of a viable weapons program. They reported so. The evidence does demonstrate that the President understood his case for war against Iraq was eroding over time, but chose to launch the war anyway.

Also, information the president had used during a key State of the Union address in January 2003 was embarrassingly discredited three months later on March 7, 2003. The president claimed he had proof Iraq was attempting to purchase uranium from Niger. However, director general of the International Atomic Energy Agency (IAEA), Mohamed ElBaradei, during his testimony to the U.N. Security Council, testified the documents to which the president so pointedly referred were "not authentic" and that the allegations of such a transaction were "unfounded."[1]

He also testified that the IAEA had conducted 218 nuclear inspections at 141 sites, including military garrisons and camps, weapons factories, truck parks, manufacturing facilities and residential areas. There was no indication of "nuclear-related prohibited activities at any inspected site," and after three months of "intrusive inspections" there was "no evidence of or plausible indication of the revival of a nuclear program in Iraq. Inspections in Iraq are moving forward, he said, and Iraq had been forthcoming in its cooperation.[2] Iraq may have been a threat in years past, but it clearly was no threat any longer.

The president and his staff claimed they had proceeded with careful deliberation against Iraq, which in essence dismissed the claims made by the IAEA and ElBaradei. Secretary of State Colin Powell appeared on NBC's *Meet the Press* two days after ElBaradei's testimony and said the information he pointed to before the U.N. Security Council in February 2003 "was provided in good faith" and if the IAEA turned out to be right, then "fine." This would not prohibit or alter in any way the administration's plans. The administration asserted that in the future it would someday be vindicated, that the WMD it was looking for in Iraq would be discovered and revealed for the world to see.

Key members of the Bush administration and the president himself have since admitted they were wrong about all those premises for war and have blamed those egregious errors on intelligence gathering and, therefore, squarely on the intelligence community. This is in sharp contrast to what many in the intelligence community claim is true. But before the attacks of 9/11, the Bush administration understood the real and imminent threat of Osama bin Laden and al Qaeda from the intelligence community it would later repudiate and ignored those warnings. After 9/11 it relied on information that was not reliable. That continued to be the case after the U.S. attack on Afghanistan in response to 9/11, as U.S. forces hunted for Osama bin Laden and in all the days and months weapons inspectors searched for WMD in Iraq up until the day of the invasion.

Many in the intelligence community and others have since gone on the record saying the president and his staff were amply warned that the intelligence they were provided was sketchy, inconclusive, and suspect, at best, and did not meet the threshold for war. According to James Bamford, one C.I.A. caseworker told him, "We had bits and pieces of things, but nothing to indicate there was this massive active program."[3] Another case officer reported that there was no evidence of WMD in Iraq.[4] The president and his administration, they said, understood the facts as they emerged in the eighteen-month run-up to the Iraq war. Those facts were disregarded and supplanted at times with other information.

Twice in September 2002 the president told reporters at Camp David and in his national weekly radio address that there was startling new evidence from the IAEA that Iraq was six months away from developing a nuclear weapon. The report he referred to was from 1996 and the program the president was describing had long been terminated. U.N. weapons inspector Hans Blix said this: "I think they had a mind set. They wanted to come to the conclusion that there were weapons. Like the former days of the witch-hunt, they are convinced that they exist. It was a reaction to 9/11 that we have to strike some theoretical, hypothetical links between Saddam Hussein and the terrorists. The Americans needed [Iraq to have] WMD to justify the Iraq War."[5]

The record shows that the president and his administration spoke publicly about Iraq with great conviction, while behind the scenes were appraised of a different emerging truth. There was ample evidence, serious enough and powerful enough available to the president, his staff, and officials high up in the intelligence community, for the president and his administration to approach the problem of Iraq differently. The evidence culled over many months and years, some of it even before 9/11, should have provided sufficient insight for the president to back off any invasion at all. A different reality had been illuminated. What was the end result? We were misguided into a war that could have been avoided.

Stephen Graubard asked how the White House became the chief purveyor of myth and falsehood and why the president wasn't controlled by Congress or the huge bureaucracy that, in theory, existed to instruct him.[6] "There had been a massive display of presidential ignorance and arrogance, and a failure of intelligence at every level. Never in the long twentieth century had so fundamental a foreign policy error been made and rarely had so much been promised and so little achieved."[7]

The failure of the intelligence community was, in part, due to its inability, for whatever reason, to speak truth to power or to go to the press with information about the pressure it was under to find intelligence to fit the policy and the case for war. One agent at the C.I.A. said his boss told about fifty of them gathered for a meeting, "If President Bush wants to go to war, ladies and gentlemen, your job's to give him a reason to do so."[8] During testimony to Congress, former C.I.A. Counterterrorism Chief, Vince Cannistraro, said the agency was under "unprecedented pressure" and that the vice president himself had come to the agency pressing analysts to "provide support" for the administration's claims of WMD.[9]

Larry Wilkerson, a retired Army colonel, and Secretary of State Colin Powell's chief-of-staff, broke ranks with the administration when Powell resigned at the end of Bush's first term in office. He told the *Washington Post* in 2006: "This is a radical administration. This is a very inept administration. I think this is probably the worst ineptitude in governance, decision-making, and leadership I've seen in fifty-plus years. You've got to go back and think about that. That includes the Bay of Pigs, that includes—oh my God, Vietnam. That includes Iran-Contra, Watergate."[10]

To this day, the Iraq war has left serious, lasting repercussions. Thousands of lives were lost and are still being lost. Foreign policy decisions were poorly developed, poorly timed, poorly executed, and ultimately ill fated. The reputation of the United States was tarnished. In sum, our ferocious aggression against Iraq was unnecessary and unwarranted. It was a war President Bush could have and should have prevented based on a thorough collection of information and intelligence gathered before the attacks of 9/11and in the eighteen months following.

This chapter will address three areas. The first is the building of support for a public policy. For a president of the United States and his staff this is standard operating procedure. How did this president and his staff orchestrate a campaign for an invasion of Iraq that would convince Congress and the news media that it was the right and best course of action for the country and for the countries of the world that subsequently would be affected by the behavior and policy of the United States?

Second, what also must be examined are the public statements made over eighteen months after 9/11 by President Bush and by those surrogates who were, in essence, deputized by the president to help him argue the case for an invasion of Iraq. Rhetoric, carefully crafted and subsequently employed to build consent for this foreign policy initiative and any political initiative, is important. Both the tone and the tenor of rhetoric, which emanates from the White House, matters. "Language is an improbably powerful thing. It's just words, after all, in a world full of noise. But certain combinations of words can move mountains and change lives."[11] Words, language, and behavior are emblematic. In this case, the words and language helped build consent for a war that was portrayed as justified, even though our nemesis in the resulting chaos and tragedy of 9/11, the elusive bin Laden, remained at large.

Third, there is the evidence, which suggested that putting a spotlight on Iraq after 9/11 was a misguided policy from the start and the administration knew it. People in the intelligence community from in and outside the White House have gone on record about their experiences with the Bush administration. Also, there are public records from the 9/11 Commission, to reports from the United Nations weapons inspectors, from others on special task forces and committees, who knew that for our leaders to move against Iraq was hubris, not sound judgment based on information that was reliable.

THE BUILDING OF CONSENT

Linguist Noam Chomsky says the "manufacture of consent" is an "Orwellian euphemism for thought control." He wrote, "Democracy permits the voice of the people to be heard, and it is the task of the intellectual to ensure that this voice endorses what leaders perceive to be the right course."[12] The invasion of Iraq and the overthrow of its leader, Saddam Hussein, happened because the George W. Bush administration ultimately was successful at convincing the Congress, the media, and the American people that it was the right and best course of action. In short, the case for war and for overthrowing a dictator was believable. Their skill at persuasion and a carefully crafted rhetoric proved to be strong and influential. Their success at building consent was even more convincing, perhaps because it came during a time of great turmoil, uncertainty, and vulnerability for Americans.

"Clearly, the national trauma inflicted by the attacks and Bush's response to the crisis radically altered the president's standing with the American people. Bush enjoyed the longest stretch of approval ratings above 60 percent of any president in forty years. Approval ratings shot up from the 50s to the highest levels ever recorded, topping 90 percent in some September and October polls."[13]

In comparison, President Franklin D. Roosevelt had an approval rating of 84 percent after the bombing of Pearl Harbor by the Japanese.[14] However, "not even the Japanese attack on Pearl Harbor in December 1941 had produced such an outpouring of support for the commander-in-chief, a president suddenly rendered invulnerable to all criticism. Bush became the hero of the nation, with few in Congress and the media prepared to question his policies."[15] The president, by virtue of a serendipitous national calamity, had inherited the political capital to act. The people of the United States were frightened. They were unfamiliar and uncomfortable with an enemy that became known to them through the news media. They understood those enemies as sinister, dark, mysterious, and lethal, who operated in a world that ordinary people could never fully comprehend. It was our leaders who could explain and make sense of it all for the rest of us.

Chomsky said that at times like this, in order for governments to act, they must "create a cloak of mystery around power. You make it look mysterious and secret above the ordinary person." People accept what governments say "out of fear that some great enemies are about to destroy them, and because of that, they'll cede their power to the president, just to protect themselves—that's the way any system of power works."[16]

It was not without precedent that President Bush built consent for war using the media as a vehicle by which to publicly dispense some of the information the administration was gathering, to explain its motives going forward, and to characterize the problems facing the people and our country after 9/11. Our president said he wanted to protect the country and her people from further harm after 9/11. He asked the people to believe and trust him. The people needed and wanted to believe and trust their president.

These types of appeals to the people from the leader of their country are not unusual. The act of building consent or building a credible case for particular programs or policies that presidents and their administrations believe are right for America is, for the most part, standard operating procedure. Many would argue it is a helpful tool for governing. Many also argue it is a necessary skill for political candidates to garner votes. In fact, the building of consent is precisely how they get elected to public office. It is a request for a vote of confidence, an appeal for belief in the candidate.

In the case of a president and key members of his administration, if they can skillfully explain and justify a policy or course of action directly to members of Congress, to the American people, and to the news media, it follows that policies may be more readily adopted or accepted. A supportive Congress, a public whose thinking has been carefully directed, and favorable media coverage, all operating in concert, increase the odds for bringing successful results for a president who wants his policies effectively implemented. A president may be considered politically agile and skillful if he can steer his policies through the intricate maize of politics and entrenched interests. This is one way he can demonstrate his leadership abilities. It gives credence to a president who says he can and will get things done. The success of programs and policies "on his watch" will both define and characterize his tenure as chief executive and commander in chief and will contribute (or not) to his legacy as will be undoubtedly later evaluated by historians, political scientists, and journalists.

The building of consent can be the fine art of persuasion, a political adeptness that may amalgamate forces, sometimes involving those who may previously have been at odds. The goal is to bring people to a singular understanding of a complex situation, to identify clearly the world vision of their leader, and to, ultimately, derive one conclusion, the only conclusion that makes the most sense. The building of consent is employed to move people and, in this case, a country in one direction with political expeditiousness. How do powerful, influential people, such as the president of the United States go about the business of building consent and support for an initiative? One method is to construct mental pictures of reality for people, who cannot or do not understand it for themselves.

Walter Lippmann, one of the most influential journalists of the twentieth century, wrote about the "pictures in our heads" which are "based not on direct and certain knowledge" but on pictures we create for ourselves or are created for us by others, which we also choose (or not) to believe.[17] Those "pictures" are convincing and based on someone else's reality or understanding of an event or chain of events, which either could be based in fact, an altered reality of the truth, or a version of the truth. In essence, people believe what they choose to believe. In some cases, people are brought along to arrive at a version of the truth or what is being offered to them as the truth.

An appropriate analogy comes from the Greek philosopher Plato and "The Allegory of the Cave." In this story, a group of people is chained together in a cave. They are situated so that they can only sit with their backs to the cave entrance where the light from behind them streams in. The only "reality" the people can experience are the shadows on the wall before them as projected from the light of the cave opening behind them. Their "reality" is a false reality because they experience only the shadows projected by the real world, which is beyond their ability to see for themselves. If they were able to turn toward the light and look out of the cave opening, they would be able to experience the real world firsthand. They would "see" differently because they would see for themselves. They would be (self) enlightened.[18]

In much the same way, Americans can only understand certain facets of politics and, necessarily, foreign policy through someone else's reality or interpretation of it. They cannot be there to experience and interpret that kind of information firsthand, for themselves, so they must depend on others, such as the president, members of his cabinet, members of Congress, and the news media to draw those so-called "pictures in our heads," according to Lippmann. "The world looks different to different people, depending not only on their own personal interests, but also on the map drawn for them by the writers, editors, and publishers of the papers they read" the radio they listen to, the television they watch, and the web sites they visit.[19] Information, particularly about foreign policy, comes to us through a series of filters, and we can only hope that the filters sustain the integrity of the information—that it is as accurate and as truthful as possible, beginning with the source of the information.

But this can also present problems. People in power can color the information, "spin it" to suit their own political visions of the world, and may use the media to that end. The public can only obtain certain knowledge through their leaders. Those leaders interpret what they impart and often explain by "framing" the information in a particular light, often with a particular bent. That information is, in turn, framed or reframed accordingly by the news media that relies on those in power for its very economic survival. At the very least, it is an interesting relationship. It can also be a dangerous one.

"The public is exposed to powerful persuasive messages from above and is unable to communicate meaningfully through the media in response to these messages. Leaders have usurped enormous amounts of political power and reduced popular control over the political system by using the media to generate support, compliance and just plain confusion among the public."[20] This was the case after 9/11. It was the case as the administration made a case for an invasion of Iraq.

It is not an overstatement to say that 9/11, certainly an event of historic proportion, was also politically transformative for the country. Our foreign policy would change. The American people's perception of our world would change. The way the news media would cover international news would change. Certainly, as a country and as a people, we began to think differently about our place in the world and about those who would and could do us real harm.

The news media became more sensitive to news about U.S. foreign policy and immediately began to cover international news more extensively. In fact, a recent Pew survey bears that out indicating there has been a 102 percent increase in the coverage of foreign news and a 135 percent increase in the coverage of terrorism.[21] The attacks of 9/11 were a defining moment for the United States as were the resulting wars that followed in Afghanistan and Iraq. It is that terrorist event and those armed conflicts that followed, which defined the emerging policies of the George W. Bush presidency.

Forever, for better, and for worse, the political framework for this president and his presidency shifted suddenly on September 11, 2001. It was the attacks that spawned the war on terror as declared by President Bush. For national security, America automatically experienced a broadening of authority in the executive branch of government, which is typical after an event of such magnitude and one that would yield consequences sometimes beyond our scope of understanding.

The president would need to act quickly. He would need to build consent for policies that were necessary in such fragile times and during a period of great angst for Americans. Mr. Bush needed to command the situation at hand beginning with his framing the event and the events to follow both for the American people and the world beyond America's borders. The ability to define those events was key in order to justify our behavior to follow, meaning the swift invasion of Afghanistan and, later, the invasion of Iraq, both of which were sanctioned by Congress.

Defining a conflict and the use of particular language to explain the conflict is not without precedent. The "rhetorical presidency" is explained as "an office, a role, a persona, constructing a position of power, myth, legend and persuasion. Everything a president does or says has implications and communicates 'something.' Every act, word, or phrase becomes calculated and measured for a response."[22] "From this point of view, the president has enormous power to set national goals and provide solutions to the nation's problems."[23] The president creates a "metanarrative" to make it easier to "construct foreign policy arguments and to take political and military action."[24]

A "metanarrative" was constructed to define our relationship with the Soviet Union during the Cold War, for example. The Soviets were described as bad or evil. America was painted as good or moral. What was defined for us was a "contest of force vs. freedom, irrationality vs. rationality, and aggression vs. defense [that permeated] the substance and style of the call-to-arms throughout American history."[25] "The primary strength of Cold War rhetoric as a *policy-making rationale* lay in its 'prevailing image of the Soviet threat.'" The perception of a threat allows the government to "characterize antagonistic states."[26] As it was in the case of the Soviet Union during the Cold War and now in the case of Afghanistan and later Iraq, "the nation's adversary is characterized as a mortal threat to freedom, a germ infecting the body politic, a plague upon the liberty of humankind, and a barbarian intent upon destroying civilization."[27] In the same way, with similar sweeping, bold, symbolic language, the Bush administration defined the times and our enemies to build consent for the invasion of Iraq in 2003 after 9/11.

The weight of decision-making on a president is a lonely job. Several former presidents have described it as such and said only those who have served before them can fully comprehend the pressure and responsibility of the office. Former President Dwight D. Eisenhower said the burden is on the president, "when one man must conscientiously, deliberately, prayerfully, scrutinize every argument, every proposal, every prediction, every alternative, every probable outcome of his action and then, all alone, make his decision."[28]

Each president must handle the job in his own way. His intellect, his skills as a public communicator, organizer, politician and his emotional intelligence—the ability "to manage emotions and turn them in to constructive purposes, rather than being dominated by them and allowing them to diminish his leadership abilities, all gage how a president will manage the challenges which he will inevitably face in the Oval Office."[29]

Historian Stephen Graubard has described the White House as a remote, solitary place, a place to which only a few have access. "The White House, a tomb even before September 11, became a fortress to which only a privileged few were admitted, generally to learn of the president's resolve that those who had perpetrated the atrocity would be taken, dead or alive. Such presidential rhetoric suited the gait of a man who seemed the quintessential American macho male, invigorated by the threat that others before him had ignored, that could no longer be denied."[30]

THE RELATIVE CALM BEFORE THE 9/11 STORM

With the election of the first President Bush's son, George W., in 2000, there was a lingering animosity about some unfinished business concerning Iraq. The president's father had ultimately decided not to remove his nemesis, Saddam Hussein, from power during the Gulf War of 1991. Also, George W. himself said of Hussein, as the United States was planning the invasion of Iraq in 2003, "After all, this is the guy that tried to kill my Dad." In fact, there was a covert operation in motion to assassinate the former president when he visited American troops based in Kuwait in 1993. The plot was discovered, and the *Washington Post* reported on June 27, 1993, that President Clinton ordered the launch of twenty-three Tomahawk missiles on the Iraqi Intelligence Service after receiving "compelling evidence" of such action. "It was an elaborate plan devised by the Iraqi government and directed against a former president of the United States because of actions he took as president," President Clinton said. "As such, the Iraqi attack against President Bush was an attack against our country and against all Americans."[31]

Washington Post reporter Bob Woodward interviewed Prince Bandar bin Sultan, Saudi Ambassador to the United States from 1983 to 2005 and a longtime friend of the Bush family, who said, "I think Bush [W.] came into office with a mission. Many people are confusing it with his faith— religious faith. I think he had a mission that was agnostic. That he was convinced that the mission had to be achieved and that he is the only one who is going to achieve it. And it started with: Injustice has been done to a good man, George Herbert Walker Bush, a man who was a hero, who served his country, who did everything right."[32]

Bush, the father, had tremendous success after the Gulf War with an approval rating exceeding 80 percent. Then to be criticized for his decision to leave Saddam in power, followed by a painful defeat in 1992 by Washington outsider, Bill Clinton, largely because of a slumping economy, was just too much. "There is no justice," Bandar said in describing the feelings of Bush the son.[33] For George W. Bush, animosity toward Iraq and Hussein was personal.

There were discussions underway to target Saddam Hussein just ten days after the second President Bush took the oath of office, months before the attacks of 9/11. It was during the first meeting of the new president's National Security Council. Vice President Cheney, Treasury Secretary Paul O'Neill, C.I.A. Director George Tenet, National Security Advisor Condoleezza Rice, Secretary of State Colin Powell, Defense Secretary Donald Rumsfeld, Chairman of the Joint Chiefs Hugh Shelton, Chief of Staff, Andy Card, and all their deputies were in attendance. The conversation quickly went from the Israeli-Palestinian conflict, a conflict the president felt he could not solve, to Iraq.[34]

Condoleezza Rice discussed Iraq and how she believed it was destabilizing the entire region. George Tenet showed some inconclusive photos that might later prove Hussein was producing chemical or biological weapons, but there was "no confirming intelligence" regarding these photographs.[35] Many of those in attendance were given assignments to gather more information about Iraq.

In a subsequent meeting several days later, there were pointed discussions about sanctions against Iraq, what the country would look like with a new regime, one that cooperated with the United States, understood and shared its strategic interests, and one that might lead a new Iraq by "freeing" the Iraqi people from the tyranny of a Hussein dictatorship and helping to establish what could be the largest democracy in the region.

Secretary of Defense Donald Rumsfeld said, "Sanctions are fine, but what we really want to think about is going after Saddam."[36] Treasury Secretary Paul O'Neill said, "From the start, we were building the case against Saddam Hussein and looking at how we could take him out and change Iraq into a new country. And if we could do that, it would solve everything."[37] This is what Rumsfeld and others had attempted to convince George H. W. Bush of during the previous Gulf War. Remove Hussein in order to help construct and install a democracy, one with which the United States could formulate a mutually beneficial, healthy, peaceful diplomatic relationship. Why? To help protect the abundant natural resources on which the United States has relied; to help protect Israel, a strong and faithful ally; and to provide another buffer against the menacing, unpredictable Iran, a theocratic Islamic republic.

There was an inherent problem in these discussions, however. The United States had no current, credible evidence against Iraq. It needed a legitimate and compelling political reason to initiate military operations against Saddam. On September 11, 2001, at approximately 8:45 a.m., there was incentive. The president remembered what he was thinking after being told by his chief of staff, Andy Card, that the country was under attack. "I made up my mind we were going to war."[38] He did not indicate with whom.

At the Emma Booker School he made a statement reminiscent of his father before the launch of the Gulf War. The first President Bush had said to reporters, "This will not stand. This will not stand, this aggression against Kuwait."[39] George W. said in a brief statement after the attacks on 9/11, "Terrorism against our nation will not stand."[40] An hour later, he said to Vice President Dick Cheney, "We're going to find out who did this and we're going to kick their asses."[41]

The president had made no mention of Saddam, but others did. Back in Washington, journalist and former intelligence analyst for the U.S. Navy, James Bamford, said, "On the afternoon of September 11th, the Pentagon is still smoking, Donald Rumsfeld dictates to one of his aides, 'We've got to see, somehow, how we can bring Saddam Hussein into this.'"[42]

But when and how did the idea of attacking Iraq seep into the public consciousness after 9/11? Who began to introduce Iraq and its president as having a role in 9/11? The case against Iraq and the intensity of the public discourse about an inevitable course of action began to creep into news stories and in television news programs. Over the next eighteen months, the president's staff and his closest advisors would build a case and make an effective public argument for attacking Iraq, whether or not the information was accurate.

RHETORIC

September 2001

In the wake of the attacks, the country and our leaders immediately were concerned with the rescue of survivors, the safety of the country, and the cleanup of the devastation in New York City and at the Pentagon. It was on the very same day of the attacks, however, when the president castigated the yet unnamed perpetrators and crucially began to "frame" the forthcoming war on terror.

Twelve hours after the attacks, at 8:30 p.m., in a brief five-minute address to the nation from the Oval Office on the evening of 9/11, the president said: "The search is underway for those who are behind these evil acts. I've directed the full resources of our intelligence and law enforcement communities to find those responsible and to bring them to justice. We will make no distinction between the terrorists who committed these acts and those who harbor them."[43]

This was an important phrase in the president's remarks—"and those who harbor them." It left a door and the country's options open. The president was reserving the right to go outside the bounds of bringing to justice those who directly attacked us, but would also target those who were involved by aiding and abetting the terrorists. He broadly framed a war on terrorism, allowing for the inclusion of other conflicts in other parts of the world, ones that may not have directly involved the United

States, but may have interested us nonetheless. It was adviser Richard Perle of the Defense Policy Board, who had pressed for this type of language in the president's remarks. He said, "We are not going to deal effectively with global terrorism if states can support and sponsor and harbor terrorists without penalty."[44]

The president also said this: "America and our friends and allies join with all those who want peace and security in the world, and we stand together to win the war against terrorism. This is a day when all Americans from every walk of life unite in our resolve for justice and peace. None of us will forget this day. Yet, we go forward to defend freedom and all that is good and just in this world."[45] He further framed our behavior going forward as seeking justice, wanting peace, and defending America's freedom and, indeed, the freedom of the world. In short, the president ultimately was defending and *defining* what is good and just in the world.

The day after the attacks, it was Richard Perle again who told C.I.A. Director George Tenet, "Iraq has to pay a price for what happened yesterday. They bear responsibility." Tenet wrote, "I was stunned but said nothing. Eighteen hours earlier I had scanned passenger manifests from the four hijacked airplanes that showed beyond a doubt that al Qaeda was behind the attacks."[46] Not Iraq, al Qaeda. They must be distinguished as having no relationship.

The manifests came by way of the Customs Office of Intelligence. It had identified the passengers aboard the planes and nineteen probable hijackers, according to The 9/11 Commission Report. Customs checked the manifests against other watch lists and could identify people who had suspicious backgrounds and had been previously involved in other terrorist attacks against U. S. interests abroad. The list was then reviewed by Dale Watson, the head of the counterterrorism division at the F.B.I. Watson would tell White House antiterrorism czar, Richard Clarke, "They're al Qaeda, Dick."[47]

Although there appeared to be broad consensus from key officials at the White House, the C.I.A., the F.B.I., and the State Department that Osama bin Laden was the likely ringleader of the attacks, behind the scenes, the notion of Iraq's involvement persisted. Richard Clarke said he thought the day after the attack would be filled with discussions about how to advance against al Qaeda, but instead "there was a series of discussions about Iraq. Since the beginning of the administration, indeed well before, they had been pressing for a war with Iraq."[48] Many in the administration who had also worked for the president's father now believed a case could be made to finish the job not completed during the Gulf War. That was regime change in Iraq.

According to Clarke, Secretary of Defense Donald Rumsfeld was talking about "getting Iraq," to which he [Clarke] responded, with support from Secretary of State Powell, "Having been attacked by al Qaeda, for us now to go bombing Iraq in response would be like our invading Mexico after the Japanese attacked us at Pearl Harbor."[49]

Clarke described an encounter with the president later that day: "Wandering alone in the Situation Room was the President. He looked like he wanted something to do. He grabbed a few of us and closed the door to the conference room. 'Look, I know you have a lot to do and all . . . but I want you, as soon as you can, to go back over everything, everything. See if Saddam did this. See if he is linked in any way. . . .' I was once again taken aback, incredulous and it showed. But, Mr. President, al Qaeda did this. 'I know, I know, but see if Saddam was involved. Just look. I want to know any shred. . . .' Absolutely we will look . . . again. But, you know, we have looked several times for state sponsorship of al Qaeda and not found any real linkages to Iraq. Iran plays little, as does Pakistan, and Saudi Arabia, Yemen. 'Look into Iraq. Saddam,' the President said testily and left us."[50]

While it may have been perfectly reasonable for the president to ask his staff to take another look at Iraq, based on the historical erratic behavior of its president, this particular exchange perhaps also gives some insight about the insistence, or at the very least, the hope of the president that Hussein was involved. To be clear, this is not an indictment of the president at this point in time. His responsibility was to learn who attacked us.

"Although at the outset the President [and press] had to respond to the immediate concerns of the American public, once the situation had stabilized, the 9/11 attacks gave the president [and the press] a unique opportunity to begin the creation of a new metanarrative and re-shape public knowledge concerning America's role in the world."[51] The building of consent began as the president and members of his administration would frame the event itself and our course of action to follow in the days and months ahead.

There was a flurry of comments from the president's national security team as they kept the public focused and the news media attentive. On September 17, 2001, during a briefing at the Pentagon where the president was announcing the call of reserve troops to active duty, he implicated Osama bin Laden by name, called him a "prime suspect," and said he wanted justice for what was done to America. "And there's an old poster out West . . . I recall that said 'Wanted: Dead or Alive.'" He also said that bin Laden was a "guest" of the Taliban in Afghanistan and called the war on terror against bin Laden and others like him a crusade. "This crusade, this war on terror, is going to take a while. And the American people are going to be patient. I'm gonna be patient."[52]

The use of the word "crusade" was unfortunate because it evoked feelings of the Crusades during the Middle Ages when the Christians of Europe waged a series of military campaigns against Muslims in the Middle East to drive them out of the Holy Land. The president continued: "We're going to find those evildoers, those barbaric people who attacked our country and we're going to hold them accountable. We're going to hold the people who house them accountable. The people who can provide them safe havens will be accountable. The people who feed them will be accountable. And the Taliban must take my statements seriously," he concluded.[53]

When being interviewed on CNN, Secretary of State Colin Powell also pointed to al Qaeda and the Taliban as he explained: "It's not one individual, it's lots of individuals and it's lots of cells. Osama bin Laden is the chairman of the holding company, and within that holding company are terrorist cells and organizations in dozens of countries around the world, any one of them capable of committing a terrorist attack."[54]

On September 16, Vice President Dick Cheney appeared with Tim Russert on *Meet the Press*, which originated from Camp David where the national security team had been meeting for the past thirty-six hours. Early in the program the vice president also implicated the group responsible for 9/11. "It looks as though the responsible organization was a group called al Qaeda. It's Arabic for "The Base." Mr. Russert asked if the organization was affiliated with Osama bin Laden. "He headed it up and organized it, but it's a very broad, kind of loose coalition of groupings," the vice president says. He also said he had no doubt that bin Laden played at least a significant role in the attacks, and he informed the public that we will be involved in this struggle—the war on terror—for the foreseeable future and that there will be no end date. Then came an interesting exchange between Russert and Cheney:

> Mr. Russert: "Saddam Hussein, your old friend, his government had this to say: 'The American cowboy is rearing the fruits of crime against humanity.' If we determine that Saddam Hussein is also harboring terrorists, and there's a track record there, would we have any reluctance of going after Saddam Hussein?"
>
> Vice President Cheney: "No."
>
> Mr. Russert: "Do we have evidence that he is harboring terrorists?"
>
> Vice President Cheney: "There is—in the past, there have been some activities related to terrorism by Saddam Hussein. But at this stage, you know, the focus is over there on al Qaeda and the most recent events in New York. Saddam Hussein is bottled up, at this point, but clearly we continue to have a fairly tough policy where the Iraqis are concerned."
>
> Mr. Russert: "Do we have any evidence linking Saddam Hussein or Iraqis to this operation?"
>
> Vice President Cheney: "No."[55]

On the same program, the vice president also began to allude to the way the administration would have to go about the dirty business of hunting down terrorists. He referred to it as "the dark side"—a place where the intelligence community would have to operate in order to be effective. "We also have to work, though, sort of the dark side, if you will. We've got to spend time in the shadows in the intelligence world. A lot of what needs to be done here will have to be done quietly, without any discussion, using sources and methods that are available to our intelligence agencies, if we're going to be successful."[56]

The tone and tenor of the vice president's explanation of the way the United States would collect and process information was precursor to the way in which the Bush administration would make its case against Saddam. The vice president intimated that for its own good the public could not know too much. The operation would have to be conducted in secret and out of public view. Reporters were kept at bay as well, in the name of national security, to keep them from reporting something that may put future operations at risk and to not inadvertently tip off the enemy about the manner in which we [the United States] would go about our business.

For now, at least publicly, Afghanistan was the focus. As the president's national security team was planning the forthcoming operation in that country, Defense Secretary Rumsfeld, one of those who felt the elder Bush should have killed Hussein during the Gulf War, asked the president why they couldn't go after Iraq as well, not just al Qaeda. "The President put Rumsfeld off, wanting to focus more on Afghanistan, al Qaeda, and Osama bin Laden."[57] This encounter was in contrast to one mentioned earlier with Richard Clarke where the President seemed preoccupied with finding a link to Hussein. Perhaps at this point he determined he would need more evidence of a substantiated link before pursuing that option.

On September 20, 2001, the president addressed a joint session of Congress and the American people in his second formal televised appearance after the attacks. In his speech the president focused on al Qaeda, but painted a broad canvas on which he gave the United States plenty of latitude to shift operations and the playing field if necessary. He made specific demands on the Taliban and requested that it meet those demands swiftly before it was too late. He spoke of "freedom under attack" and terrorist groups that had "global reach." He described our future actions as "civilization's fight" for "progress, pluralism, tolerance and freedom" and called this era the "age of liberty" that would spread across the world.[58]

"Tonight I announce the creation of a cabinet-level position reporting directly to me, the Office of Homeland Security. And tonight, I also announce a distinguished American to lead this effort, to strengthen American security: a military veteran, an effective governor, a true patriot, a trusted friend, Pennsylvania's Tom Ridge." The president prepared the nation for a long campaign after "an act of war" committed on the United States.[59]

In closing the forty-one-minute address he concluded: "I will not forget this wound to our country or those who inflicted it. I will not yield. I will not rest. I will not relent in waging this struggle for freedom and security for the American people."[60] Almost overnight, the president's approval rating spiked from 55 to 90 percent. He told Karl Rove that this event would define a generation just as World War II defined his father's. "I'm here for a reason, and this is how we are going to be judged."[61] The Afghanistan and Iraq wars would indeed ultimately define the president's tenure in office.

After Vice President Cheney appeared on *Meet the Press* and the president had addressed the American people on television in prime time, the administration's hawks and conservatives fanned out across the media landscape for interviews discussing the issue head-on at the end of the month. They began to mention Iraq. Richard Perle, of the conservative American Enterprise Institute, was on ABC News: "Weapons of mass destruction in the hands of Saddam Hussein, plus his known contact with terrorists, including al Qaeda terrorists, is simply a threat too large to continue to tolerate."[62] CNN's John King interviewed Perle the following day on *War Room* with Wolf Blitzer. John King: "Next phase Saddam Hussein?" Perle: "Absolutely." Perle went on to say that should the United States topple the Hussein regime, "We would be seen as liberators in Iraq."[63]

William Kristol, editor and founder of *The Weekly Standard*, said on Fox News: "One person close to the debate said to me this week that it's no longer a question of if, it's a question of how we go after Saddam Hussein." He was asked by Fred Barnes of the *Beltway Boys* on Fox, "What are the consequences if the U.S. does not finish off this Saddam Hussein as a second step in the war on terrorism?" Kristol replied, "It would mean that the President, having declared a global war on terrorism, didn't follow through, didn't take out the most threatening terrorist state in the world."[64]

Former C.I.A. Director under President Clinton and adviser to George W. Bush, James Woolsey, was interviewed by Ted Koppel on *Nightline*. Koppel to Woolsey: "You are probably the hawkiest of the hawks on this [Saddam Hussein]. Why?" Woolsey answers: "Well, I don't know that I accept that characterization, but it's probably not too far off. I think the Baghdad regime is a serious danger to world peace."[65]

October 2001

During his weekly radio address to the nation on October 6, 2001, President Bush repeated the demands he had made of the Taliban. "The Taliban has been given the opportunity to surrender all the terrorists in Afghanistan [including bin Laden and all members of his al Qaeda network] and to close down their camps and operations. Full warnings have been given and time is running out."

In response, the Taliban's representative to Pakistan, Abdul Salam Zaeef, made an offer to try suspected terrorist bin Laden under Islamic law if the United States provided them with evidence. Zaeef said, "America has given evidence to other countries, we do not say anything. If Americans are convinced that they have solid evidence, we are ready for his trial in Afghanistan, and they have to produce that evidence." The United States summarily rejected the offer. [66]

On the morning of October 7, 2001, William Kristol appeared with Tim Russert on *Meet the Press*. He said in part, "The biggest mistake we have made—it's our mistake, it's not the mistake of the Arabs, was not finishing off Saddam Hussein in 1991." [67] While Kristol was discussing our options in Iraq, the United States had only just begun a military campaign in Afghanistan to hunt down Osama bin Laden. Later that same day, the president went on national television from the Treaty Room in the White House and said:

> On my orders, the United States Military has begun strikes against al Qaeda terrorist training camps and military installations of the Taliban regime in Afghanistan. These carefully targeted actions are designed to disrupt the use of Afghanistan as a terrorist base of operations, and to attack the military capabilities of the Taliban regime. Today we focus on Afghanistan, but the battle is broader. Every nation has a choice to make. In this conflict there is no neutral ground. If any government sponsors the outlaws and killers of innocents, they have become outlaws and murderers themselves. And they will take that lonely path at their own peril. The battle is now joined on many fronts. We will not waiver; we will not tire; we will not falter; and we will not fail. Peace and freedom will prevail. [68]

Meanwhile, an un-named spokesman for al Qaeda released a cryptic and confusing statement, which said, "America knows that the battle will not leave its land until America leaves our land, until it stops supporting Israel, until it stops the blockade of Iraq. The Americans must know that the storm of airplanes will not stop and there are yet thousands of young people who look forward to death, like the Americans look forward to living." [69]

On October 10, 2001, Secretary of State Colin Powell made the rounds on numerous news programs reinforcing our commitment to the mission in Afghanistan. About the threat from the terrorist spokesperson he said, "Chilling words from a terrorist. It is a chilling challenge, but I assure you, we will meet that challenge." [70] With ABC *World News* anchorman Charles Gibson he said the immediate goal was to destroy the terrorist operations in Afghanistan, but continued, "Let's not deceive ourselves into thinking that if we get rid of one individual or one network then this campaign is over. It is not. It is a campaign that is directed at all terrorism. That is why President Bush's leadership challenge to the world is that we have to see this as a long-term campaign that will go on in many dimensions for years to come."

A final exchange between Gibson and Powell was rather prophetic:

> Mr. Gibson: "One other thing I wanted to ask you about, which is the letter that the US Ambassador to the United Nations delivered in recent days. He said, 'We may find that our self-defense requires further action with respect to other organizations and other states.' What is he saying there?
>
> Secretary Powell: "It's just a statement of the obvious. It's a statement of what President Bush said from the beginning: that we will seek out wherever they are located; we will work with other nations that have terrorist problems and if we find nations who are providing havens for terrorists or support terrorists, they will have to pay the consequences of such support."[71]

Secretary Powell concluded by saying the United States "understands our obligations under Article 51 of the United Nations charter," but that the president and the United States has to retain the authority to do what is necessary to protect U.S. citizens." This was a clear statement of intent should the United States be attacked again or suspect the real threat of another attack.

The discourse in the coming days and months would focus on Afghanistan, but also it would be punctuated with questions and answers about Iraq, keeping Americans mindful that Iraq was equally dangerous and may eventually require the involvement of American soldiers as well. This repeated message was sustained by the administration through its surrogates and through the president himself. The message was that we will find our attackers, whom we know to be in Afghanistan, but Iraq is a place of interest, and Hussein is a man who had done unspeakable harm in the past. This would give the president and his administration wide latitude to maneuver. There were to be no surprises for the Congress, the press, and the American people.

In a prime time news conference on October 11, 2001, Helen Thomas, veteran White House correspondent for *United Press International* and the grand dame of the Washington press corps, asked the president: "We understand you have advisers who are urging you to go after Iraq, take out Iraq, Syria and so forth. Do you really think that the American people will tolerate you widening the war beyond Afghanistan?"

He replied: "Our focus is on Afghanistan. But we're looking for al Qaeda cells around the world. We're making progress. You mentioned Iraq. After all he gassed his own people. We know he's been developing weapons of mass destruction. And I think it's to his advantage to allow inspectors back in his country to make sure that he's conforming to the agreement he made after he was soundly trounced in the Gulf War. And so we're watching him very carefully. We're watching him carefully."[72]

The Arabic Al Jazeera television network interviewed National Security Advisor Condoleezza Rice a week later and asked her to comment on the perception that she is a person in the Bush administration who wanted to "enlarge the war on terrorism to include Iraq." She replied, "Iraq has been a problem not just for U.S. policy, but for policy in the region as well. This is a country that could not even acknowledge the right of Kuwait to exist. This is a country that has threatened its neighbors, that has been harmful to its own people." The interviewer then asked if Iraq is next for "military mobilization" in the "second stage of the war on terrorism." She answered, "The President has made it clear that the war on terrorism is a broad war on terrorism. You can't be for terrorism in one part of the world and against it in another part of the world. We worry about Saddam Hussein. We worry about his weapons of mass destruction that he's trying to achieve. There's a reason he doesn't want U.N. inspectors—it's because he intends to acquire weapons of mass destruction. But for now, the President has said that his goal is to watch and monitor Iraq; and certainly the United States will act if Iraq threatens its interests."[73]

Later in October came the anthrax attacks in New York and Florida. A British newspaper, *The Guardian*, reported that hawks in Washington, DC, were gunning for Saddam Hussein and believed he was responsible for the anthrax scare. It reported that Iraq had the technology and the supplies of anthrax "for terrorist use." The article quoted a C.I.A. source, which said, "They aren't making this stuff in caves in Afghanistan. This is prima facie evidence of the involvement of a state intelligence agency. Maybe Iran has the capability. But it doesn't look likely politically. That leaves Iraq." For senior White House and Pentagon officials, an attack against Iraq, the newspaper continued, was becoming "irresistible."[74]

Secretary Powell publicly did not mention Iraq with regard to the anthrax scare when asked who might be responsible. Bob Schieffer of *Face the Nation* on CBS asked if there was a connection to Osama bin Laden. Powell replied, "There might be, but I don't know, Bob. I think our intelligence, law enforcement, law enforcement agencies are hard at work trying to get to the bottom of this, the source of the anthrax, how it's being distributed, the persons responsible, and what linkages may exist with terrorist organizations such as al Qaeda."[75]

Behind the scenes there was evidence of some military intrigue. The hunt was intensifying for Osama bin Laden in the intricate and dangerous mountains on the Afghan border with Pakistan in an area called Tora Bora. The directive to an elite, secretive military unit called Delta Force was to "kill bin Laden," but to make it look like the Afghanis were responsible.[76] It would appear as if the Afghans were supporting the American war effort by killing U.S. public enemy number one and in our efforts to eradicate or substantially marginalize the Taliban, who by this point had mercilessly overrun the country, terrifying and intimidating its citizens.

The plan of Delta, so mysterious a unit that there are many who say it does not exist, was to come across the treacherous mountains of Pakistan from behind where bin Laden and his men were hiding to launch a surprise attack. They wanted to leave no room or possibility for the elusive and clever bin Laden to escape. Once they hit bin Laden, they would disappear as quietly as they arrived, leave him to die, and for the Afghanis to collect his body. No one would know Delta Force had ever been there. The force was convinced it would be successful. It had ascertained by radio transmission that bin Laden was, in fact, hiding in a cave waiting for the cover of darkness to make his move into the safe-haven of neighboring Pakistan where local tribesman would hide him, and protect and defend his secret location.

Delta asked permission to execute its plan. The request was "disapproved" as it traveled up the chain of command. Acknowledging that order, the unit then asked permission to plant landmines along a mountain path that would be bin Laden's only escape route. That request was also "disapproved." The commander of Delta Force, known as Dalton Fury, a fictitious name used to protect his identity, asked whether his orders not to attack came from "Central Command or from the President of the United States." He never learned the answer, but he did tell the CBS news magazine program *60 Minutes* that in the five years he had been with Delta Force, the unit had never been refused such an operation. Hampered by other factors and with the mission now compromised, Fury said he believed the Force wounded bin Laden in a subsequent intense firefight that lasted many hours.[77] Nonetheless, Osama bin Laden escaped. This begs the question. Was it the president who ultimately "disapproved" the request to kill bin Laden? There is evidence to suggest he did, which will be discussed later.

The director of the C.I.A. told another version of the story, perhaps to protect the delicate and secretive operation of Delta and not expose President Bush if he did, in fact, disapprove a request to kill bin Laden. "We had sensitive intelligence that strongly suggested bin Laden was in the Tora Bora area," wrote George Tenet, "and likely was plotting a quick escape through soon-to-be completed tunnels. U.S. air power was brought to bear on this very difficult terrain."[78] The United States and Pakistani military failed to seal an impossible border, and Osama bin Laden escaped to Pakistan. George Tenet: "The Pakistani military did manage to capture hundreds of al Qaeda members slipping across the border, but not the one we wanted most."[79]

The news media was also in the area searching for information about the world's most wanted fugitive. International correspondent for CNN, Amanda Kibel, said her news crew, comprised of three people, paid a

Pakistani interpreter to take them to the house where bin Laden was believed to have been hiding in Tora Bora. Kibel was informed by local Afghani tribesmen that he had indeed escaped, but the house was filled with a cache of weapons and the landscape was dotted with caves that were connected to an intricate network of tunnels leading in and out of the country.[80] The public understood the difficulty and danger of the mission. It was also assured the military would continue the intense hunt for the outlaw until the day he was located, captured and brought to justice, or killed.

By the end of the month, the administration was now "stepping up efforts" to nail down a tangible link between Saddam Hussein and 9/11. Some in the news media were reporting that a meeting had taken place in Prague between Iraqi agents and the 9/11 ringleader, Mohammed Atta.[81] The report was leaked from a source inside the White House who we would later learn was Vice President Cheney.

Defense Secretary Donald Rumsfeld was asked about the link between Hussein and 9/11 by CNN's Wolf Blitzer. Rumsfeld said, "What we do know about Iraq is that Iraq has been a nation that has been involved in terrorist acts. We know they have been a nation that has harbored terrorists, facilitated and financed, and fostered those kinds of activities. We know they have occupied their neighbor Kuwait. That regime is a bad regime. It is a regime that is a dangerous regime. What the meaning was in this particular instance is something that I think will have to unfold and learn more about."[82]

On November 10, 2001, President Bush delivered an impassioned speech to the United Nations. He spoke about the attacks on the United States, how the world must come together to fight terrorism, and that the battle is just beginning against rogue countries that shun the mission of the United Nations and with deliberation throw the world into chaos through violence. He made an appeal to the world body, asking for its support and participation in the war on terror. He focused on Afghanistan, a military mission well underway, and promised to rebuild that nation, which had historically suffered under occupying forces and religious fanaticism. Again, he made it clear the United States would keep its options open. The war on terror would be lengthy, he said, and it had tentacles that would unfurl to include other nations if and when necessary.

He said, "We're taking new measures to investigate terror and prepare against threats. The leaders of all nations must now carefully consider their responsibilities and their future. Terrorist groups like al Qaeda depend on the aid or indifference of governments. They need the support of financial infrastructure, and safe havens to plan and hide. Some governments, while pledging to uphold the principles of the U.N., have cast their lot with the terrorists. For every regime that sponsors terror, there is a price to be paid. And it will be paid. The allies of terror are equally guilty of murder and equally accountable to justice."[83]

The day before Thanksgiving, the president determined he was ready to move in earnest against Iraq. "Let's get started on this," he told Donald Rumsfeld.[84] "On this day, Bush formally set in motion the chain of events that would lead to the invasion of Iraq 16 months later." According to Bob Woodward, Bush's inner circle, led by Christopher DuMuth of the American Enterprise Institute, a conservative Washington think tank, wrote with a group of advisers, who were Beltway insiders, some from academia and the news media, on the condition of absolute secrecy, a document called "Delta of Terrorism." The document concluded that in order to bring stability to the Middle East and cleanse the region of fascism and fanaticism, Saddam Hussein would have to be confronted. It was "inevitable." He [Hussein] would have "to leave the scene before the problem could be addressed."[85]

The day after Thanksgiving, the president called Defense Secretary Donald Rumsfeld into a private meeting and asked what kind of war plan the Pentagon had for Iraq. Rumsfeld told the president it was not at all current and reflected the Gulf War launched by the former President Bush. He asked Rumsfeld not to disclose their discussion that day with anyone, but requested that he quietly begin to prepare an updated Pentagon plan to confront Iraq.

General Tommy Franks, the commander of U.S. forces in Afghanistan, busy with his soldiers hunting down bin Laden, had "only a vague indication there had been discussion in Washington about the Iraq war plan."[86] Now the president of the United States, through the Secretary of Defense, was asking Franks, through his deputies at central command headquarters (CENTCOM) in Tampa, Florida, to start looking at their "Iraq planning in great detail" and provide a "new commander's estimate."[87]

While speaking to his deputies in Florida through a secured phone line from Afghanistan, Franks was said to be incredulous and responded, "Goddamn, what the fuck are they talking about?"[88] The military was squarely focused on Afghanistan and bringing to justice the man responsible for 9/11, not creating a new conflict simultaneously in another part of the Middle East.

December 2001

As the year was coming to a close the rhetoric was increasing about inspectors being allowed back into Iraq to search for weapons of mass destruction. There is no dispute that Hussein had these weapons at one time, used these weapons against his own people, and may have wanted to amass them again. However, there was no credible evidence that indicated he was making anything or was hiding anything at this point in time. This will be addressed in more detail later, but early in December, in an exchange with a reporter, the president had this rather provocative, cryptic response to a question about the inspectors, Iraq, and Saddam:

> Bush: "In order to prove to the world that he is not developing weapons of mass destruction, he ought to let the inspectors back in. Yes."
>
> Reporter: "If he does not do that sir, what will be the consequences? If he does not do that what will be the consequences?"
>
> Bush: "That's up for him. He'll find out."
>
> Reporter: "He'll find out?" (The president did not answer as he walked away.)[89]

The president continued to remind America and the world, very broadly, of the dangers that lurked in the shadows of our war on terror. On Pearl Harbor Day, aboard the U.S.S. *Enterprise*, he compared the attack in 1941 to the attack of 9/11 by saying the attacks came on quiet mornings, they were plotted in secret, waged without mercy, and killed thousands. We are still fighting, he reminded the crowd. "We are fighting to protect ourselves and our children from violence and fear. We're fighting for the security of our people and success of liberty. We're fighting against men without conscience, but full of ambition—to remake the world in their own brutal images. For all the reasons we're fighting to win—and we will win."[90]

In a photo opportunity with the Prime Minister of Norway, the president said his job is to protect America from further attack and that is what he intended to do. "There are still real threats. I will not jeopardize the people of the United States. I will not show our secrets. I will not tip our hand. I will not let the world at large—particularly our enemy—understand how we put a case together."

A reporter at the event asked the president if we might consider the use of troops elsewhere in the world. The president replied: "I will not tip our hand in any way, shape or form, but I will tell you this: Those who want to commit terror against the United States or our friends and allies must beware that they will be hunted down. And those nations which harbor a terrorist or feed a terrorist or hide a terrorist or clothe a terrorist better be aware of the United States and our friends, because they will be brought to justice. Now is a time for the free world to stand up and defend the freedoms that these evil ones hate."[91]

While the president spoke in broad terms, meaning not of Iraq specifically, those in his immediate circle did speak pointedly about Iraq and weapons of mass destruction as a horrible year for America [2001] was coming to a close. Osama bin Laden was still at large. There was a painful awareness of that fact and his responsibility for the attacks of 9/11. On NBC in early December, Vice President Dick Cheney told interviewer Tim Russert that he had seen a tape of Osama bin Laden where he took responsibility for the attacks of September 11. "There's no doubt about his responsibility for the attack on 9/11," the vice president asserted.[92]

In the same interview, Russert turned to Iraq. He quoted an article, which reported that a Czech Interior Minister confirmed a meeting of an Iraqi intelligence officer and Mohammed Atta, one of the ringleaders of the 9/11 attacks in Prague five months before the attack. Before he let Cheney respond, Russert also quoted former C.I.A. Director James Woolsey, who asserted that three Iraqi defectors and U.N. inspectors had evidence that airplanes were used to train hijackers, including "non-Iraqi hijackers" to take over airplanes with knives. This purportedly happened at a place called Salman Park, at the southern edge of Baghdad.

Cheney: "That report has been well confirmed that he [Atta] did go to Prague and he did meet with a senior official of the Iraqi intelligence service in Czechoslovakia last April. The evidence is pretty conclusive that the Iraqis have indeed harbored terrorists. The situation, I think, that leads a lot of people to be concerned about Iraq had to do not just with their past activity of harboring terrorists, but also with Saddam Hussein's behavior over the years and with his aggressive pursuit of weapons of mass destruction." Cheney concluded by saying the president had made it clear that U.N. inspectors should go back into Iraq, even though Hussein has rejected the notion.[93]

Secretary of Defense Rumsfeld appeared on *Meet the Press* and was also asked about Iraq. There had been an article in the *Los Angeles Times*, which quoted Egyptian sources who claimed the United States had plans to attack Iraq. Here is the brief exchange between the host of *Meet the Press* and Secretary Rumsfeld:

> Mr. Russert: "Will we insist, demand, that Saddam Hussein allow in United Nations inspectors to find out just how developed his biological, chemical, and perhaps nuclear weapon systems are?"
>
> Mr. Rumsfeld: "There ought to be inspections. The U.N. resolutions call for inspections. He is violating the U.N. resolutions. We know that man is determined to have those weapons. He has them, and he's used them against his own people."[94]

Secretary of State Powell also appeared on *Meet the Press* and said the ten years since the Gulf War had been an "untidy" ten years dealing with Saddam, but that we have "not totally been able to keep him from trying to pursue these weapons of mass destruction. And that is why it is important to try to get the inspectors back in and that's why we continue to believe that a regime change is a sensible US policy."[95]

Weapons inspectors had been in and out of Iraq since the Gulf War, but left the country in 1998 after UNSCOM (United Nations Special Commission) accused Iraq of not being cooperative.

The Bush administration began to focus the public's attention toward Saddam Hussein as a clear and present danger to the world and away from the reality that bin Laden remained at large. The lack of concrete progress on bin Laden was clearly a failure of the administration. There was speculation, made public, that he was hiding in Pakistan, protected by villagers and tribal leaders. The rhetoric was that while bin Laden remains public enemy number one, he is crafty and difficult to pursue, given the political and practical terrain. Saddam, on the other hand, thumbed his nose at the world, by defying inspectors. We knew where he was. We defeated him once, and we could defeat him again, this time with definition and finality. Our fight with Saddam was a conflict we were familiar with and one at which we could be successful. The American people would need to be convinced. The president declared at the end of the year that the New Year (2002) would be a year of America on the alert. He also promised "a great [new] year" ahead.

2002: A PIVOTAL STATE OF THE UNION ADDRESS

The stage was set for a defining State of the Union Address on January 29, 2002. The president himself, as opposed to his proxies, who had spoken of Iraq across the spectrum of news channels, would essentially come out against Iraq with reasons why it was both an adversary and an imminent threat. He made a convincing case to the American people.

While the ashes at ground zero in New York City were still smoldering, the president acknowledged the evil political forces in the world, stating that he understood the nature of the enemy, and reinforced what the very existence of America represented to the world. The president began to frame his case against Iraq in stark, dramatic terms: good versus evil; freedom versus tyranny; peace versus terror and violence; the civilized world versus a primitive one; justice versus lawlessness; hatred versus understanding and tolerance. We Americans, according to the president, pursued peace and represented goodness in the world, but there were "the evil ones" out there lurking, who were bent on our destruction. His goal was for Americans to internalize this argument.

The president announced our "partnership" with Afghanistan in rooting out terrorist elements in the form of the ideological Taliban and declared that the United States was "winning the war on terror." He said: "The men and women of our armed forces have delivered a message now clear to every enemy of the United States: Even seven thousand miles away, across oceans and continents, on mountaintops and in caves you will not escape the justice of this nation."[96]

The president's rhetoric was building to a flourishing crescendo as he introduced the world to his justification for future military action in Iraq. It was what the news media most adopted as a major talking point in newscasts, talk shows, and newspapers across the globe. The president first spoke of the "enemies' hatred" and the "madness of the destruction they design." He specified that it was the terrorists who view the entire world as their battlefield, that they brought the fight to us, and that we must now "pursue them wherever they are." As long as nations are harboring terrorists, he said, "freedom is at risk and America and our allies must not, and will not, allow it." He continued: "First, we will shut down terrorist camps, disrupt terrorist plans and bring terrorists to justice. And second, we must prevent the terrorists and regimes who seek chemical, biological or nuclear weapons from threatening the United States and the world."[97]

While the president reminded America that it was fighting a very public war in Afghanistan, he also informed the country that on his orders, our military was also "acting elsewhere." Our net would swing wide and target those countries we could identify as culpable in committing or supporting terrorism. He named the Philippines, Bosnia, Somalia, and Pakistan as areas of both interest and concern and then, pointedly, indicted the countries of North Korea and Iran as "grave and growing dangers" to the world.

But it was Iraq on which he spent more time. Iraq, the third nexus in that triad of evil, was where the president gave a much more detailed account of the danger it posed, saying: "Iraq continues to flaunt its hostility toward America and to support terror. The Iraqi regime has plotted to develop anthrax and nerve gas and nuclear weapons for over a decade. This is a regime that has already used poison gas to murder thousands of its own citizens, leaving the bodies of mothers huddled over their dead children. This is a regime that agreed to international inspections then kicked out the inspectors. This is a regime that has something to hide from the civilized world."[98]

It was because of this address to the nation and to the world that we would, for months and years to come, associate the terms "axis of evil" and "weapons of mass destruction" (WMD) with Iraq. It was on the basis of those inflammatory buzz words, like a mantra repeated over and over again by the president and his minions, that we would come to believe that Iraq was the most dangerous of countries, that its nefarious leader was a madman who posed an imminent risk to the planet, and that something must be done about both or choose to sit idly by at our own peril. We were warned that we could experience another 9/11 or something far worse. The president said these enemies were "arming to threaten the peace of the world, they could provide arms to terrorists, attack our allies, or attempt to blackmail the United States. In any case, the price of indifference would be catastrophic."[99]

The Bush Doctrine was born as the president put the world on notice: "America will do what is necessary to ensure our nation's security. We'll be deliberate, yet time is not on our side. I will not wait on events while dangers gather. I will not stand by as peril draws closer and closer. The United States of America will not permit the world's most dangerous regimes to threaten us with the world's most destructive weapons. Our war on terror is well begun, but it is only begun. This campaign may not be finished on our watch, yet it must be and it will be waged on our watch."[100]

Americans had yet not realized the implications of this speech. But according to Arthur Schlesinger, our country would adopt a new foreign policy going forward, which is military in scope and embodies the notion of "striking a potential enemy, unilaterally if necessary, before he has a chance to strike us. Unilateralism reached its grand climax when President George W. Bush repudiated the strategy that won the Cold War, the combination of containment and deterrence carried out through such multilateral agencies as the U.N., NATO, and the Organization of American States."[101]

Scott Ritter a former U.N. weapons inspector calls it "The Right of Pre-Emptory Self-Defense." He said, "If a nation expresses hostile intent and it is accumulating the means to strike you, you're not obligated to sit back and wait for them to strike. You can find support for this in article 51 of the United Nations charter." Ritter claims this was the excuse the Germans used to attack Poland and that Israel uses it frequently.[102] President Franklin Roosevelt invoked this doctrine when the U.S.S. *Greer* was fired upon by a German submarine in the north Atlantic on September 4, 1941.

It is fair to say that such a political strategy and diplomacy would not work with rogue terrorists whose religious fundamentalist beliefs and fanaticism drive their behavior. Terrorists are often not affiliated with an established, sovereign nation but only may be protected and harbored in a country by those who share beliefs. It is fair to say, however, that Iraq was a suspected target because as a state it had "terrorized" by violent means in the past and was allegedly preparing to do so in the future against other nations. As a country with diplomatic and political relationships with other nations, containment and deterrence could be effective.

After the State of the Union Address, Saddam Hussein's alleged nuclear ambitions would be at the front and center of the debate about the level of danger he actually posed. The "axis of evil" was widely quoted and discussed, but it was Iraq and Saddam that made headlines as the most problematic and our greatest cause for concern and fear. Many in the Bush administration would say the United States was not looking for a war, but that it would have no choice in the matter should Saddam choose *not* to show the world what Iraq was up to inside its own country or in alliance with other countries or people acting on behalf of those countries. The United States would advocate for U.N. weapons inspectors to be allowed back into Iraq.

In February, Secretary of State Powell said, "Let the inspectors in. They threw them out in 1998. They ought to be allowed back in. If Iraq is not a member of the 'axis of evil' club, let the inspectors in to establish it and prove it." He added, "We suspect they are developing weapons of mass destruction. We more than suspect it. We know it."[103]

On *Meet the Press* two weeks later, the Secretary would claim that there was no proven linkage of Iraq to the events of 9/11 and that Saddam was "bottled up" as Vice President Dick Cheney had earlier suggested. He meant that Saddam was operating in an environment that was being closely monitored. The vice president said, "We know he continues to find the means to develop weapons of mass destruction—nuclear programs, chemical programs, biological programs—that we should be fearful that these weapons he is developing could fall into the hands of terrorists who might be able to use them."[104]

Also in the same month, Secretary of Defense Donald Rumsfeld appeared on PBS to echo the sentiments emanating from the White House. Hussein was a threat to the world and to the Middle East. He also defended the Bush Doctrine and preemption as policy by saying we would attack those who are plotting terror. "We've already been attacked so what we're doing is in self-defense."[105]

Vice President Cheney called Saddam Hussein "a man of great evil" and reinforced to Americans that he had weapons of mass destruction and could use them in the region against our allies. "The issue is that he has chemical weapons and he's used them. The issue is that he is developing and has biological weapons. The issue is that he is pursuing nuclear weapons." Cheney also left open the possibility of taking action against Iraq even if the inspectors were let back in the country saying, "A return of inspectors would provide no assurance whatsoever of [Saddam's] compliance with U.N. resolutions."[106] But on May 3, 2002, the United Nations Monitoring, Verification and Inspections Commission (UNMOVIC), headed by Hans Blix, began to speak with Iraq about inspectors coming back into the country. This was the first time there were discussions since inspectors left in 1998. These negotiations would be ongoing until November 2002.

Meanwhile, on May 19, 2002, the vice president appeared on *Meet the Press* to say that Saddam is "working on nuclear."[107] The same day National Security Advisor Condoleezza Rice appeared on CNN and was interviewed by Wolf Blitzer. The conversation was about 9/11, but Rice's message was broader. She spoke about an expanded war on terror, which would involve both the F.B.I. and C.I.A. Eight months after 9/11, Rice said she believed bin Laden had been killed, although there was no conclusive evidence of this, and also that America was far from safe. Before 9/11, she said, America was faced with a "covert war on terrorism" and since 9/11 was now engaged in an "overt war on terrorism."[108]

President Bush, on June 1, 2002, gave the commencement address to the graduating class of the United States Military Academy at West Point. Several major themes ran through his address, but he explained his belief in preemptive engagement with an enemy who might later prove a threat to America.

> Deterrence—the promise of massive retaliation against nations—means nothing against shadowy terrorist networks with no nations or citizens to defend. Containment is not possible when unbalanced dictators with weapons of mass destruction can deliver those weapons on missiles or secretly provide them to terrorist allies. We cannot defend America and our friends by hoping for the best. We cannot put our faith in the word of tyrants who solemnly sign non-proliferation treaties and then systematically break them. If we wait for threats to fully materialize, then we've waited too long. [109]

The president compared 9/11 to other great military and political struggles in history, mentioning World War II.

> The gravest danger to freedom lies at the perilous crossroads of radicalism and technology. When the spread of chemical and biological and nuclear weapons, along with ballistic missile technology—when that occurs, even weak states and small groups could attain a catastrophic power to strike great nations. Our enemies have declared this very intention, and have been caught seeking these terrible weapons. [110]

The Bush administration stayed on message. These words: nuclear, biological, chemical, tyrant, unbalanced dictator, and weapons of mass destruction were being used routinely, it seemed even uniformly, by those in the Bush administration when referring to President Hussein of Iraq. Twice in August, during an address to the California Commonwealth Club in San Francisco and to the V.F.W. (Veterans of Foreign War) National Convention in Washington, DC, Vice President Cheney again referred to the events of 9/11, Saddam Hussein, and his pursuit of nuclear weapons. [111]

The sustained message from the White House seemed to have had an effect on the American people. According to a Gallup Poll, 86 percent believed Saddam was supporting terrorist groups aimed at attacking the United States, 65 percent believed he was involved in 9/11, 94 percent said they believed Saddam had weapons of mass destruction and would use them to attack the United States. [112]

In early September, Condoleezza Rice appeared on CNN's *Late Edition* with Wolf Blitzer. The tone of her rhetoric was sharp and unambiguous. She said Saddam Hussein was a clear and present danger to the United States, our allies, and our interests. She said the danger was gaining momentum and that "given what we experienced on 9/11, I don't think anyone wants to wait for the 100 percent surety that he has weapons of mass destruction that can reach the United States, because the only time we may be 100 percent sure is when something lands on our territory." She pushed for weapons inspectors to be allowed back into Iraq. Then came this exchange:

Blitzer: "Based on what you know right now, how close is Saddam Hussein's government, how close is that government to developing a nuclear capability?"

Rice: "We do know he is actively pursuing a nuclear weapon. We do know that there have been shipments going into Iran, for instance, into Iraq, for instance, of aluminum tubes that are only really suited for nuclear weapons programs, centrifuge programs. We do know that he has the infrastructure, scientists to make a nuclear weapon. The problem here is that there will always be some uncertainty about how quickly he can acquire nuclear weapons. But we don't want *the smoking gun to be a mushroom cloud.*" [113]

On the same day, the vice president returned to *Meet the Press* and said this, revisiting the possibility that Saddam might have been connected to the 9/11 attacks:

I want to be very careful about how I say this. I'm not here today to make a specific allegation that Iraq was somehow responsible for 9/11. I can't say that. On the other hand, since we did that interview, new information has come to light. And we spent time looking at that relationship between Iraq, on the one hand, and the al Qaeda organization on the other. And there has been reporting that suggests that there have been a number of contacts over the years. We've seen in connection with the hijackers, of course, Mohamed Atta, who was the lead hijacker, did apparently travel to Prague on a number of occasions. And on at least one occasion, we have reporting that places him in Prague with a senior Iraqi intelligence official a few months before the attack on the World Trade Center. [114]

America's attention, it seemed, was effectively diverted from Afghanistan and the failure to capture Osama bin Laden to Iraq and Saddam Hussein. September 11, 2001, had been held up as the reason for our behavior, our rhetoric, and our future actions. In his address to the United Nations on September 12, 2002, President's Bush speech was squarely focused on Iraq, Saddam, weapons inspectors, and disarmament. He traced the historic behavior of Iraq with Iran, with Kuwait, and with the United Nations, as it ignored several resolutions to allow weapons inspectors in the country saying: "The history, the logic, the facts lead to one conclusion: Saddam Hussein is a grave and gathering danger. All the world now faces a test and the United Nations a difficult and defining moment." [115]

The president issued Iraq a number of ultimatums, which included the destruction of weapons of mass destruction and the end to all support for terrorism. The president asked for those resolutions involving inspections and the confiscation of weapons to be enforced by the United Nations, mentioning 9/11 as a prophetic event in the world, "a prelude to far greater horrors," and then issued a threat of his own if the resolutions were not enforced.

"We cannot stand by and do nothing while dangers gather. We must stand up for our security and for the permanent rights and the hopes of mankind. By heritage and by choice, the United States of America will make that stand. And, delegates to the United Nations, you have the power to make that stand as well."[116]

The pressure on Saddam Hussein was working, which should have given the administration pause. It was diplomatic pressure on Iraq from a coalition of countries comprised of our closest allies and other member nations in the United Nations, which resulted in weapons inspectors being allowed back in to Iraq. In a letter from Naji Sabri, the Foreign Minister of Iraq to the United Nations, dated September 16, 2002, Iraq would accept the return of inspectors without condition. Inspectors, in fact, returned to resume their mission on November 18, 2002, led into Baghdad by Hans Blix.

Would these inspections prove the relentless claims made by the United States that Saddam had not destroyed his cache of weapons, but rather was procuring more of them and was actively plotting to use them? In any case, the stage was set. These inspections, presumably, would settle the matter for the public and pave the way for further options. The Bush administration would now discount them. War with Iraq seemed inevitable, despite the reentry of weapons inspectors, despite continuing diplomatic efforts by the United Nations, and despite the fact that Saddam Hussein was diplomatically engaged and militarily monitored. The Bush administration launched the same preemptive war that it did, even with these initiatives well underway.

At the conclusion of 2002, the Security Council unanimously adopted U.N. Resolution 1441, which outlined a so-called "enhanced inspection regime" and the road to disarmament. Iraq provided a twelve thousand-page document with "a complete declaration" of the country's chemical, biological, and nuclear weapons programs and asserted that it had no weapons of mass destruction.

Before the next State of the Union in January 2003, Blix reported that the dense report Iraq had provided was nothing more than a "reorganized version" of what was submitted in 1997 to UNSCOM (United Nations Special Commission). This was not a serious charge. He also asserted there were no "smoking guns" in the search for those weapons of mass destruction. Meanwhile, a cache of twelve (empty) warheads had been discovered by the inspectors. They had been used for carrying chemical weapons, but these warheads had not been accounted for in Saddam's twelve thousand-page audit. A spokesman for the Iraqi government said the "stocks were old weapons and had been mentioned in its declaration" the previous month.[117] Blix verified this claim and said the Iraqis were cooperating fully with the inspections.[118] This also could have been a turning point in the behavior and attitude of the Bush administration.

It received what it had been asking for. Weapons inspectors were finally back in the country. Hussein was being carefully monitored. The United Nations had successfully convinced him to cooperate with inspectors. The slow and steady wheel of diplomacy was turning and proving to be effective. No weapons of mass destruction, to this point, had been discovered, but the United States persisted.

If not found now, WMD would someday be discovered, hidden in some obscure place not yet discovered, according to the Bush administration. A war would presumably be launched, not for hard evidence of WMD, but for the promise of their manifestation at some future date. The administration was dismissive, unrelenting, threatening war, and issuing an exit strategy for Hussein. War could be averted only if he vacated his own country. Also, he was promised immunity if he complied.

According to a Gallup poll, 86 percent of Americans believed the United States should prevent Iraq from developing weapons of mass destruction. Twenty-five percent described Iraq's military capabilities as a "crisis," and another 56 percent said they were a "major problem." A *Los Angeles Times* poll, published in December 2002, said 90 percent of the respondents said there was no doubt Iraq was developing weapons of mass destruction, but also 72 percent said the United Nations had not produced enough new evidence of those weapons to justify a war. At the end of the year, a Gallup/*USA Today* poll reported the president's approval rating at about 60 percent. *The Los Angeles Times* said three-quarters of the respondents approved of the way the president was handling the threat of terrorism, and three in five generally approved of the way he was handling the country's affairs.

2003: THE YEAR OF THE IRAQ INVASION

Forty-eight hours before the State of the Union Address in January 2003, Secretary Powell and White House Chief of Staff Andrew Card were articulating what the White House called its "final phase" with Iraq. Powell was in Davos, Switzerland, and said this:

> The United States believes that time is running out. We will not shrink from war, if that is the only way to rid Iraq of its weapons of mass destruction. We will continue to reserve our sovereign right to take military action against Iraq, alone or in a coalition of the willing. As the President has said, "We cannot defend America and our friends by hoping for the best." History will judge us harshly as those who saw the coming danger but failed to act.[119]

The same day, Card was a guest on *Meet the Press* and said:

> Should Saddam Hussein have any thought that he would use a weapon of mass destruction, he should anticipate that the United States will use

whatever means necessary to protect us and the world from a holocaust.[120]

Saddam was, metaphorically speaking, surrounded. His military
forces were being carefully monitored by the United States and so were
his activities, public statements, and statements through his proxies, yet
the Bush administration continued to use language which could be interpreted as provocative and incendiary. First, Secretary Powell spoke with
foreboding about history and its lessons. Then, Card warned of a possible
"holocaust" with the mental image that very term invokes. The State of
the Union Address would be a pivotal speech designed as much for the
American people as it was for the people of the world and for their
leaders.

According to Gallup, the president's approval rating had decreased
from a stunning 90 percent after 9/11, to a modest, but respectable 58
percent. Fifty-two percent of Americans favored an invasion of Iraq with
ground troops. Interestingly, 76 percent of those polled also said the U.N.
inspectors were doing a "good job," having found nothing of great suspicion or alarm.

On January 28, 2003, in prime time television, the President devoted a
healthy part of his state of the union address to Iraq and issued warnings
to its leader Hussein. These warnings came despite the fact that the
U.N.'s chief weapons inspector Blix was satisfied with the progress of
inspections. How could Saddam disarm if there were no weapons to
speak of? How could the president speak of Saddam being deceptive
when Blix reported that he was cooperative?

Nonetheless, in his address the President said:

> The dictator of Iraq is not disarming. To the contrary; he is deceiving.
> From intelligence sources we know, for instance, that thousands of
> Iraqi personnel are at work hiding documents and materials from the
> U.N. inspectors. Saddam Hussein has gone to elaborate lengths, spent
> enormous sums, taken great risks to build and keep weapons of mass
> destruction. Before September 11th, many in the world believed that
> Saddam Hussein could be contained. Imagine those 19 hijackers with
> other weapons and other plans—this time armed by Saddam Hussein.
> Trusting in the sanity and restraint of Saddam Hussein is not a strate-
> gy, and it is not an option. We will consult. But let there be no mis-
> understanding: If Saddam Hussein does not fully disarm, for the safety
> of our people and for the peace of the world, we will lead a coalition to
> disarm him.[121]

The president announced that Secretary Powell would present information and intelligence "about Iraq's illegal weapons programs, its attempt to hide those weapons from inspectors, and its links to terrorist
groups." The United States would ask the U.N. Security Council to con-
vene in special session on February 5, 2003. And then, the president

spoke these words, which are now familiarly known as "the sixteen words." He said: *"The British government has learned that Saddam Hussein recently sought significant quantities of uranium from Africa.* Our intelligence sources tell us that he has attempted to purchase high-strength aluminum tubes suitable for nuclear weapons production."[122] This sixteen-word-passage will be discussed later in great detail, but it was a line in the speech, which never should have appeared. Later, it would be embarrassingly discredited.

The Gallup polls after the national address painted a fluctuating and interesting portrait of the mood of the public. Of those who heard or read about the president's speech, 50 percent received it in a "very positive" light and another 34 percent in a "somewhat positive" light. Seventy-one percent said that Bush's policies were moving the country in the "right direction," and 67 percent of those polled said the president had "made a compelling case for war in Iraq."

On February 4, 2002, Tony Benn, a former Labour MP (Member of [British] Parliament) and Cabinet Minister, was granted an exclusive interview with Saddam Hussein for British Channel 4. Hussein stated through an interpreter that Iraq was committed to its own rights as much as it was to the rights of others. He said that there is "one truth," which is that his country possesses "no weapons of mass destruction whatsoever" and that Iraq is "free of such weapons; nuclear, biological and chemical."

About his country's alleged links with bin Laden's al Qaeda, Hussein said he would be transparent about the relationship if there was one, but said "we have no relationship with al Qaeda." With regard to the weapons inspectors in his country, Hussein said he wanted the world to understand the suffering of the Iraqi people under the sanctions that had been imposed over the years and that while he understood the "motivations" of the Security Council and its mission, he only objected to the "conduct" of some of the inspectors. He said the inspectors have found no weapons of mass destruction and that they would be easy to find if Iraq had them. They do not fit into someone's "pocket," he said. They would be obvious. Hussein claimed his country had "no interest in war" and he had "no wish to go to war," but that some are "looking for a pretext for war to justify war."[123]

Secretary of State Powell addressed the U.N. Security Council on February 5, 2003, a presentation he would later regret. It was a sobering event that included evidence reportedly characterized by C.I.A. Director, George Tenet, as a "slam dunk," which further solidified our national will to take action against Iraq. Tenet has since said that some in the Bush administration used him as a scapegoat, ruined his reputation, and took the term "slam dunk" completely out of context.[124]

Tenet wrote, "Many people believe that my use of the phrase 'slam dunk' was the seminal moment for steeling the president's determination to remove Saddam Hussein and to launch the Iraq war. It certainly makes for a memorable sound bite, but it belies the facts." Tenet said the decision to invade Iraq had been made before he made those remarks in December 2002.[125] He does not deny the use of the phrase. He says the phrase was used in the context of "sharpening the argument" to "Joe Public," as the president referred to the American people, that an invasion of Iraq was necessary. The day Tenet used that phrase, "Everyone in the room believed Saddam possessed WMD."[126] That may have been the case, but "slam dunk," as Tenet explains his use of the phrase, still seems unclear.

That belief was based on a National Intelligence Estimate (NIE), which Tenet was asked to produce in September 2002 by the Senate Select Committee on Intelligence before Congress voted to authorize the use of force against Iraq. Tenet was being pressed to come up with better information to add to the debate, information that would later be declassified to the extent that it would "help the public understand what we believed to be true." Tenet said he explained to the president "that strengthening the public presentation was a 'slam dunk.'"[127] In any case, Tenet's explanation of his use of the term "slam dunk" is as confusing as it reads.

According to another account of the "slam dunk" remark, the president turned to Tenet and asked if the information they had on WMDs was "the best we've got." It's a "slam dunk case," Tenet was to have confidently said. The president later said Tenet's assurance about WMD was key. "In fact, it provided a firewall for the President on the most serious charge history might level at him: taking the country to war under false pretenses. It was Tenet's fault. The SLAM DUNK sign would hang forever around Tenet's thick neck and be the first sentence of his obituary."[128]

George Tenet is a complex character in the drama of the Iraq war as the story unfolded. The president and Tenet each have been described as a man's man. They were the same kind of personalities, operating on instincts from the gut, visceral in their approach to the world. They enjoyed each other's company, and Tenet relished his close relationship with the president. Tenet has been described as a pleaser and certainly did not want to disappoint the president of the United States.

A loyal soldier who served at the pleasure of President Bush, Tenet was with Secretary Powell at the U.N. while he made a final argument against the Hussein regime. Tenet sat directly behind Powell, in full view of the television cameras. Powell had told Tenet he wanted him there for his testimony to symbolically give it more weight and gravitas.

Ray McGovern, a veteran C.I.A. analyst for over thirty years, said, "My first visual impression here, watching George Tenet, the head of the Central Intelligence Agency back there as a prop almost like a potted plant, as if to say that the Central Intelligence Agency stands behind, or in this case sits behind everything that Colin Powell says."[129] Tenet would later say the race to invade Iraq on the basis of WMD and the sale of yellowcake took on a life of its own. He said, "A careful reading of the NIE gives a more nuanced impression of its comments than the public has been led to believe."[130] This will be discussed in more detail later.

The information Powell dispensed was compelling. He said it came from "a variety of sources" which included the United States and those from other countries. He said some people had risked their lives to bring evidence against Iraq to light. Powell described "an accumulation of facts and disturbing patterns of behavior." He contended that Hussein was not disarming, but was concealing and, in fact, hiding by moving caches of weapons of mass destruction. "Saddam Hussein and his regime are busy doing all they possibly can to ensure that inspectors succeed in finding absolutely nothing. Every statement I make today is backed up by sources, solid sources. These are not assertions. What we're giving you are facts and conclusions based on solid intelligence."[131]

This testimony at the United Nations marked another definitive moment. Powell asserted that the United States had photos to back up claims of Iraq stashing and moving weaponry, that he had evidence of a relationship between Hussein and people from al Qaeda who orchestrated and carried out the 9/11 attacks, and that Hussein was actively shopping on the world market for materials to create a nuclear bomb. Powell was at the center stage of the world stage as he built a final public case for war. The information Powell cited would later be proven to be either misleading or false.

Later that day, with Secretary Powell at his side, the president reinforced the Secretary's points at the United Nations during a televised statement the following day at the White House. He urged the Security Council to back a new resolution that would demand again that Saddam disarm and fully declare its weapons programs or else the United Nations would sanction military action as a body against Iraq. He asked that the United Nations stand by its words and make good on its implied threats and said, "The United Nations can renew its purpose and be a source of stability and security in the world." The president also said the lack of such a resolution would not preclude action on the part of the United States. Again, he associated Iraq with the attacks of 9/11:

> On September the 11th, 2001, the American people saw what terrorists can do by turning four airplanes into weapons.
>
> Saddam Hussein has the motive and the means and the recklessness and the hatred to threaten the American people.
>
> Saddam Hussein will be stopped.[132]

Of those Americans who heard Powell's speech, 57 percent favored an invasion of Iraq, 42 percent said Powell made a "very strong case" for war with Iraq, and 37 percent said he made a "fairly strong case." Interestingly, they indicated they trusted Powell more than the president on

Iraq 56 to 39 percent. Perhaps this was because the public was familiar and comfortable with Secretary Powell on both a national and international stage. He had been a four star general with a distinguished record of service. He had served as national security advisor and as the chairman of the joint chiefs of staff.[133]

On February 14, 2003, Dr. Hans Blix, the Executive Chairman of UNMOVIC briefed the U.N. Security Council. He said the following:

> Since we arrived in Iraq [in January 2003], we have conducted more than 400 inspections covering more than 300 sites. All inspections were performed without notice, and access was almost always provided promptly. In no case, have we seen convincing evidence that the Iraqi side knew in advance that the inspectors were coming.

> Through the inspections conducted so far, we have obtained a good knowledge of the industrial and scientific landscape of Iraq, as well as of its missile capability but, as before, we do not know every cave and corner.

> The total number of staff in Iraq now exceeds 250 from 60 countries. This includes about 100 UNMOVIC inspectors, 15 IAEA (International Atomic Energy Agency), inspectors, 50 aircrew, 65 support staff.

> We note that access to sites have so far been without problems, including those that had never been declared or inspected, as well as Presidential sites and private residences.

> How much, if any, is left of Iraq's weapons of mass destruction and related proscribed items and programmes? So, far, UNMOVIC has not found any such weapons, only a small number of empty chemical munitions, which should have been declared and destroyed. Another matter—and one of great significance—is that many proscribed weapons and items are not accounted for. If they exist, they should be presented for destruction. If they do not exist, credible evidence to that effect should be presented.

> UNMOVIC is not infrequently asked how much more time it needs to complete its task in Iraq. The answer depends upon which task one has in mind—the elimination of weapons of mass destruction and related items or programmes, which were prohibited in 1991—the disarmament task—or the monitoring that no new proscribed activities occur. The latter task, though not often focused upon, is highly significant and not controversial. It will require monitoring, which is 'ongoing,' that is, open-ended until the Council decides otherwise. [134]

Also, weapons inspector and director general of the IAEA (International Atomic Energy Agency) Mohamed ElBaradei, addressed the Security Council and said, "We have to date found no evidence of ongoing prohibited nuclear activities in Iraq" and that there are "a number of issues under investigation, and we're not in a position to reach a conclusion about them."[135]

Subsequently, a progress report issued by the U.N. Security Council, reinforced Blix's testimony, saying no weapons of mass destruction had been located, and encouraged Iraq to continue to be cooperative.[136] The foreign ministers of China, Russia, and France, all permanent Security Council members, as are the United States and Great Britain, encouraged restraint and to give inspectors more time. French Foreign Minister, Dominique de Villepin said, "The option of inspections has not been taken to the end. The use of force would be so fraught with risk for the people, for the region, and for international stability that it should only be envisioned as a last resort."[137] Iraq's Deputy Prime Minister, Tariq Aziz, said, "Iraq doesn't have weapons of mass destruction" and "doesn't have any relationship with any terrorist group." A war against Iraq, he said, "would be interpreted in the Arab world as a crusade against Arabs and Muslims."[138]

Meanwhile, in mid-February, while millions around the world marched and protested in the streets against a military response to the problem of Iraq, an interesting story broke on CBS about the weapons inspectors. According to veteran correspondent Mark Phillips, U.N. inspectors told CBS News that various U.S. tips about the location of various weapons of mass destruction were "garbage after garbage after garbage."[139]

> Example: The United States provided satellite photographs purporting to show new research buildings at Iraqi nuclear sites. U.N. inspectors found nothing.

> Example: The U.S. supplied specific satellite coordinates on where to locate incriminating evidence Saddam's palaces. U.N. Inspectors found nothing.

> Example: The U.S. claimed that Iraq had imported aluminum tubes for enriching uranium. Iraqi scientists countered that they were used for making rockets. Inspectors, after interviewing the scientists, said the Iraqi response was "air tight."[140]

The Bush administration dismissed these reports and the testimony of Blix and ElBaradei by saying that "Saddam Hussein was used to deceiving the world" and that he "would be disarmed one way or another." National Security Advisor, Condoleezza Rice, appeared on both *Meet the Press* and *Fox News Sunday*. She urged the U.N. National Security Council to "carry out its obligations" and insisted that President Bush would not "back down." She directed one comment to Hussein himself by saying he was not going to "get away with it again," referring to "the game" he was playing with inspectors, letting them in one day, kicking them out another, and the primary contention of the United States, that he was moving and hiding weapons of mass destruction.[141] Secretary Rice was correct in her statement that inspectors were being toyed with by Hussein, but there is no evidence to suggest he was hiding or moving WMD.

The president and Secretary of Defense Donald Rumsfeld were discussing what they termed the "coalition of the willing," a cohort of countries that would join the United States in a military offensive. The coalition, Rumsfeld said, "will very likely be as large or larger than the coalition that existed in the Gulf War. The United States will not go it alone, it will go with a great many countries."[142] Secretary of State Colin Powell named thirty countries and said there were an additional fifteen that did not declare support, but would provide assistance. They included: Afghanistan, Albania, Australia, Azerbaijan, Bulgaria, Colombia, the Czech Republic, Denmark, El Salvador, Eritrea, Estonia, Ethiopia, Georgia, Hungary, Italy, Japan, South Korea, Latvia, Lithuania, Macedonia, the Netherlands, Nicaragua, the Philippines, Poland, Romania, Slovakia, Spain, Turkey, United Kingdom, and Uzbekistan.[143]

In early March, the president held a televised press conference, which was entirely devoted to Iraq. He called it an "important moment" in the war on terror. The world was expecting an update from the weapons inspectors about whether Hussein had "fully disarmed." Bush was telling the nation and the world that according to the intelligence the United States had received, Hussein had not disarmed and was conducting a "willful charade." Yet again, the president made the connection between Hussein and the terrorist attacks of 9/11:

> Saddam Hussein and his weapons are a direct threat to this country, to our people, and to all free people. The attacks of September 11, 2001 show what the enemies of the America did with four airplanes. We will not wait to see what terrorists or terrorist states could do with weapons of mass destruction. I will not leave the American people at the mercy of the Iraqi dictator and his weapons.[144]

Mr. Bush described this time as "the last phase of diplomacy." His intention, he said during the press conference, was to disarm Iraq, and encourage a regime change. The president said that Iraq had the previous twelve years to disarm itself, but that it had repeatedly failed to do so. At this point, it seemed that no matter what the U.N. report indicated, the Bush administration had made up its mind to invade.[145]

Vice President Cheney appeared on *Meet the Press* to discuss a war effort and the war itself, which now seemed a foregone conclusion. While the vice president said the administration was still in a diplomatic mode, he mostly described what a war would look like with Iraq. "We would be greeted as liberators," he said, and he laid out the objectives of the United States, which included, "taking down Saddam Hussein, eliminating weapons of mass destruction, preserving the territorial integrity of Iraq, and standing up a broadly representative government of the Iraqi people."[146] The vice president, like the president, insisted on connecting

Hussein with 9/11, repeatedly reminding the American people that the one pertained to the other, that an event as spectacular as 9/11 could happen and implied that, in fact, it would happen again should we leave in power a man like Saddam Hussein.

> Cheney: "We saw on 9/11 men hijack aircraft with airline tickets and box cutters, kill 3,000 Americans in a couple of hours. That attack would pale in comparison to what could happen, for example, if they [Iraq] had a nuclear weapon and detonated it in the middle of one of our cities. The cost would be much greater in a future attack if the terrorists have access to the kinds of capabilities that Saddam Hussein has developed."[147]

The very top leadership of our government was implying and, at times, was explicit in warning the American people that the action we were about to undertake was necessary because danger to the country was or could be imminent. How else could we believe? We had no choice *but* to trust the judgment of those who were allegedly educated about the intelligence, having been briefed by the sharpest minds in the intelligence community.

On March 17, 2003, in a fifteen-minute national address from the White House, President Bush issued Saddam Hussein an ultimatum. In forty-eight hours, be gone or face an attack from the United States "at a time of our choosing." The president was dissatisfied with diplomatic efforts by the United Nations and frustrated by the attitudes of those skeptical members of the U.N. Security Council.

He said, "The United Nations Security Council has not lived up to its responsibilities, so we will rise to ours." The president put our country on heightened alert in case there were reprisals. He warned American civilians, including journalists, to leave Iraq immediately. To the Iraqi people he offered assurances that the United States would not abandon them. "We will tear down the apparatus of power, and we will help you build a new Iraq that is prosperous and free. In a free Iraq, there will be no more wars of aggression against your neighbors, no more poison factories, no more executions of dissidents, no more torture chambers and rape rooms," he promised. [148]

To the American people the president provided yet another reminder of our vulnerability and the real possibility of another attack on U.S. soil:

> The danger is clear. Using chemical biological or, one day, nuclear weapons, obtained with the help of Iraq, the terrorists could fulfill their stated ambitions and kill thousands or hundreds of thousands of innocent people in our country or any other.

> We will set a course toward safety before the horror can come.

> Saddam Hussein and his terrorist allies could choose the moment of deadly conflict when they are strongest. We choose to meet that threat

now where it arises before it can appear suddenly in our skies and cities.[149]

Forty-eight hours later, the war was indeed a reality, and the so-called "Operation Iraqi Freedom" was already underway. The president defended our behavior in the name of liberty, freedom, justice, and the peace of the world he believed was hanging in the balance:

> My fellow citizens, at this hour, American and coalition forces are in the early stages of military operations to disarm Iraq, to free its people and to defend the world from grave danger.

> The people of the United States and our friends and allies will not live at the mercy of an outlaw regime that threatens the peace with weapons of mass murder.

> The dangers to our country and the world will be overcome. We will defend our freedom, we will bring freedom to others and we will prevail.[150]

From September 11, 2001, to March 19, 2003, within a period of just eighteen months and eight days, the Bush administration built public support that would alter beliefs and change behaviors. The American public essentially believed and trusted that its personal safety and our national security were imminently threatened. Another attack like the one on 9/11 could be at hand and could be even more devastating if the United States did not act decisively and expeditiously. It seemed we could not afford to leave the situation to chance.

Before 9/11, the president's job approval rating hovered between 55 and 60 percent. At the time of the February 2002 State of the Union, it had climbed to 86 percent and a year later, by the time the United States launched its attack, it was at a robust 71 percent.[151]

Despite what the American people believed about the purported danger of Iraq and how well they may have thought the president was doing his job, the facts surrounding the invasion and the president's self-created, rather insular reality were incongruous at best. Here is why.

Did Osama bin Laden and Saddam Hussein have a "diplomatic" relationship of convenience? Did Hussein have any involvement in 9/11? Hussein had no involvement in 9/11, and a relationship between the two, for all practical purposes, was nonexistent and, at that point in time, rather implausible. This was widely known and well understood. There was evidence that Iran may have provided support to al Qaeda and the Saudis as well, but "any Iraq 'link' to al Qaeda is a minor footnote when compared to the 'links' with other regimes. Not one of the possible 'links' between Iraq and al Qaeda rise to the level of noteworthy assistance and support," according to Richard A. Clarke, the counterterrorism expert who worked at the White House at the time of 9/11.[152] Also, Intelligence analysts said the information was not substantive enough to bolster the president's case for war and was more a point of information rather than instrumental in any way.

Scott Ritter, a member of UNSCOM's weapons inspection team in Iraq, said, "It would be ludicrous for Iraq to support al Qaeda, to give it weapons of mass destruction. Saddam is the apostate, the devil incarnate. He's evil in the eyes of these people. There are no facts to back up claimed connections between Iraq and al Qaeda. Iraq had no history of dealing with terrorists of this nature. It does have a history of using terrorism as a tool, but it's been used by Iraqi terrorists primarily focused on Iran, Syria and Iraqi opposition leaders abroad."[153]

Greg Thielmann, a former weapons analyst at the State Department's Bureau of Intelligence and Research (INR), said, "Saddam would have seen al Qaeda as a threat, and al Qaeda would have opposed Saddam as the kind of secular government they hated."[154] According to the 9/11 Commission, bin Laden "had explored possible cooperation with Iraq," but "Iraq never responded." There was never any "collaborative relationship" and according to two senior bin Laden "associates," there was no meaningful tie between Iraq and al Qaeda.[155]

There was some evidence of contact between the two between 1994 and 1996, but it was out of self-interest, perhaps even self-preservation, rather than for any tactical, long-term goals. For example, in 1997, bin Laden was invited to Kandahar, Afghanistan, by Taliban leader Mullah Omar for [bin Laden's] "own security." It was around then that bin Laden "put out feelers" to Iraq offering a non-descriptive "cooperation," but Hussein, according to reports, shunned the overtures as he was trying to re-establish a relationship with Saudi Arabia and other governments in the Middle East after the Gulf War.[156]

In 1998, when bin Laden ordered a "fatwa" against the United States, two al Qaeda officials met with Iraqi intelligence, and bin Laden was offered a safe haven in Iraq. Reportedly, bin Laden declined and considered his safety was better assured in Afghanistan, perhaps assuming "that his circumstances in Afghanistan remained more favorable than the Iraqi alternative."[157] It was clear that to surmise a relationship between Iraq and al Qaeda was a stretch and Iraq had no hand whatsoever in 9/11.[158]

Despite a comprehensive report from the trusted 9/11 Commission, which was impaneled to investigate the attacks and the government's response to it, Vice President Cheney had insisted in various media interviews that the evidence was "overwhelming" indicating a relationship between bin Laden and al Qaeda and Iraq and Saddam Hussein. "We don't know," if Iraq was involved with the attacks of 9/11, he said on CNBC. He tried to clarify his interpretation of the 9/11 Commission report explaining, "What the commission says is that they can't find evidence of that."[159]

The vice president referred to a meeting in Prague to help prove a link between al Qaeda and Iraq. The meeting allegedly occurred between Mohamed Atta, the lead hijacker in the 9/11 attack on the World Trade Center in New York, and an Iraqi diplomat, Ahmad Khalil Ibrahim Samir al Ani, at the Iraqi Embassy in Prague in April 2001. The Commission Report states, "No evidence has been found that Atta was in the Czech Republic in April 2001."[160] The report also states that "only some anecdotal evidence linked Iraq to al Qaeda," there was no "compelling case" that Iraq had either planned or perpetrated the attacks," bin Laden "resented" the secularism of the Hussein regime, and there was nothing confirmed that Hussein had cooperated with bin Laden on "unconventional weapons."[161] The vice president's use of the word "overwhelming" was both inaccurate and misleading.

A Congressional Research Service (CRS) Report prepared for Congress in February 2004 by Dr. Kenneth Katzman, a specialist in Middle East Affairs, wrote, "The F.B.I and C.I.A. eventually concluded the meeting probably did not take place, and there was no hard evidence of Iraqi regime involvement in the 9/11 attack."[162] Also, according to the report, Secretary of State Colin Powell stopped using those claims in future key speeches, once the claims were seriously questioned, but the vice president continued to use them on television news talk programs and in speeches.

Former C.I.A. counterterrorism specialist Vincent Cannistraro said the vice president's "willingness to use speculation and conjecture as facts in public presentations is appalling. It's astounding."[163] Very recently, however, on June 1, 2009, the former vice president conceded the information was not true this way: "I do not believe and have never seen any evidence to confirm that [Hussein] was involved in 9/11. We had that reporting for a while, [but] it eventually turned out not to be true."[164] Also, Cheney said, despite the facts, now contrary to what the Bush administration had reported to the American people, the removal of Saddam from power was the right thing to do and made the world a safer place. "What we did in Iraq was exactly the right thing to do. If I had it to recommend all over again, I would recommend exactly the same course of action."[165]

In a press conference on August 21, 2006, President Bush answered a question from a reporter who asked him why he had attacked Iraq in the first place. Bush first responded by saying "We thought he [Hussein] had weapons of mass destruction. Imagine a world in which Saddam Hussein was there, stirring up even more trouble in a part of the world that has so much resentment and so much hatred that people came and killed 3,000 of our citizens. The terrorists attacked us and killed 3,000 of our citizens before we started the freedom agenda in the Middle East."[166]

Reporter Question: "What did Iraq have to do with that?"

Bush: "What did Iraq have to do with what?"

Reporter: "The attack on the World Trade Center?"

Bush: "Nothing, except for its part of—and nobody's ever suggested in this administration that Saddam Hussein ordered the attack. The lesson of September the 11th is take threats before they fully materialize, Ken."[167]

After being briefed on classified information about "the relationship between Iraq and al Qaeda," Senator Joseph Biden (D-DE), reported, "credible evidence had not been presented."[168] Our European allies could find "no evidence of links" between Iraq and al Qaeda, which included information from "investigative magistrates, prosecutors, police, and intelligence officials."[169] Overall, claims that there was a partnership between Iraq and al Qaeda were unproven and slim, but there was insistence upon linking the two. "It was as if the Bush White House had adopted Walter Lippmann's recommendation to decide in advance what policies it wanted to follow and then to construct a propagandistic mass persuasion campaign to 'manufacture' the consent of the people to do what the 'specialized governing class' had already made up its mind to do."[170]

Richard Clarke, the antiterrorism expert, claimed that the president ignored a terrorist threat months before 9/11. When interviewed on the CBS news magazine *60 Minutes*, he said he made numerous requests to brief the president about the threat Osama bin Laden posed to the United States. "He [the president] ignored it. He ignored terrorism for months, when maybe we could have done something to stop 9/11."[171]

Immediately after 9/11, the president was pushing for strikes against Iraq, even though al Qaeda was in Afghanistan, Clarke said. "The President wanted me to find out whether Iraq did this. Now he never said 'make it up.' But the entire conversation left me with absolutely no doubt that George Bush wanted me to come back with a report that Iraq did this." The administration wanted there to be a connection between Iraq, 9/11, and Osama bin Laden, according to Clarke. The F.B.I. and the C.I.A. were sending reports to the president and to the National Security Advisor showing that Iraq had nothing to do with 9/11, and they were continually "bounced back." Clarke said we were not giving them the answer they wanted. "Do it again. The C.I.A. was sitting there, the F.B.I. was sitting there, I was sitting there saying we looked at this issue for years. For years we've looked, and there's just no connection."[172]

According to Michael Scheuer, who was a C.I.A. agent from 1982 to 2004, Director Tenet asked the agency to go back ten years to see if there was any connection between al Qaeda and Iraq. "I led the effort. And we went back 20 years. We examined 20,000 documents, probably along the line of 75,000 pages of information. And there was no connection between al Qaeda and Saddam." Tenet delivered this information directly to the president.[173]

In a secret Downing Street Memo, which contains top secret minutes taken during a meeting with British Prime Minister Tony Blair, one person said of the American approach to the terrorist attacks and its posture toward Iraq, "Intelligence and facts are being fixed around the policy." This overarching mentality, this "group-think," is also corroborated by Lawrence Wilkerson, chief of staff for Secretary of State Colin Powell. He publicly discussed the reasons for the use of so-called "enhanced interrogation techniques," which are classified as torture and a violation of Geneva Convention saying this method of interrogating detainees and other suspected terrorists from the time between 9/11 and the Iraq War in 2003 "was not aimed at preempting another terrorist attack on the U.S., but discovering a smoking gun linking Iraq and al Qaeda."[174]

U.S. Army Psychiatrist Major Paul Burney is quoted in a 261-page Senate Armed Services Report, issued in 2009. He was assigned to "support questioning of suspected terrorists at the Guantanamo Bay prison camp in Cuba."[175] He said, "This is my opinion. Even though they were giving information and some of it was useful, while we were there a large part of the time, we were focused on trying to establish a link between al Qaeda and Iraq and were not being successful in establishing a link between al Qaeda and Iraq. The more frustrated people got in not being able to establish this link . . . [the] more pressure to resort to measures that might produce more immediate results."[176]

Did Saddam Hussein possess weapons of mass destruction (WMD)? This was the primary pretext for war with Iraq and perhaps the most incendiary claim. None have been discovered in Iraq to date. In fact, in a recent October 2009 news report on ABC *World News*, the only weapons found in Iraq are those remnants left by the United States and coalition forces, many of whom are still there protecting the population from rogue insurgent tribal warriors, although fighting has substantially diminished. The president laid out his case for war based on the "fact" that Iraq was an "imminent threat" against the United States, although there was evidence disproving these charges. For example, in 2002 around the first anniversary of 9/11, the president had referred to a report by the International Atomic Energy Agency (IAEA) claiming that Iraq was "6 months away from developing a weapon." Such a report did not exist.[177]

Based on information that the Bush administration was releasing to the American public and the press, five busloads of reporters went in search of weapons of mass destruction in Iraq at a site used in the past to manufacture weapons. Reporters found no evidence to support a viable, active weapons program. Trained U.N. inspection teams dispatched to Iraq in November of 2002 discovered nothing of any import. Early the following year, in 2003, the British government published a report on its Downing Street website. It stated that the evidence that Iraq concealed its weapons and its overall deception about them was found to be based on the work of a postgraduate student. The information was a dozen years old.[178]

Early on, in 2002, when the British government understood that the United States was serious about ousting Saddam Hussein, the British agreed to support military action, but would only do so under certain conditions. Both governments would seek the reentry of U.N. weapons inspectors, and the Security Council would have to authorize the war, if Saddam was not cooperative. The British acknowledged, at the time, that the case for war was "thin."[179]

The biggest selling point, what most would convince the American people to accept a war with Iraq, was the evidence of weapons of mass destruction and the presumed intention of the Iraqi regime to use them against Americans. Americans were forced to consider this sobering information from the Bush administration in the wake of the 9/11 attacks. Greg Thielmann said, "Well, he [President Bush] was trying to build a case that Iraq posed an imminent danger, and there's no better way to scare the American people that to conjure up mushroom clouds."[180]

What most stuck in the minds of Americans was not that inspectors were not successful in finding evidence of WMDs; but that they were there somewhere, and inspectors eventually would find them. David Albright, president of the Institute for Science and International Security in Washington, DC, said, "I think that it's one of the mysteries, is why the administration could not change its assessment as new information became available. And you're left to conclude, unfortunately, that perhaps the WMD was somewhat an excuse, that they made up their mind they were going to attack Iraq and they needed a reason. This was the sellable reason. This is why people would get behind a war."[181]

The chief U.N. inspector in Iraq, Hans Blix, said that Washington's "virtual reality" about Iraq was in sharp contrast to "our old-fashioned reality." He wrote, "inspections and monitoring by the IAEA, UNMOVIC and its predecessor UNSCOM, backed by military, political and economic pressure, had indeed worked for years, achieving Iraqi disarmament and deterring Saddam from rearming. Containment had worked."[182]

David Kay, a scientist, veteran weapons inspector, and the head of the Iraq Survey Group, "a 1,400 plus person fact-finding mission set up by the Pentagon and C.I.A. to search for WMD in Iraq," resigned his post after reporting to Congress that there were no stockpiles of WMD. He said, "It turns out that we were all wrong, probably, in my judgment."[183]

On October 10, 2004, former National Security Advisor and Secretary of State Condoleezza Rice said in an interview on FOX, "We thought they [Iraq] had a more active weapons of mass destruction program than they had. We believed at the time that Saddam Hussein had reconstituted this biological and chemical weapons program and was likely making progress on his nuclear program. That was the assessment of the intelligence community." [184]

Former Secretary of State Colin Powell also blamed the intelligence community by saying, "The intelligence community did not work well. There were some people in the intelligence community who knew at the time that some of those sources were not good, and shouldn't be relied upon, and they didn't speak up." Powell was more circumspect, however, saying his speech to the United Nations indicting Iraq for a nonexistent weapons program was "a blot on his record" and "painful" because it was he who presented it "to the world." [185]

C.I.A. Director Tenet characterized the National Intelligence Estimate, which provided Secretary Powell with some of his testimony for the United Nations, as a rush job. "A production process that normally stretched for six to eight months, had to be truncated to less than three weeks." [186] Tenet said Congress wanted the report instantly. He admitted that some of the analysis provided to Powell was flawed, but that the report was also restrained and nuanced in its findings. The document was ninety pages long. "The phrase 'we do not know' appears some thirty times. The words 'we know' appear in only three instances." An estimate, he said, does not connote certifiable knowledge. He also accused many in Congress of not reading the entire report and of missing or ignoring the nuance in many of the findings. As the report was declassified and being discussed publicly, many went way "beyond what was in the estimate." Tenet suggested the report should have been written differently to make it clear that the evidence was a "matter of dispute among some analysts." [187] He wrote, "We should have said, in effect, that the intelligence was not sufficient to prove beyond a reasonable doubt that Saddam had WMD." Tenet said, however, the war was not only about the weapons of mass destruction and believed the administration probably would have gone to war anyway, no matter what the report indicated.

During a *Meet the Press* interview, former Secretary Powell had a different view and had this comment: "I think without the weapons of mass destruction case, the justification would not have been there. Even though Hussein was a terrible person, human rights abuses abounded, he was cheating on the U.N. Oil for Food Program. But I think it's doubtful that without the weapons of mass destruction case, the President and Congress, and the United Nations and those who joined us in the conflict—the British, the Italians, the Spanish, the Australians—would've found a persuasive enough case to support a decision to go to war." [188]

The vice president has remained defiant in his belief that weapons or not, the United States did the right thing by invading Iraq and overthrowing it leader. "Clearly, the intelligence was wrong. He [Saddam] had produced chemical weapons before and used them. He had produced biological weapons. He had a robust nuclear program in '91." [189]

Interestingly, according to Patricia Wald, a member of the Commission on the Intelligence Capabilities of the U.S. Regarding Weapons of Mass Destruction, a group impaneled by order of the president in 2004, the vice president had meetings with C.I.A. analysts "ten times" through mid-2002. The findings of the Commission report, later issued in 2005, concluded that those intelligence analysts "worked in an environment that did not encourage skepticism about the conventional wisdom" regarding Saddam having WMD and his relationship to 9/11 and those responsible.[190]

The president has said that the main reason the country went to fight in Iraq was the belief that Saddam was harboring weapons of mass destruction with the intent to use them. "It turns out he didn't have them," the president admitted during a press conference in 2006, but insisted instead, "he had the capacity to make weapons of mass destruction." This claim is faulty.

After the Gulf War, Saddam and his country were sufficiently weakened, unable to reconstitute a weapons program of any consequence, and by the time George W. Bush took office, the C.I.A. reported that there was "no direct evidence" Baghdad was rebuilding a weapons program. Not much had changed after 9/11. Any evidence weapons inspectors found was old, and after inspecting thirteen major "facilities of concern" in Iraq, the U.N. and the IAEA (International Atomic Energy Agency) reported no signs of weapons making.[191]

> Since 1998, Iraq has been fundamentally disarmed: 90-95% of Iraq's weapons of mass destruction capability has been verifiably eliminated. This includes all of the factories used to produce chemical, biological, and nuclear weapons and long-range ballistic missiles; the associated equipment of these factories; and the vast majority of the products coming out of these factories," according to Scott Ritter. The missing five to ten percent does not constitute a threat, or a weapons program, which means, "it doesn't amount to much.[192]

Former C.I.A. official Tyler Drumheller, a twenty-six-year veteran of the agency, spoke out on the CBS News magazine *60 Minutes* in April 2006 and corroborated that information. He said the administration became no longer interested in the "intel" about Iraq; it was interested in "regime change" in Iraq. "It just sticks in my craw every time I hear them say it's an intelligence failure. This was a policy failure."[193]

Mel Goodman, a thirty-four-year C.I.A. veteran who also worked as an intelligence analyst said, that though it was clear Iraq had no nuclear weapons program, "over and over again, President Bush, Secretary of Defense Rumsfeld, particularly Vice President Cheney, but also National Security Advisor Condi Rice drummed up the idea of reconstituted nuclear capability." It had "resonance" with the American people.[194]

On February 7, 2004, when asked by NBC's Tim Russert whether the war in Iraq was a war of necessity or a war of choice, now in light of finding no WMDs, the president said "In my judgment, we had no choice, when we look at the intelligence I looked at, that says the man was threat." The president's press secretary, Scott McClellan, later said the president was "puzzled" after the interview and did not understand what Russert was "getting at" with his question.[195]

When the president was interviewed by ABC's Diane Sawyer on December 16, 2003, he said whether or not there were any WMDs in Iraq, "Saddam Hussein was a danger, and the world is better off because we got rid of him." Sawyer pressed the president to clarify the distinction between Hussein actually having weapons of mass destruction and the possibility that he may have them at some future point in time. The president responded, "So what's the difference?"[196]

One of the most disconcerting episodes for the president came a year after the Iraq war began. Former Press Secretary McClellan wrote, "I could feel the muscles in my body tensing up as I listened to the president's tortured response to a straightforward question."[197] The question was from John Dickerson of *Time* magazine. He asked, "In the last campaign you were asked about the biggest mistake you've made in your life. You've looked back before 9/11 for what mistakes might have been made. After 9/11, what would your biggest mistake be, would you say, and what lessons have you learned from it?"[198]

McClellan said the president began with a "lighthearted quip" then there was an "an agonizingly long pause." He wrote, "I found myself thinking, 'come on, sir, this one is not difficult.'[199] The president finally came out with a rambling, incoherent response" as he spoke in broad terms about 9/11, Afghanistan, Iraq, and Hussein, but he could not articulate a response to a question about any mistake he had made since 9/11. He said, "I hope I—I don't want to sound like I've made no mistakes. I'm confident I have, I just haven't—you put me under the spot here, and maybe I'm not as quick on my feet as I should be in coming up with one."[200] McClellan: "There were many other times, in private and in public, when the president defended the most fateful decision of his administration. But few will be remembered as vividly as the one he made that night. It became symbolic of a leader unable to acknowledge that he got it wrong, and unwilling to grow in office by learning from his mistake—too stubborn to change and grow."[201]

Did Saddam Hussein purchase significant quantities of yellowcake from Niger from which could be later be used for a nuclear weapon? The simple answer is no. This was the third claim lodged for the case to war with Iraq made in the January 2003 State of the Union address. This claim was referred to as "the sixteen words." The administration claimed that the evidence of this purchase, in part, came from a document, referred to as "The Italian Letter" that will be discussed more fully in chapter 4. It supposedly "proved" the exchange of such product from Niger to Iraq. However, this bogus information became the "nexus of the controversy that delivered a near fatal blow to the credibility of the president and his administration."[202]

The genesis of the letter and the subsequent handling of the information included in the dossier was a quintessential case of ineptitude on the parts of many who were involved in what now might be described as a complicated international caper which actually began in 1998. The letter itself rose to prominence five years later and helped to precipitate the devastating consequences of the Iraq War. It is unnecessary here to chart the complexities of the politics and tension between those in the intelligence community, the State Department, and the White House about this information. It really detracts from the nub of the issue, which is this: Information, known to be false, made it to the lips of the president during an important State of the Union address at a time of great uncertainty for the country.

"Perhaps no single document has had such an impact on US policy and opinion since the detection of the Zimmerman Telegram in 1917, a secret communication from Germany to Mexico that helped draw the United States into World War I. But in that case, there was at least one fundamental difference: The Zimmerman Telegram, written by the German foreign minister, was intercepted by British intelligence. It was real."[203] The Italian Letter turned out to be a phony document with forged signatures. To date, no one knows for certain who forged it and who planted it in the dossier. More detail about The Italian Letter will be discussed later in the final chapter about the news media.

Most intelligence analysts concluded that the claim of such a business deal between Iraq, an unpredictable dictatorship, and Niger, one of the world's leading producers of uranium oxide, a form of uranium ore known as yellowcake, was not credible.[204] During the time after 9/11 and before the Iraq war, however, such information proved useful and a point of interest, but was used irresponsibly as it made its way to American officials.

Early in 2002, as the administration was weighing its options regarding Iraq, Joseph Wilson, who was the American Ambassador to Gabon from 1992 to 1995, was dispatched to Niger by the C.I.A. on a fact-finding mission to verify this alleged activity between Niger and Iraq. "I spent the next eight days drinking sweet mint tea and meeting with dozens of people: current government officials, former government officials, people associated with the country's uranium business. It did not take long to conclude that it was highly doubtful that any such transaction had ever taken place."[205] Wilson went on to explain that there were only two mines that were operated by a consortium of international interests. To move any such product, the consortium would have to sign off and would have to be monitored by the IAEA (International Atomic Energy

Agency). "There's simply too much oversight over too small an industry for a sale to have transpired."[206] Wilson reported his findings to the C.I.A. The White House was fully aware of what he discovered.

But, later that year, in the fall 0f 2002, Congress requested a National Intelligence Estimate (NIE). It was entitled "Iraq's Continuing Programs for Weapons of Mass Destruction" where the claim was made about the purchase of "yellowcake" by the Iraqis from Niger. "Based partly on this NIE, Congress voted overwhelmingly and across party lines on October 11, 2002, to authorize military action against Iraq by the commander in chief."[207]

Meanwhile, around the same time, Secretary of State Colin Powell and C.I.A. Director George Tenet appeared before a closed hearing of the Senate Foreign Relations Committee to discuss the Niger-Iraq connection. At the time, the information "was judged serious enough to include in the President's Daily Brief (PDB), one of the most sensitive intelligence documents in the American system."[208] Despite this, however, C.I.A. Director George Tenet, who was skeptical about the information, asked that any reference about the "yellowcake" sale be taken out of any speeches the president might give in the coming weeks. "The facts were too much in doubt," he said, and he had told Congress the day before the British had exaggerated the issue.[209] In sum, the intelligence about the purchase of uranium by Iraq from Niger could not be trusted, he argued.

One C.I.A. official said in fact "everybody knew at every step of the way that they were false—until they got to the Pentagon, where they were believed."[210] Another official said, "It's not a question as to whether they were marginal. They can't be 'sort of' bad, or 'sort of' ambiguous. They knew it was a fraud—it was useless."[211] Scott McClellan, the president's former press secretary, said that even though by this time everyone inside the White House understood the Niger claim was no good, the president and the State Department continued to cite it anyway.[212]

Analysts at the Bureau of Intelligence and Research (INR), a part of the State Department, did not even bother to have the documents officially translated from the French they were written in. "It was bullshit. It was clear it was bullshit," said one analyst.[213] They concluded that a sale of this magnitude in a country the size of Niger by a tightly managed French state-owned company that operated the mines could not have taken place. Also, they noted the sloppiness of the documents and a "funky" Nigerian seal, which had been altered "to make it look official." One of the letters in the dossier had been signed by a Nigerian "minister of foreign affairs and cooperation, who had been out of office since 1989. Another letter, allegedly from Tandja Mamadou, the president of Niger, had a signature that had obviously been faked and a text with inaccuracies so egregious, 'they could be spotted by someone using Google on the Internet.'"[214]

Analysts tried to get word up the chain to others in the State Department, but "few paid attention to its analytical product, much of which clashed with the hawks' assumptions."[215] Journalist Seymour Hersh reported that the Secretary of State had never seen the Niger documents and that C.I.A. Director Tenet was "ambivalent" about the information, but was successful in preventing the president from discussing it in an October 7, 2002, speech he gave in Cincinnati.[216] "But then Tenet seemed to give up the fight, and Saddam's desire for uranium from Niger soon became part of the administration's public case for going to war."[217]

In December 2002, the Bush administration made public that Niger was the seller of the nuclear materials to Iraq. Both countries denied the charge.[218] The next month, for a January 23, 2003, edition of the *New York Times*, Condoleezza Rice wrote an op-ed column entitled "Why We Know Iraq Is Lying." On January 26, 2003, in Davos, Switzerland, at the World Economic Forum, Secretary of State Powell addressed the issue of Iraq and its purchase of uranium from Africa. Two days later the president included the information in his January 28, 2003, State of the Union address, but the story immediately began to fall apart.[219]

George Tenet, who had argued that the language be purged from anything the president might say, admitted he had not read the final draft of the State of the Union speech and, in fact, said he had gone to bed long before the president's live televised address. He said he repeatedly said the allegation about "yellowcake" being sold to Iraq "was worthy of investigation." He also said "based on what we found, it was not worthy of inclusion in a presidential speech."[220] He did not believe he had to worry about it at that point and had no reason for concern regarding the president's speech specifically.

Two months after the war was launched, Nicolas Kristof, a Pulitzer Prize–winning columnist for the *New York Times*, reported that an unnamed "former U.S. Ambassador to Africa" [Joseph Wilson] had been sent to Niger to investigate the claims about the uranium from Niger. "The envoy reported to the C.I.A. and State Department that the information was unequivocally wrong and that the documents had been forged. The envoy's debunking of the forgery was passed around the administration and seemed to be accepted—except that President Bush and the State Department kept citing it anyway."

Mr. Wilson eventually went public in an op-ed in the *New York Times* entitled "What I Didn't Find in Africa" and also appeared on *Meet the Press* the same day it was published. The ambassador said he believed the Bush administration had deliberately deceived the American public in building its case for war. In response, the vice president and his staff made a concerted effort to discredit the ambassador, his trip to Niger and, through his Chief of Staff Lewis "Scooter" Libby, publicly identified his wife, Valerie Plame, by name as a C.I.A. operative, in essence destroying her long career with the agency.[221]

Despite statements made by the president and those in his administration asserting they acted based on what they believed to be true at the time, and although the former C.I.A. director himself subsequently admitted to some intelligence failures, many have said the president knew that information he came to understand over time was suspect and striking enough to change course. "He greatly exaggerated the dangers and opted for a do-it-yourself policy. Critics, especially those abroad, thought him a reckless gambler, departing from traditions that had given the United States its unique position among the world's democracies." The president "hermetically sealed off the White House and dispensed information to the public that reflected mostly what he wanted them to learn and believe." [222]

There is serious evidence enough to support the following claim. The president of the United States and key members of his administration progressively learned the information and intelligence was not credible enough to support a war, but insisted on circulating false claims, weak evidence, and information out of context to promote their agenda for an invasion of Iraq. This information gave the run-up to war some traction and provided those in Congress, the American people, and the news media enough apprehension and suspicion about Iraq to support the war, internalizing a better-to-be-safer-than-sorry mentality, particularly in the wake of the 9/11 attacks. It is clear, however, that since the information coming into the White House was evolving, the policy being developed in tandem should have been reviewed and reviewed again, especially when war was at hand and the lives of thousands were at risk.

Since the Iraq invasion, many have come forward in books and in the news media to say the president was briefed about such information and chose, despite it, to press forward, building a case of his own for a war based on the thinnest of evidence. There has been sufficient evidence from both the F.B.I. and the C.I.A., before 9/11 and after, that Iraq was not the source of our problems when we were attacked on 9/11. The president and his administration understood this to be the case and either ignored it, spun it to their advantage, or chose to believe a different reality. The president bolstered what little information was available to him about Iraq's connection to 9/11, WMD, and the Niger connection to build a case on false premises. Also, there are two reports to support claims that misinformation was circulated for the benefit of the Congress, the news media, and the public so that all would join the Bush administration in supporting an invasion.

Representative Henry Waxman, a Democrat from California, requested that an examination be conducted of statements made by the "five administration officials most responsible for providing public information and shaping public opinion on Iraq." They are President George Bush, Vice President Richard Cheney, Defense Secretary Donald Rumsfeld, Secretary of State Colin Powell, and National Security Advisor Condoleezza Rice. The Minority Staff Special Investigations Division compiled a database of statements made, which did not "include statements that in hindsight appear to be erroneous, but were accurate reflections of the views of intelligence officials at the time."[223]

It found that "the five officials made misleading statements about the threat posed by Iraq in 125 public appearances. The report further identified "237 specific misleading statements by the five officials." Also noted, the president specifically, made "55 misleading statements about the threat by Iraq in 27 separate public statements or appearances."[224]

According to another report by The Center for Public Integrity, "President George W. Bush and seven of his top administration officials, including Vice President Dick Cheney, National Security Adviser Condoleezza Rice, and Defense Secretary Donald Rumsfeld made at least 935 false statements in the two years following September 11, 2001, about the national security threat posed by Saddam Hussein."[225] The report shows that the statements were part of an "orchestrated campaign to galvanize public opinion." The country was led to war "under false pretenses" on the basis of "erroneous information" which the administration "methodically propagated."[226] The report also "calls into question the repeated assertions of Bush administration officials that they were the unwitting victims of bad intelligence."[227]

The president and his administration have repeatedly claimed the intelligence on which they built a case for war was faulty. However, many in the intelligence community have since come forward, breaking with their former director George Tenet, and at great risk to their reputations, to say the intelligence was sound and clear on the points the president cited to go to war in the first place. Many have said he was directly advised the intelligence was not sound enough to launch a war. And if the president of the United States were to admit that he left much of his foreign policy decisions to the vice president and others in the cabinet, thus pleading ignorance, this would be both a preposterous and damaging admission, one surely the president would not make.

It would also be absurd for the president to admit that he did not understand the historical implications of war with such an enemy given his father's experiences with Iraq and a well-documented trail of evidence all concluding that Iraq had no business with al Qaeda. Also, the president must have pondered the instability of the Middle East, the possibility of a new Iraq in turmoil with an unfamiliar leader at the helm of power. Though Vice President Cheney believed and promoted the notion that U.S. forces would be greeted as liberators should Saddam be toppled, given history and emerging evidence to the contrary, this was clearly an optimistic view and an overstatement.

With respect to the intelligence community itself, if it believed that the president and those high up in his administration were deliberately misleading the nation while crucial policy was being formulated, why did it keep silent? Many in the intelligence community understood that fraudulent intelligence was deliberately and publicly being touted as fact, and no weapons of mass destruction were turning up anywhere in Iraq, as many knew months before, that none ever would be. Although not necessarily surprising, they never came forward to publicly dispute the president or those in his administration at the time, even if at the expense of their jobs. It was not until many months later, and not until after the fact, that they came forward.

It is true that there were also institutional failures at many levels, but the buck, as Harry Truman once so aptly put it, stops at the desk of the president. There were too many clues obvious for the president to have simply missed them or been misled about them over eighteen long months. The president may have wanted to protect the country after 9/11, but he disregarded and marginalized emerging evidence and facts because they were contradicting his early objectives.

"Every detail of the proposed remedy—to protect the nation against terrorism—was mistakenly represented. The threats posed by terrorists and rogue states—the administration chose to link the two—were unlikely to be as immediately threatening to the survival of United States as those posed by Nazi Germany and the Communist Soviet Union."[228] Like those two periods in our history, what was required by the president was a deliberative "calculated policy over time" drawing strategic allies near to defeat the real enemy, proven to have been a violent menace around the world and for years. That was Osama bin Laden and his band of terrorists called al Qaeda.

To date, the story of the Iraq war and the political fallout continues. Osama bin Laden was finally killed by an elite team of Navy Seals on May 1, 2011, in Pakistan, but al Qaeda remains a threat, operating in Afghanistan, Pakistan, Yemen, and from terrorist cells in other parts of the world. According to a report issued in November 2009 by the U.S. Senate Foreign Relations Committee, prepared at the request of its Chairman, Senator John Kerry of Massachusetts, Osama bin Laden was definitely within the grasp of U.S. military forces shortly after 9/11. His escape has "laid the foundation for today's reinvigorated Afghan insurgency and inflamed the internal strife now endangering Pakistan."[229]

After the publication of the report, Representative Maurice Hinchey, a Democrat from New York, appeared on MSNBC and said: "Look what happened with regard to our invasion into Afghanistan, how we apparently intentionally let bin Laden get away. That was done by the previous administration because they knew very well that if they would capture al Qaeda, there would be no justification for an invasion in Iraq. There's no question that the leader of the military operations of the U.S. called back our military, called them back from going after the head of al Qaeda." Hinchey was asked if he thought President Bush deliberately let him get away. "Yes, I do," said the congressman.[230] President Bush was personally advised in November 2001 to mobilize U.S. troops in Tora Bora so he wouldn't lose his prey, Osama bin Laden. U.S. Special Forces had him in their sights. "Bush didn't heed the advice."[231]

Former President Bush did not see it this way. In his memoir, he wrote that the "intelligence never panned out" and that the information about bin Laden's whereabouts was conflicting. "Critics charged that we allowed bin Laden to slip the noose at Tora Bora. If we had ever known for sure where he was, we would have moved heaven and earth to bring him to justice," he wrote.[232]

In Great Britain, a special inquiry began in November 2009 in an effort to explain its own involvement in the Iraq War. Testimony revealed that members of the Bush administration wanted to topple Saddam Hussein after Bush was elected in 2000, before the 9/11 attacks, and had approached Britain's Tony Blair government about doing so. The Blair administration at first distanced itself from such a prospect because it knew any such invasion was "unlawful." Later, Britain joined the war effort against Iraq.

Former Prime Minister Blair has since repeatedly stated in news reports that Britain also believed at the time Iraq possessed WMD and was a threat. In his memoir, "A Journey," Blair stated he does not regret the decision to go to war. "Based on what we do know now, I still believe that leaving Saddam in power was a bigger risk to our security than removing him and that, terrible though the aftermath was, the reality of Saddam and his sons in charge of Iraq would at least arguably be much worse."[233]

However, Sir Peter Ricketts, a former member of the British Joint Intelligence Committee (JIC) and now head of its Foreign Office, testified that the then U.S. National Security Adviser, Condoleezza Rice, had written a paper pushing for regime change in Iraq before 9/11. Also, during the course of his testimony, he said, British intelligence had no evidence of a relationship between bin Laden and Hussein and that there was neither any evidence connecting Hussein to the attacks of 9/11.[234]

The next chapter will address the role of Congress in the run-up to war with Iraq. It bears some responsibility for our actions between 9/11 and March 19, 2003. How did it respond to the claims made by the Bush administration? What was the response of Congress to the attacks of 9/11 in the short term, and in the run-up to the war with Iraq in the long term? What did members of Congress say on the record about the role of Congress as the Bush administration anticipated and prepared for a war with Iraq?

NOTES

1. Official Transcript, March 7, 2003, U.N. Security Council

2. Ibid.

3. Bamford, James. *A Pretext for War* (New York: Doubleday, 2004), 340.

4. Ibid., 337.

5. Ibid., 360.

6. Graubard, Stephen. *Command of Office* (New York: Basic Books, 2004), 549.

7. Ibid., 549–50.

8. Bamford, James. *A Pretext for War* (New York: Doubleday, 2004), 334.

9. Ibid., 336.

10. Risen, James. *State of War* (New York: Free Press, 2006), 226–27.

11. Suskind, Ron. *The One Percent Doctrine* (New York: Simon & Schuster, 2006), 341.

12. Chomsky, Noam. "Propaganda System: Orwell's and Ours." *Propaganda Review*, no. 1 (1987–1988): 14–18.

13. Jacobson, Gary C. "The Bush Presidency and the American Electorate." *Presidential Studies Quarterly* 33, no. 4 (2003): 701.

14. *The Washington Post* by Jennifer Agiesta, July 24, 2007, Gallup Poll.

15. Graubard, Stephen. *Command of Office* (New York: Basic Books, 2004), 542.

16. Chomsky, Noam. *Understanding Power* (New York: W. W. Norton & Company, Inc., 2002), 11.

17. Lippmann, Walter. *Public Opinion* (New York: Macmillan, 1949), 16.

18. Plato. *The Allegory of the Cave, Book VII, The Republic*, 360 BC, (taken from the Benjamin Jowett translation (Vintage, 1991), pp. 253-261.

19. Cohen, Bernard Cecil. *The Press & Foreign Policy* (Princeton: Princeton University Press, 1963), 13.

20. Bennett, Lance W. *News: The Politics of Illusion* (New York: Longman, 1988), 178–79.

21. Kuypers, Jim A. *Bush's War* (Lanham, MD: Rowman & Littlefield Publishers, Inc., 2006), 2.

22. Ibid.

23. Ibid.

24. Pew Research Center Project for Excellence in Journalism, "How 9/11 Changed the Evening News," September 11, 2006.

25. Ivie, Robert L. "Images of Savagery in American Justifications for War," *Communication Monographs* 47 (1980): 279–94.

26. Kuypers, Jim A. *Bush's War* (Lanham, MD: Rowman & Littlefield Publishers, Inc., 2006), 3.

27. Ivie, Robert L. "Cold War Motives and the Rhetorical Metaphor: A Framework of Criticism," in *Cold War Rhetoric: Strategy, Metaphor, and Ideology* (New York: Greenwood Press, 1990), 72.

28. Official transcript, President Dwight D. Eisenhower speech in Pittsburgh, sponsored by the Allegheny County Republican Executive Committee, November 4, 1960.

29. Greenstein, Fred I. *The Presidential Difference* (Princeton: Princeton University Press, 2001), 5–6.

30. Graubard, Stephen. *Command of Office* (New York: Basic Books, 2004), 542.

31. Drehle, David Von, and R. Jeffrey Smith. "US Strikes Iraq for Plot to Kill Bush." *The Washington Post*, June 27, 1993, A01.

32. Woodward, Bob. *State of Denial* (New York: Simon & Schuster, 2006), 16.

33. Ibid.

34. O'Neill, Paul. *The Price of Loyalty: George W. Bush, The White House and the Education of Paul O'Neill* (Waterville, ME: Thorndike Press, 2004), 72.

35. Ibid.

36. Ibid., 85.

37. Ibid., 86.

38. Woodward, Bob. *State of Denial* (New York: Simon & Schuster, 2006), 16.

39. www.margaretthatcher.org/archive.

40. www.whitehouse.gov/news/releases/2001/09/2001/20010911.

41. Woodward, Bob. *State of Denial* (New York: Simon & Schuster, 2006), 19.

42. PBS, WGBH, *Frontline* transcript, "Bush's War," March 24 2008.

43. www. whitehouse.gov/news/releases/2001/09/2001/20010911.

44. PBS, WGBH, *Frontline* transcript, Bush's War, March 24 2008.

45. www.whitehouse.gov/news/releases/2001/09/20010911.

46. Tenet, George. *At the Center of the Storm, My Years at the CIA* (New York: Harper-Collins Publishers, 2007), xviiii.

47. Clarke, Richard A. *Against All Enemies* (New York: Free Press, 2004), 30.

48. Ibid., 30–31.

49. Ibid., 32.

50. Ibid.

51. Kuypers, Jim A. *Bush's War* (Lanham, MD: Rowman & Littlefield Publishers, Inc., 2006), 19.

52. www.archives.cnn.com/2001/US/09/17/bush.powell.terrorism.

53. Ibid.

54. Ibid.

55. wwW. W.hitehouse.gov/vicepresident/news/-speeches/vp20010916.

56. Ibid.

57. Woodward, Bob. *State of Denial* (New York: Simon & Schuster, 2006), 77.

58. www.whitehouse.gov.news/releases.2001/09/20010920.

59. Ibid.

60. Ibid.

61. Woodward, Bob. *State of Denial* (New York: Simon & Schuster, 2006), 81.

62. ABC News, *This Week* with George Stephanopoulos, September 18, 2001.

63. CNN, *War Room* with Wolf Blitzer, September 19, 2001.

64. FOX NEWS, September 24, 2001.

65. ABC, *Nightline* with Ted Koppel, November 28, 2001.

66. www.archives.cnn.com/2001/US/10/07.

67. NBC, *Meet the Press* with Tim Russert, October 7, 2001.

68. wwW. W.hitehouse.gov/news/2001/10/20011007.

69. Official transcript, PBS, OnLine *NewsHour*, October 9, 2001.

70. NBC, *Today Show* with Katie Couric and Matt Lauer, October 10, 2001.

71. ABC, *Good Morning America* with Charles Gibson, October 10, 2001.

72. wwW. W.hitehouse.gov/news/2001/10/20011007.

73. *Al Jazeera* television network, October 16, 2001.

74. www.guardian.co.uk.world/2001/oct/14/terrorism/afghanistan.

75. CBS, *Face the Nation* with Bob Schieffer, October 21, 2001.

76. CBS, *60 Minutes*, October 5, 2008.

77. Ibid.

78. Tenet, George. *At the Center of the Storm, My Years at the CIA* (New York: Harper-Collins Publishers, 2007), 225.

79. Ibid., 226.

80. Interview with Amanda Kibel, former correspondent for CNN, November 22, 2007.

81. PBS, *Buying the War*, Bill Moyers Journal, April 8, 2007.

82. www.defenselink.mil.transcripts/transcript.aspx.

83. Official White House transcript, November 10, 2001.

84. Woodward, Bob. *State of Denial* (New York: Simon & Schuster, 2006), 81.

85. Ibid., 84–85.

86. Woodward, Bob. *Plan of Attack* (New York: Simon & Schuster, 2004), 8.

87. Ibid.

88. Ibid.

89. Official State Department transcript, December 6, 2001.

90. Official White House transcript, December 7, 2001.

91. Official White House transcript, December 20, 2001.

92. Official White House transcript, December 9, 2001.

93. Ibid.

94. Official Department of Defense transcript December 2, 2001.

95. Official State Department transcript, December 16, 2001.

96. Official White House transcript. January 29, 2002.

97. Ibid.

98. Ibid.

99. Ibid.

100. Ibid.

101. Schlesinger, Arthur M. *War and the American Presidency* (New York, London: W. W. Norton & Company, 2004), 21.

102. Pitt, William Rivers, with Scott Ritter. *War on Iraq: What Team Bush Doesn't Want You to Know on Iraq* (New York: Context Books, 2002), 27.

103. Official transcript, CBS, *Face the Nation* with Bob Schieffer, February 3, 2002.

104. Official transcript, NBC, *Meet the Press* with Tim Russert, February 17, 2002.

105. Official transcript, PBS, *Newsmakers* February 4, 2002.

106. Official transcript, CNN, *Late Edition* with Wolf Blitzer, March 24, 2002.

107. Official transcript, NBC, *Meet the Press* with Tim Russert, May 19, 2002.

108. Official transcript, CNN, *Late Edition* with Wolf Blitzer, May 19, 2002.

109. Official White House transcript, June 1, 2002.

110. Ibid.

111. Rich, Frank. *The Greatest Story Ever Sold* (New York: The Penguin Press, 2006), 239–40.

112. Ibid.

113. Official transcript, CNN, *Late Edition* with Wolf Blitzer, September 8, 2002.

114. Official transcript, NBC, *Meet the Press* with Tim Russert, September 8, 2002.

115. Official CNN archival transcript, September 12, 2002.

116. Ibid.

117. Official transcript, *The Guardian*, January 17, 2003.

118. Interview with CNN correspondent Christianne Amanpour at UC Berkeley, March 18, 2004.

119. www.geneva.usmission.gov/press/2003/2601Powell.

120. Official transcript, NBC, *Meet the Press* with Tim Russert, January 26, 2003.

121. Official White House transcript, January 28, 2003.

122. Ibid.

123. British Channel 4, February 4, 2003. (From YouTube.)

124. CBS, *60 Minutes* interview with Scott Pelley, April 30, 2007.

125. Tenet, George. *At the Center of the Storm, My Years at the CIA* (New York: Harper-Collins Publishers, 2007), 357.

126. Ibid., 361.

127. Ibid., 362.

128. Suskind, Ron. *The One Percent Doctrine* (New York: Simon & Schuster, 2006), 188.

129. Official transcript, Fox News, "Uncovered: The War on Iraq," 2004, Carolina Productions.

130. Tenet, George. *At the Center of the Storm, My Years at the CIA* (New York: Harper-Collins Publishers, 2007), 327.

131. Official White House transcript, February 5, 2003.

132. Official White House transcript, February 5, 2003.

133. Gallup poll.

134. Official transcript, Briefing of the (U.N.) Security Council, February 14, 2003.

135. Ibid.

136. CNN transcript, U.N. Security Council proceedings, February 14, 2003.

137. Ibid.

138. Official transcript, Fox News, February 14, 2003.

139. Official transcript, CBS News, January 18, 2003.

140. Ibid.

141. Official transcript, NBC, *Meet the Press* with Tim Russert, February 17, 2003.

142. Official transcript, CNN, February 14, 2003.

143. Official transcript, BBC News, March 18, 2003.

144. Official transcript, CBC News, March 3, 2003.

145. Ibid.

146. Official transcript, NBC, *Meet the Press* with Tim Russert, March 16, 2003.

147. Ibid.

148. Official transcript, CNN, March 17, 2003.

149. Ibid.

150. Official White House transcript, March 19, 2003.

151. Gallup.

152. Clarke, Richard A. *Against All Enemies* (New York: Free Press, 2004), 270.

153. Pitt, William Rivers, with Scott Ritter. *War, What Team Bush Doesn't Want You to Know on Iraq* (New York: Context Books, 2002), 51.

154. Official transcript, PBS, *Frontline*, "Bush's War," March 24, 2008.

155. Pincus, Walter, and Dana Milbank. "Al Qaeda-Hussein Link Is Dismissed," *Washington Post*, June 17, 2004, A1.

156. Final Report of the National Commission on Terrorist Attacks Upon the United States. *The 9/11 Commission Report* (New York: W. W. Norton & Company, 2004), 65–66.

157. Ibid., 66.

158. Ibid.

159. Official transcript, CNN, June 18, 2004.

160. Final Report of the National Commission on Terrorist Attacks Upon the United States. *The 9/11 Commission Report* (New York: W. W. Norton & Company, 2004), 66.

161. Ibid., 334.

162. Katzman, Kenneth. *CRS Report for Congress*. Library of Congress, February 5, 2004, pg. 8.

163. Kornblut, Anne E., and Bryan Bender. "Cheney Link of Iraq, 9/11 Challenged." *Boston Globe*, September 16, 2003.

164. Official transcript, CNN, June 1, 2009.

165. Nichols, Bill. "Barbs Fly as No. 2's Try to Inflict Damage." *USA Today*, October 5, 2004.

166. Official White House transcript, August 21, 2006.

167. Ibid.

168. Fisher, Louis. "Deciding on War against Iraq: Institutional Failures." *Political Science Quarterly* 118 (2003): 399.

169. Ibid.

170. Gore, Al. *The Assault on Reason* (New York: Penguin Group, 2007), 44.

171. Official transcript, CBS, *60 Minutes* with Lesley Stahl, March 3, 2004.

172. Ibid.

173. Offical transcript, PBS, "Bush's War," March 24, 2008.

174. Official transcript, CNN, March 14, 2009.

175. Ibid.

176. Ibid.

177. Fisher, Louis. "Deciding on War against Iraq: Institutional Failures." *Political Science Quarterly* 118 (2003): 399.

178. Ibid.

179. Hanley, Charles J. "Piecing together the story of the weapons that weren't." *USA Today*, September 2, 2005.

180. Official transcript, PBS, "Chasing Saddam's Weapons" January 22, 2004.

181. Official transcript, PBS, "Bush's War," March 24, 2008.

182. Lewis, Patricia. "Why We Got It Wrong: Attempting to Unravel the Truth of Bioweapons in Iraq." *UNU Iraq* 2, ch. 8, pg. 12.

183. McClellan, Scott. *What Happened* (New York: Public Affairs, 2008), 202.

184. Official transcript, FOX *News Sunday*, with Chris Wallace, October 15, 2006.

185. Associated Press report, September 8, 2005.

186. Tenet, George. *At the Center of the Storm, My Years at the CIA* (New York: Harper-Collins, 2007), 323.

187. Ibid., 327.

188. Official transcript, NBC, *Meet the Press* with Tim Russert, June 10, 2007.

189. Official transcript, NBC, *Meet the Press* with Tim Russert, September 10, 2006.

190. Hanley, Charles J. "Piecing together the story of the weapons that weren't." *USA Today*, September 2, 2005.

191. Ibid.

192. Pitt, William Rivers, with Scott Ritter. *War on Iraq: What Team Bush Doesn't Want You to Know About* (New York: Context Books, 2002), 28–29.

193. Official transcript, CBS, *60 Minutes* with Ed Bradley, April 23, 2006.

194. Official transcript, "Uncovered: The Whole Truth About the Iraq War," 2004.

195. McClellan, Scott. *What Happened* (New York: Public Affairs, 2008), 203.

196. Ibid., 200.

197. Ibid., 203.

198. Ibid., 204.

199. Ibid., 205.

200. Ibid., 205–6.

201. Ibid., 207.

202. Ibid., 5.

203. Eisner, Peter, and Knut Royce. *The Italian Letter* (New York: Rodale, 2007), 5.

204. Hersh, Seymour M. *Chain of Command* (New York: HarperCollins Publishers, 2004), 204.

205. Wilson, Joseph. "What I Didn't Find in Africa." *New York Times*, July 3, 2003.

206. Ibid.

207. Ibid.

208. Hersch, Seymour M. *Chain of Command* (New York: HarperCollins Publishers, 2004), 204–5.

209. Tenet, George. *At the Center of the Storm, My Years at the CIA* (New York: Harper-Collins Publishers, 2007), 449–50.

210. Hersh, Seymour M. *Chain of Command* (New York: HarperCollins Publishers, 2004), 233.

211. Ibid.

212. McClellan, Scott. *What Happened* (New York: Public Affairs, 2008), pg. 7

213. Eisner, Peter, and Knut Royce. *The Italian Letter* (New York: Rodale, 2007), 39.

214. Hersh, Seymour M. *Chain of Command* (New York: HarperCollins Publishers, 2004), 206.

215. Eisner, Peter, and Knut Royce. *The Italian Letter* (New York: Rodatel, 2007), 40.

216. Hersh, Seymour M. *Chain of Command* (New York: HarperCollins Publishers, 2004), 233.

217. Ibid.

218. Ibid., 205.

219. Ibid., 233–34.

220. Tenet, George. *At the Center of the Storm, My Years at the CIA* (New York: Harper-Collins Publishers, 2007), 451.

221. Ibid., 168–69.

222. Graubard, Stephen. *Command of Office* (New York: Basic Books, 2004), 545–47.

223. United States House of Representatives. Committee on Government Reform, Minority Staff, Special Investigations Division. "Iraq on the Record, The Bush Administration's Public Statements on Iraq," prepared for Rep. Henry Waxman, 2004.

224. Ibid.

225. The Center for Public Integrity. "False Pretenses." Charles Lewis and Mark Reading-Smith. January 23, 2008.

226. Ibid.

227. Ibid.

228. Graubard, Stephen. *Command of Office* (New York: Basic Books, 2004), 545.

229. *Associated Press,* November 29, 2009.

230. Official transcript, MSNBC, November 29, 2009.

231. Suskind, Ron. *The One Percent Doctrine* (New York: Simon & Schuster, 2006), 351.

232. Bush, George W. *Decision Points* (New York: Crown Publishers, 2010), 202.

233. Today.MSNBC.msn.com, September 1, 2010.

234. Norton-Taylor, Richard. "Iraq war inquiry: Britain heard US drumbeat for invasion before 9/11," *The Guardian,* November 24, 2009.

THREE

The United States Congress and Iraq

Checks, Balance, and Oversight

Allow the president to invade a neighboring nation, whenever he shall deem it necessary to repel an invasion, and you allow him to do so, whenever he may choose to say he deems it necessary for such a purpose—and you allow him to make war at pleasure. . . .

If, today, he should choose to say he thinks it necessary to invade Canada, to prevent the British from invading us, how could you stop him? You may say to him, "I see no probability of the British invading us" but he will say to you, "Be silent. I see it if you don't."

—Congressman Abraham Lincoln, Letter to William H. Herndon, February 15, 1848

The Congress was intimidated after 9/11. People were afraid to get in the way of a strong executive who was talking about suppressing a vicious enemy, and we were AWOL for a while, and I'll take the blame for that. We should have been more aggressive after 9/11 in working with the executive to find a collaboration, and I think the fact that we weren't probably hurt the country. I wish I had spoken out louder and sooner.

—Lindsay Graham, (R) South Carolina

INTRODUCTION

What was the role of Congress during the run-up to the war with Iraq after the attacks of 9/11? What was the role of congressional committees that should have provided the necessary oversight? How did Congress react as an institution and how did particular members of the leadership, on both sides of the aisle, direct their parties? Did it ask enough questions before agreeing to sanction a war, the justifications for which were not accurately vetted? Was it disempowered for lack of credible intelligence? Was it deliberately kept in the dark? What other factors affected its behavior as an institution?

Many since the attacks of 9/11 have criticized Congress for being docile and malleable as a war with Iraq was being orchestrated by an executive branch that was clearly emboldened after the crisis on 9/11. In a detailed and reflective *New York Times* magazine cover story about President Bush, entitled "After the Imperial Presidency," author Jonathan Mahler quoted framer James Madison who said: "Ambition must be made to counteract ambition." Mahler continued: "America's divided system of government would depend on both the president and Congress forcefully pursuing their respective roles and in doing so, acting as a natural check on each other." Those prescribed institutional checks and balances "failed" during the Bush administration.[1]

Journalist Thomas E. Ricks referred to members of Congress and its collective behavior, in advance of the invasion of Iraq, as "the silence of the lambs." He wrote, "The role of Congress in this systematic failure was different, because its mistakes were mainly of omission. In the months of the run-up to war, Congress asked very few questions."[2]

Congress shares responsibility for the country's military actions after 9/11. It voted to authorize the attack on Afghanistan to avenge those who attacked us on 9/11. Arguably, that military action was justified. It was a quid pro quo. The United States understood, without doubt, that Osama bin Laden launched the 9/11 attacks from Afghanistan. The intelligence community had been forewarned of such attacks. Shortly after, bin Laden himself, on behalf of Al Qaeda, the organization he leads, directly claimed responsibility for them.

Congress also voted to authorize the invasion of Iraq, but this military action was different. Much different. Members of Congress in both the House and Senate were remiss in not asking more questions and demanding more evidence to justify a war for which "the potential costs, risks, and consequences" would produce a "dangerous gamble that could be damaging to American and (Western) interests" and could both undermine and escalate the war on terror.[3] "For its part, Congress seemed incapable of analyzing a presidential proposal and protecting its institutional powers. The decision to go to war cast a dark shadow over the health of U.S. political institutions and the celebrated system of democratic debate and checks and balances."[4]

It was years after the start of the war that Congress acknowledged Iraq had no weapons of mass destruction, that Saddam Hussein had no relationship of any meaningful consequence with Osama bin Laden, and that he (Saddam) had not purchased uranium from Niger. It was not until 2005, too late and long after the fact, that members became more vocal in opposition to the war and more openly critical of the president, his staff, and decisions, which had already been implemented. Why?

Just prior to the launch of the Iraq war, Congress seemed overwhelmed by what had befallen the country and appeared quieted by a forceful executive in the president, who vowed that his administration and his party would keep America safe going forward. In large measure, opinion polls indicated the public supported the president with a 71 percent approval rating.[5] The day of 9/11, the president's approval ratings went from mediocre to astronomical almost overnight. Matthew Dowd, President Bush's pollster, said, "I had done a poll that finished the morning of 9/11. [Before the attacks.] I was going to go to Washington that day to present the findings to Karl [Rove]. The amazing thing about that is: not a single question was asked about foreign policy, terrorism, national security. In the poll I'd been sitting on, Bush's approval was 51 or 52 percent. Twenty-four hours later [after the attacks] his approvals are 90 percent."[6]

Support of the president of the United States is essential after a crisis such as 9/11. However, what the country also requires is a stabilizing force in the so-called "first branch of government," which is the Congress. After 9/11, the role of Congress could have been this: "Powerful, independent, representing a large and diverse republic, to deliberate on important policy questions, and to check and balance the other branches."[7] The point is more questions were necessary, more debate was imperative, increased oversight was sorely lacking, and answers to questions should have been demanded by Congress before it agreed to fund another war while the first one had not yet yielded a successful result. Success would have been the apprehension of the person and persons responsible for the murder of three thousand Americans on 9/11.

Louis Fisher wrote that "the dismal performance of the executive and legislative branches raise[s] disturbing questions about the capacity and desire of the United States to function as a republican form of government. A republic means giving power to the people through their elected representatives, trusting in informed legislative deliberation rather than monarchical edicts, and keeping the war power in Congress instead of transferring it to the president."[8]

The Bush administration and, especially, veteran politician Vice President Richard Cheney, were "contemptuous of congressional hand-wringers" and so "felt the urge to move fast" on many fronts. He encouraged the president to do so. Congress was also encouraged to rush through decision-making. It is not that Congress did nothing in response to being pressured, but rather it did not do enough. It should not have been distracted from its duty because of politics, and it should not have been influenced or paralyzed by the forces of fear and apprehension resulting from the attacks.[9]

Over time, from the attacks of September 11, 2001, to March 19, 2003—day one of the Iraq invasion—Congress should have more carefully weighed its moral obligation or could have better exercised its influence through more and better oversight to slow an aggressive presidential/executive agenda that was in perpetual motion forward in the months following the attacks. It chose not to. And even if it had decided, as a body, to demand restraint in the country's approach to the problem, admittedly, the results might have been the same. We should ask the question, however, had there been more probing, more questions, and better answers, could the war itself have been averted? Should it have been averted based on several keys facts that emerged over time? Within weeks of the launch of the war, there was reason to shift course and members of Congress knew it.

Also, if an overwhelming sense of fear and overall discomfort gripped the populace and shook the administration to its core, so too must have the same fear and discomfort affected members of Congress. No matter, said the late democratic Senator Robert Bryd from West Virginia, who was the Senate's longest serving member. He said the Congress should never hurry a piece of legislation, and especially not hurry it during a time of panic. Congress needs to rise above pressure, political and otherwise, in order to do the work it was elected to do. "Congress's primary purpose lies in its unique capacity to publicly, and under the hot lights of media scrutiny, sort through competing interests. Congress alone can deliberate, reconcile, apportion public treasure, and forge laws, compromises, solutions, and priorities which are compatible with our general national objectives and which promote the public good."[10]

Finally, and perhaps even most influential when analyzing the role of Congress, were political factors. Politics itself, divided along party lines, drove congressional behavior. A mid-term election was looming when Congress sanctioned war with Iraq. Democrats could not afford to appear weak on national security and defense of the homeland or they would cede even more power. Senator Byrd wrote, "The country looked to Bush for protection. All dissenting voices were stilled. Vast foreign policy pronouncements went unquestioned. What the White House requested was quickly provided by the Congress. The Constitution's careful separation of powers has been breached, and its checks and balances circumvented."[11] Congress did not rise to the occasion, and the president rushed to war with seemingly little regard for the process of governing.

Senator Byrd wrote that Congress did not do its job, nor did the president do his while deliberating about the Iraq War. He questioned the integrity of the president and that of the Congress in which he served for fifty-one years. Writing about the two branches, he said, "Two constitutional power centers set up by the framers to check and balance one another, and do battle over politics, policies and priorities, occupy their distinct ends of Pennsylvania Avenue. What makes it all work for the good of the nation is the character of the individuals who serve."[12]

CONGRESS, 9/11, AND THE ROAD TO IRAQ

We must evaluate the performance of Congress, vis-à-vis the Iraq war, through the prism of its constitutional role, the character of the people who serve, and the political parties to which those people belong. Congress is but one leg of a tripod on which stands America's co-equal branches of government, which also includes the executive and judicial. "If one leg gets weak, the tripod begins to not supply the support the country needs," explained former Virginia Senator John Warner.[13]

Senator Robert Byrd said the legislative branch is charged "with keeping an eye on all the enormous power" of the executive branch. Only 435 members of the House and 100 members of the Senate, 535 in total, plus its adjuncts in other offices are tiny with approximately some 32,000 employees compared with the enormous "White House controlled federal bureaucracy" with over two million employees.[14]

Despite the vast difference in numbers, "legislators have been given by the framers in their wisdom one extraordinary tool: the power of the purse. This control over the purse is the people's sturdiest hammer to beat back any usurpation of their liberties by the executive."[15] The other part of Congress's responsibility is oversight, to watch, check, and question the executive. "Legislators are expected to have expertise on every subject, which may flash across the headlines on any given day. Is there a scandal? Congress must hasten to investigate it. Is there a problem? Congress must hustle through legislation to address it."[16] The pre-eminent Congress, the first branch of government, was placed "at the Center, not the periphery, of a strong federal government and empowered with democratic legitimacy and institutional authority."[17]

The wheels of Congress, as it debates and makes the laws by which we live, often move cautiously and carefully forward, so that clear-headed decisions emerge and ultimately prevail. That is why it is divided in two, House from Senate, each with two distinct institutional dispositions. Members in the people's House represent their constituencies at a local level, "providing an important link between citizens and their government."[18] Members of the Senate represent an entire state and have broader interests, both nationally and internationally. This division of Congress was designed to cool passions.

In fact, there is a famous story of lore, about Thomas Jefferson, who after returning from France, took George Washington to task for agreeing to a second chamber of Congress. Why, Jefferson asks Washington, did he agree to that? This second chamber, he admonished him, will bog down the wheels of our government. Washington then asked Jefferson why he pours milk into his coffee. To cool it, Jefferson answered. And that is why Washington said he advocated for a second chamber. To cool the legislative saucer.[19]

While it is the executive branch that dominates in the formulation of foreign policy, Congress also has a vital role to play. "The making of sound U.S foreign policy depends on a vigorous, deliberative, and often combative process that involves both the executive and the legislative branches. The country's founding fathers gave each branch both exclusive and overlapping powers in the realm of foreign policy, according to each one's comparative advantage—inviting them, as the constitutional scholar Edwin Corwin has put it, 'to struggle for the privilege of directing American foreign policy.'"[20]

The point is that as Congress and the executive branch were deliberating various courses of action in the days, months, and years following 9/11, passions were indeed flaring. Those passions needed to be cooled, and clearer heads should have predominated so that sound judgments could emerge from the chaos, certainly before attacking a country that had nothing to do with it and posed no imminent threat. Immediately following 9/11, with the sympathy and support of much of the world, we certainly were emboldened to act. Militarily, we were sufficiently fortified to take on any enemy, anywhere in the world. There was certainly cause for measured, but immediate action, but no room for haste as the administration considered the most important foreign policy decisions of its tenure.

James Wilson, considered "one of the most penetrating constitutional theorists of the founding generation," said during the 1787 Philadelphia Constitutional Convention that the new country's system of checks and balances "will not hurry us into war; it is calculated to guard against it. It will not be in the power of a single man, or a single body of men, to involve us in such a distress, for the important power of declaring war is invested in a legislature at large."[21] It was the legislature that assumed the initial burden of the Iraq war. Congress did authorize the president's plans to attack Iraq.

It is both important and necessary to chronicle what events paved the way to that crucial vote in Congress, and to explain that Congress had a pivotal role to play. The run-up to the war, including the initiatives in which Congress was involved, demonstrated a pattern of acquiescence and spoke to "the degree to which members of Congress were interested in opposing the president and the haste by which congressional leaders" pushed through particular initiatives, said Northeastern University political science professor Christopher Bosso. These events would characterize Congress in both the short and long term and would lead some scholars, historians, and politicians to ponder and question its effectiveness as an institution, which will be discussed in some detail later in this chapter.

The Bush administration, the executive branch, and Congress all were compelled to move quickly after 9/11. In a period of just eighteen months, America's military flooded into Afghanistan, Congress hastily passed the expansive USA Patriot Act, voted to authorize a war in Iraq, and failed to thoroughly probe the validity of disturbing information about a sale of uranium to Iraq, which ultimately paved the road on which the United States toppled a foreign government.

It was not as if Congress did not understand what was happening. As the president became aware of changing information over time, so too did Congress. Journalist Jonathan Mahler wrote, "Congress was hardly unaware of what was going on. Many of the most aggressive positions that the Bush administration staked out after 9/11 were a matter of public record. Not only did Congress not flinch at such unilateral actions, but it also helped enable the expansion of the presidential authority."[22] Senator Robert Byrd wrote, "A crisis like 9/11 can practically flatten the congressional 'will to watch.' An emergency tends to weaken the spine of the legislative branch."[23]

According to former democratic Representative Lee Hamilton of Indiana, Congress had been ceding its responsibility to the president all through his thirty years serving in the House of Representatives. He said its power was further diminishing and at an accelerated pace after he left office in 1999. "Times have changed," he wrote. "As complex as the affairs of state must have seemed in 1789, they are exponentially more complicated now. I fully understand Woodrow Wilson's claim that the presidency is the 'vital place of action in the system.' Often the cumbersome separation of powers does not work in the challenges of the day, and the president needs to take the initiative."[24]

Hamilton also blamed politics for the diminishing influence of Congress. He said, "Congress does not work smoothly. It can be difficult and time consuming to develop a legislative consensus among 535 representatives and senators who have many competing interests and agendas."[25] But this is not wise, Hamilton warned, because it causes an erosion of checks and balances and oversight. The framers intended that the legislative and executive branches are co-equal.

Arthur Schlesinger made an argument for an "imperial presidency" when there is a crisis that confronts the nation. "The more acute the crisis, the more power flows to the president," he wrote.[26] He also made a case for a "strong system of accountability" within which a strong presidency operates.[27] When it comes to foreign affairs, however, there is a hesitancy to exercise those appropriate checks on power. Schlesinger continued, "Congress and the courts, [along with the press and the citizenry, too], often lack confidence in their own information and judgment and are likely to be intimidated by executive authority. The inclination in foreign policy is to let the president have the responsibility and the power—a renunciation that results from congressional pusillanimity as well as from presidential rapacity."[28]

There was no question that the country had to respond immediately and decisively to 9/11. It was clear, based on reliable intelligence going back to the Clinton administration, that Osama bin Laden was a dangerous man. He had ties to the U.S. Embassy bombings in Tanzania and Kenya in 1998 and also to the attack in 2000 on the U.S.S. *Cole*, which was docked in Yemen at the time. Bin Laden was the "mastermind" behind 9/11 and had taken up residence in Afghanistan to train his forces and plan the attacks. This interesting country—sad, desperate, war torn—has been in decline for decades. It is where the fundamentalist Taliban had taken root, destroyed civil society, imposed Islamic religious traditions and law (Sharia), and permitted the establishment of training camps for aspiring jihadists. There is no dispute that this is where the plot for 9/11 was hatched and operationally from where it was orchestrated.

But there was haste in the decisions to follow and disregard, some even said contempt, for those who would question the president during this time or attempt to alter the conversation about what was the best course of action to follow and in what time frame. The problem was, no doubt, compounded by the fact that the House of Representatives was controlled by the Republican Party, the president's party, in 2000. The precarious Senate wobbled from republican control after the 2000 election back to democratic control when Senator Jim Jeffords of Vermont fled the party to caucus with Democrats, and then swung back decisively to republican control at the mid-term election in 2002, a year and two months after the attacks. National security featured prominently at the ballot box, and the incumbent administration exploited the issue to its advantage.

While the nation was in "deep shock" and "traumatized" by the events, the president would use his political capital to make decisions as he saw fit. According to Stephen Graubard, Bush was "rendered invulnerable to all criticism" and became "the hero of the nation with no one in Congress and the media prepared to question his policies. The White House became a fortress to which only a privileged few were admitted, generally to learn of the president's resolve."[29]

President Bush, according to Lee Hamilton, "pursued a definition of executive power more all-encompassing than any of his immediate predecessors." Congress, he said, handed off war-making powers to the president. Congress declaring war, he said, has become a "nullity" and instead has become "presidential prerogative."[30] It follows that there were also failures of congressional committees on intelligence as they sought to justify an invasion of Iraq rather than analyze, question, and thoroughly vet the information they were evaluating.

The unique and isolating environment of the presidency has been experienced by relatively few individuals. In times of crisis, an already impervious circle tends to close in tighter. Many who have held the presidency have described it as solitary and often lonely. The people who intimately understand the office and the actual job of being the president of the United States are those who have held it previously and on whom the full weight of decisions ultimately rests. While constitutionally compelled to be accountable to Congress, and to the people, this president perhaps believed this moment in history, dealing with a crisis of this magnitude, may have redefined his responsibilities.

The president himself, in an interview with *Washington Post* reporter Bob Woodward, said "I'm the commander—see, I don't need to explain—I do not need to explain why I say things. That's the interesting thing about being the president. I don't feel like I owe anybody an explanation."[31] This statement was of great concern to Senator Robert Byrd, who asked, did he [the president] not feel he needed to explain to Congress either? According to the senator, trust was abused. "Behind closed doors schemes have been hatched, with information denied to the legislative branch and policy makers shielded from informing the people or Congress. In fact, there appears little respect for the role of the Congress."[32]

Twenty-four hours after the 9/11 attacks, President Bush asked the Congress for "such sums as may be necessary to respond to the terrorist attacks on the United States." "No amounts or purposes were mentioned, and no reporting notification requirements listed." The House and Senate Appropriations committees rejected the request.[33] But on September 14, 2001, Congress approved $40 billion to be allocated by the president after "consultation" by the Appropriation Committees in both chambers, but with no formal notification required.[34] Senator Byrd said the money was for "unspecified missions related to the war on terrorism," and the monies would be in an "unallocated fund" rather than in a "traditional appropriation account," something the senator would make sure would happen in later months after the invasion of Iraq.

Also, on September 14, 2001, as money was being allocated to any future war effort, the self-proclaimed "war president" declared a national state of emergency "by reason of the terrorist attacks at the World Trade Center, New York, New York, and the Pentagon, and the continuing and immediate threat of further attacks on the United States."[35] The 107th Congress voted to give the president the power to engage our military in Afghanistan. The legislation, S.J Res. 23, entitled "Authorization for Use of Military Force," cleared the Senate by a vote of 98–0 and passed the House 420–1. "This joint resolution authorizes the president 'to use all necessary and appropriate force against those nations, organizations, or persons he determines planned, authorized, committed, or aided terrorists attacks that occurred on September 11, 2001, or harbored such organizations or persons, in order to prevent any future acts of international terrorism against the United States by such nations, organizations or persons.'"

The one lone voice to oppose the measure was Representative Barbara Lee, a Democrat from the 9th Congressional District of California. If for no other reasons, her testimony is noteworthy because she stood completely alone in her vote of opposition.

> I know this use of force resolution will pass although we all know that the president can wage war even without this resolution. However difficult this vote may be, some of us must urge the use of restraint. There must be some of us who say, let's step back for a moment and think through the implications of our actions today—let us more fully understand their consequences.
>
> We are not dealing with a conventional war. We cannot respond in a conventional manner. I do not want to see this spiral out of control. This crisis involves issues of national security, foreign policy, public safety, intelligence gathering, economics and murder. Our response must be equally multifaceted.[36]

As Congresswoman Lee concluded her remarks, she reminded the chamber of another time in American history when Congress gave President Lyndon Johnson the power in 1964 to authorize further and deeper military involvement in Vietnam. She harkened back to Senator Wayne Morse of Oregon, a Republican turned Democrat, who stood with democratic Senator Ernest Gruening of Alaska, mavericks in their time, voting in opposition to the Gulf of Tonkin Resolution. Morse said the vote was a mistake because the president alone could not be in charge of America's foreign policy, certainly not when sending troops to fight without an official declaration of war by Congress.[37] Lee agreed with those sentiments expressed thirty-seven years earlier, saying we should heed the lessons of history, and concluded, "as we act, let us not become the evil that we deplore.'"

The same day, the president issued this brief two-line statement regarding the vote: "I am gratified that the Congress has united so powerfully by taking this action. It sends a clear message—our people are together, and we will prevail."[38] Would this vote set a tone for a future military engagement in Iraq? Was the authority granted to the president too broad, too sweeping? Just days later the *New York Times* published an article reporting that the resolution was broad and cautioned that it could not limit the president in any significant way. The article quoted Professor Harold H. Koh of Yale Law School: "I think it is extremely broad because no nations are named, the nations are to be determined by the president and the president could theoretically name lots of nations. There is also no time limit."[39]

The newspaper also reported that Congress "seemed eager to show unity in the face of the attacks" and that discussions with members of Congress "were largely over whether to include a reference to the War Powers Resolution (it was retained) and whether to delete a reference authorizing the president to deter 'future acts' of terrorism (it remained)." Representative Peter A DeFazio, a Democrat of Oregon, was quoted in the same article, expressing concerns that "earlier drafts 'authorized the use of force in an unprecedented open-ended manner,'" but that he was ultimately satisfied that the authority of Congress would be recognized and respected.[40]

On October 7, 2001, the president addressed the nation in a televised address to announce "Operation Enduring Freedom." The initiative would target "al Qaeda training camps and military installations of the Taliban regime" in Afghanistan. The president said in part:

> Today we focus on Afghanistan, but the battle is broader. Every nation has a choice to make. In this conflict, there is no neutral ground. If any government sponsors the outlaws and killers of innocents, they have become outlaws and murderers themselves. And they will take that lonely path at their own peril. I'm speaking to you from the Treaty Room of the White House, a place where American presidents have worked for peace. We're a peaceful nation. Yet, as we have learned, so suddenly and so tragically, there can be no peace in a world of sudden terror. In the face of today's new threat, the only way to pursue peace is to pursue those who threaten it. We did not ask for this mission, but we will fulfill it.[41]

Two days later the president sent a letter to Congress. It served as a formal notification of his decision to deploy troops in Afghanistan. Also, it said that the operation was in direct response to 9/11 and in defense of the American people. He wrote in part: "I have taken these actions pursuant to constitutional authority to conduct U.S foreign relations as Commander in Chief and Chief Executive."[42]

Next on the list for congressional approval was the proposed United and Strengthening America by Providing Appropriate Tools Required to Intercept and Obstruct Terrorism Act. This was the USA Patriot Act. This legislation was first considered by the Clinton Administration in 1996, a year after the bombing of the Alfred P. Murrah Federal building in Oklahoma City, in which dozens of people were killed. Now, five years later, Attorney General Ashcroft was proposing a revamped and enlarged bill, sweeping legislation, the first draft of which had been introduced to Congress on September 19, 2001. He urged Congress to pass it within forty-eight hours. He said the bill was essential to protect the country from further terrorist attacks.

Senate Judiciary Chairman Patrick Leahy (D-VT) said he would take the matter under advisement and promised to work on a bill that could pass both houses. He expressed concern about the constitutionality of the proposal and the encroachment on civil liberties. "If the Constitution is shredded," he said, "the terrorists win. We want to do this carefully."[43]

Days later, on September 24, 2001, Attorney General Ashcroft appeared before the House Committee on the Judiciary. In stark and urgent, yet in vague terms, here is how he characterized his twenty-one-page proposal, which was now on a fast track to passage:

> First, law enforcement needs strengthened and streamlined ability for our intelligence-gathering agencies to gather the information necessary to disrupt, weaken and eliminate the infrastructure of terrorist organizations.
>
> Second, we must make fighting terrorism a national priority in our criminal justice system. We would make harboring a terrorist a crime.
>
> Third we seek to enhance the authority of the Immigration and Naturalization Service to detain or remove suspected alien terrorists from within our borders.
>
> Fourth, law enforcement must be able to follow the money in order to identify and neutralize terrorist networks. Our proposal gives law enforcement the ability to seize the terrorist's assets.
>
> Finally, we seek the ability of the president of the United State and the Department of Justice to provide swift emergency relief to the victims of terrorism and their families. [44]

Ashcroft concluded his remarks by urging Congress to act swiftly because the nation was vulnerable, and the threat of another attack could be imminent. Before they became targets of the infamous anthrax letters, which came later in the month, and before the Patriot Act was passed, Senate Majority Leader Tom Daschle and Senate Judiciary Committee Chairman Patrick Leahy, along with Senator Russ Feingold, voiced their concerns about the bill while Attorney General John Ashcroft grew impatient, accusing the Senate of dragging its feet. [45] There was pressure on the Congress. Seventy-four percent of Americans believed another attack was very or somewhat likely, and Ashcroft himself has a 77 percent approval rating for his handling of the war on terror. [46]

Senator Leahy and his counterpart in the House Judiciary Committee, James Sensenbrenner (R-WI), decided with their congressional colleagues to draft their own versions of the Patriot Act, which became S. 1520 and H.R. 2975 respectively. The House bill passed on October 12, 2001, and the Senate bill passed the day previous. The final bill, H.R. 3162, passed the House by a vote of 357 to 66 and passed the Senate the following day, 98 to 1. In the House, voting yes were 211 Republicans, 145 Democrats, and one Independent. Voting no were three Republicans, 62 Democrats, and one Independent. In the Senate, there was one Democrat who abstained from voting and another Democrat who voted no.

Senator Robert Byrd wrote, "The customary conference between the two bodies to resolve differences never occurred, despite a preexisting understanding between the House and Senate Leadership that there would be a conference on the bill. The House leadership incorporated the product of only certain informal House-Senate agreements, instead of gathering the full conference—both houses—to hammer out the differences. Few committee hearings had been held."[47]

Again, it is worth noting the testimony of the lone dissenting voice from the Senate floor the day before the president signed the bill into law. Russ Feingold, Democratic senator from Wisconsin and the chairman of the Constitution Subcommittee of the Judiciary Committee, noted other difficult times in our history—times when civil liberties were trampled in the name of national security, which he denounced. He acknowledged the fear of Americans after 9/11 and said he understood the extreme reactions from the people and the government. He was bothered by the rush of this particular legislation to passage because it contained "vast new powers for law enforcement, some seemingly drafted in haste and others that came from the F.B.I.'s wish list that Congress had rejected in the past."

He continued: "You may remember that the Attorney General announced his intention to introduce a bill shortly after the September 11 attacks. He provided the text of the bill the following Wednesday, and urged Congress to enact it by the end of the week. That was plainly impossible, but the pressure to move on the bill quickly, without deliberation and debate, has been relentless ever since. It is one thing to shortcut the legislative process in order to get financial aid to the cities hit by terrorism. We did that, and no one complained that we moved too quickly. It is quite another to press for the enactment of sweeping new powers for law enforcement that directly affects the civil liberties of the American people without due deliberation by the people's elected representatives."[48]

Although there were some "non-controversial" provisions in the bill, which Feingold supported, overall he was "troubled by the broad expansion of government power." It threatened the First Amendment to the Constitution, he said. He also said he did not trust the F.B.I., the Attorney General, nor did he trust the Justice Department to do the right thing, even though they had given Congress verbal assurances they would not target lawful, legal immigrants from Arab, Muslim and South Asian countries in the wake of the attacks perpetrated by people exactly from those areas.

Feingold again: "The Congress will fulfill its duty when it protects *both* the American people and the freedoms at the foundation of American society. So let us preserve our heritage of basic rights. Let us practice as well as preach that liberty. And let us fight to maintain that freedom that we call America."[49]

On October 26, 2001, the president signed the bill, a huge document at over three hundred pages. In such a short time, how well did Congress understand the implications of the bill? Later, it would open the door to the government looking into the personal lives of its citizens, and allowed for cruel places to operate behind a wall of secrecy at Guantanamo Bay, Cuba, redesignated as a special prison for "detainees" suspected of terrorism and those deemed "enemy combatants." The same was true for Abu Ghraib (prison) in Iraq where, under the authority of the United States, some people were tortured and humiliated, others denied due process and held without charge. Both places, we would later learn, violated the Geneva Conventions in the treatment of those suspects and so-called "enemy combatants" they held.

The swift passage of the expansive USA Patriot Act set the tone for the rush to war with Iraq in months to come and speaks to the lack of appropriate and vigorous congressional oversight. The Patriot Act had been "rushed to passage without hearings or committee reports forty-five days after 9/11." Before passage of the bill, Attorney General Ashcroft appeared only once before the Senate Judiciary Committee. He promised to answer in writing any subsequent questions members may have had, "but he never did, not a word, after the bill's final passage."[50]

This was serious legislation for a serious time, but the implications would be far-reaching and long lasting. "The Patriot Act increases the discretionary power of federal agents to collect information about individuals, to search their homes, to inspect their reading habits and their Internet queries, to view their credit reports, to conduct wiretaps without warrants and overhear lawyer-client telephone conversations without court orders, to reduce judicial supervision, and to spy on domestic organizations and advocacy groups."[51]

Senator Feingold commented, "The new law goes into a lot of areas that have nothing to do with terrorism and have a lot to do with the government and the F.B.I. having a wish list of the things they want to do."[52] Democratic Congressman Jerrold Nadler from New York said the bill is "little more than the institution of a police state."[53]

The president, however, defined the legislation in very different terms. On October 26, 2001, upon signing the bill at the White House, he struck a different tone: "This legislation is essential not only to pursuing and punishing terrorists, but also preventing more atrocities in the hands of the evil ones. This government will enforce this law with all the urgency of a nation at war. The elected branches of government and both political parties, are united in our resolve to fight and stop and punish those who would do harm to the American people."[54]

And about Congress and the bill the president said this: "This bill was carefully drafted and considered. Led by the members of Congress on this stage, and those seated in the audience, it was crafted with skill and care, determination and a spirit of bipartisanship for which the entire nation is grateful. This bill met with an overwhelming—overwhelming— agreement in Congress, because it respects and upholds the civil liberties guaranteed by our constitution."[55]

In stark contrast there was a flurry of criticism in days to follow. Some press weighed in to say, "The law passed without any public debate."[56] "There was no hearing or congressional debate."[57] Democratic Massachusetts Congressman Barney Frank, who voted "nay" on the Patriot Act, said, "This was the least democratic process for debating questions fundamental to democracy that I have ever seen. A bill drafted by a handful of people in secret, subject to no committee process comes before us immune to amendment."[58] One congressman from the president's home state and party, Texas Republican Ron Paul, voted against the bill. He implied that the administration was using tactics to hasten a vote without allowing Congress careful study of the bill saying, "It's my understanding the bill wasn't printed before the vote—at least I couldn't get it. They played all kinds of games, kept the House in session all night, and it was a very complicated bill. Maybe a handful of staffers actually read it, but the bill was definitely not available to members before the vote."[59] "Only two copies of the bill were made available in the hours before its passage and most House members admit they voted for the act without actually reading it first."[60] *The Los Angeles Times* reported, "Few in Congress were able to read summaries, let alone the fine print before voting on it."[61]

Representative Brian Baird, a Democrat from Washington, says none of this is unusual. He wrote in an op-ed piece for the *Washington Post*, "If forced to tell the truth, most members of Congress would acknowledge that they did not fully, or in many cases, even partially read these bills before casting their votes."[62] Members are usually briefed by staffers regarding changes and updates to a bill. Senator Byrd wrote that the problem was that the process was rushed. He cited the example of the Patriot Act as a "case study in the perils of speed, herd instinct and lack of legislating in the face of crisis. The Congress basically got stampeded by Attorney General John Ashcroft. I voted for it [the Patriot Act of 2001]. I have come to wish I had not."[63]

An America on edge about another attack and a Congress hyperaware of the patriotism that had swept the nation, rendered many unsympathetic to what would be the emerging encroachment on civil liberties on which the country had long prided itself. The same was true in varying degree during both World Wars. Many have said this is necessary and that people understand legislation that might curb civil liberties to some degree if it kept them safe. Stephen Graubard wrote that in this case, "No one conscious of the patriotism that had become the nation's most distinctive trait, dared question the excessive controls on aliens, non-citizens who might one day be discovered as undercover terrorists."[64]

There was certainly no doubt the executive branch had become emboldened and strengthened. History teaches that this is predictable during times of national crisis. There was Lincoln and the Civil War, Franklin Roosevelt during World War II, Truman and Korea, Johnson and Viet-

nam. All "took acts they knew to be beyond the Constitution."[65] September 11, 2001, the day of an attack on the homeland like never seen before,
a pervading threat of terrorism by an enemy not represented by any
government or country, made this time in history different. Also, this
presidency came to "see itself in messianic terms" and put the Constitution under "unprecedented, unbearable strain."[66] According to former
Commerce Secretary Don Evans, a close personal friend of the president
who spoke to him every day, the president believed this was his time to
lead—that he was called by God to this period in history.[67]

Congress was aware of the news of the day, which may have prevented any measurable resistance. Congress was also aware of the mood of
the people, which was reflected in opinion polls regarding the president's
job performance. Those polls also reflected the perceptions of the people,
which evolved over time, about Osama bin Laden and Saddam Hussein.

Jack Goldsmith, former legal adviser to the Department of Defense,
said:

> After 9/11 the administration faced two sharply conflicting impera-
> tives. The first was fear of another attack. This permeated the adminis-
> tration. Everyone felt it and it led to the doctrine of pre-emption, which
> has many guises, but basically means that you can't wait for the usual
> amounts of information before acting on a threat because it may be too
> late. They were really scared. They were afraid of what they didn't
> know. They were afraid they didn't have the tools to meet the threat.
> And they had this extraordinary sense of responsibility—that they
> would be responsible for the next attack. They really thought of it as
> having blood on their hands, and that they'd be forgiven once, but not
> twice. On the other hand, there was this counter-veiling imperative,
> and that was the law.[68]

The point is the executive branch perceived it had a mandate. This, in
effect, would trump any obstacle the Congress may have presented. So it
made great strides forward, under the current circumstances, and could
sustain a highly charged climate in the country over the next year.

In November 2001, two things would have tremendous impact and
subsequent political fallout. The president signed an executive order that
would alter the presidential Records Act of 1978. Instead of records being
released after twelve years, as the law requires, now the records of the
vice president and whoever else the president designates, would be exempt from review in perpetuity. Second, another executive order that
would later have painful ramifications was one that instituted the closed,
secret military tribunal that would try accused terrorists. John Bellinger
III, former legal adviser to the National Security Council, said "A small
group of administration lawyers drafted the president's military commis-
sions, but without the knowledge of the rest of the government, including the national security adviser, me, the secretary of state, or even the

C.I.A. director."[69] Congress could have challenged both of these initiatives. It did not.

The president ended the year (2001) with an 87 percent approval rating according to a joint poll by ABC News and the *Washington Post*. There was strong support for this president as he prepared for a crucial midterm election the next fall and an important State of the Union address the next month. On January 19, 2002, before the State of the Union address, Karl Rove, the White House's chief political strategist, traveled to Austin, Texas, for a meeting of the Republican National Committee. He told the group that the war on terror would be the key to winning elections in November. Polls suggested that Americans trusted Republicans to keep them safer than Democrats, and Rove reinforced the point to his audience by saying, "Americans trust the Republicans to do a better job of keeping our community and families safe. We can also go to the country on this issue because they trust the Republican Party to do a better job of strengthening America's military might and thereby protecting America."[70] Congressional Democrats certainly took note of the political climate that surrounded them, which was diminishing their influence.

Ten days later during a momentous State of the Union address, the president would introduce the people of the United States and the world to three other nations, North Korea, Iran, and Iraq, specifically, as potential targets of the United States in the war on terror. Americans supported by three to one the expansion of the war to other countries where terrorists were believed to be operating.[71] Interestingly, there was not one single mention of bin Laden, despite that by two to one Americans believed the war on terrorism would only be successful with "the death or capture of bin Laden." For at least one U.S. senator this speech was disconcerting.

"What did the president mean?" asked Senator Robert Byrd. "What did he know and not share with Congress? Was he signaling to the world—for the world does watch—a plan to attack one or more of these countries? The speech begged the question, where was this president taking us? We had just bombed the Afghanistan mountains into rubble. We had struck at the bin Laden hiding places, the caves and the camps of terrorism. We had so far spent $7 billion in Afghanistan, and yet uncovered no sign of bin Laden. So what was our goal now?"[72]

A senior member of the House Armed Services Committee, Representative Ike Skelton, from the 4th District in Missouri, was also "alarmed" by the president's speech, the same night, telling his staff that in essence it was a "declaration of war." He was concerned as well that the Truman Democrats were about to be a dying breed, "run over by the "21st century Republicans."[73] "In the following months, Skelton would begin asking questions and got few answers. His unhappy role would be that of a Congressional Cassandra, his foresight accurate but disregarded."[74]

Most Americans, however, received the president's speech positively and by a wide margin—62 percent of the people believed the threat of terrorism should be the country's priority wherever it might be lurking. They also wanted the president to have more influence over the direction of the country than the Democrats and believed by 61 to 23 percent that the Republicans could better handle the issue of terrorism than Democrats.[75]

There were some interesting polls conducted about three weeks after the president's address worth noting:

79% of the American people believed the United States should prevent the "Axis of Evil" countries, Iran, Iraq, and North Korea, from developing weapons of mass destruction (WMD).

77% of Americans believed the United States should destroy terrorist operations outside of Afghanistan.

68% of Americans believed capturing or killing Osama bin Laden should be a priority.

64% of Americans believed Saddam Hussein should be removed from power.

82% of Americans believed Iraq had an "evil" government.[76]

These numbers are revealing because the United States had not accomplished its primary mission, which was the capture or killing of bin Laden, the principal architect of 9/11, and the destruction of his training camps, hideouts, and safe havens within Afghanistan and adjacent to Afghanistan. The president and his party were successful at helping to migrate the public's attention to include not only bin Laden in Afghanistan, but now also Saddam Hussein and Iraq.

Members of Congress were being given some confusing information. In February 2002 Senator Bob Graham, a Democrat from Florida and chairman of the Senate Foreign Intelligence Committee, had been briefed by Central Command (CENTCOM) in Tampa, Florida. Commanding General Tommy Franks asked the senator into a private meeting in which he told the senator "we were no longer fighting a war in Afghanistan." The senator said, "Some of the key personnel, particularly some special-operations units and some equipment, specifically the Predator unmanned drone, were being drawn down in order to get ready for a war in Iraq."[77]

The same month during a Senate Budget Committee hearing, Senator Robert Byrd asked Secretary of State Colin Powell whether there was a plan to attack any of the countries the president had mentioned in the "axis of evil," to which the secretary replied no, there were no plans on his desk.[78] Byrd did not say that the secretary was lying to the committee, but did characterize his appearance as guarded. "I could read between the lines. I felt that the administration was indeed considering an attack on Iraq as one of its options." Byrd went on to ask Secretary Powell if there was evidence of any of the countries in the "axis of evil" having any role whatsoever in the attacks of 9/11. "Powell filibustered my question," Byrd said.[79]

These meetings occurred at approximately the same point in time when the president signed yet another executive order that would render some terrorist suspects and detainees exempt from the protections of the Geneva Conventions while they were being held and interrogated. "The president has maintained the United States commitment to the principles of the Geneva Convention simply does not cover every situation in which people may be captured or detained by military forces, as we see in Afghanistan today," press secretary Ari Fleischer said during a press briefing.

By March 2002, Osama bin Laden, while still an object of revulsion, did not seem as much of an interest as before when he was public enemy number one. The bigger issue was the war on terror, which had broadened now to focus on Iraq. "Terror is bigger than one person," Bush would later say in a 2004 presidential debate. He may be dead, the president said, but if he were still alive, "I truly am not that concerned about him."

Unbeknownst to the public at the time, and as noted in the previous chapter, an elite military force had bin Laden in its sights and reported they could have killed him. In a 2009 report to the Senate Committee on Foreign Relations [Tora Bora Revisited: How We Failed to Get bin Laden and Why It Matters Today], Senator John Kerry of Massachusetts wrote, "This failure and its enormous consequences was not inevitable."[80] The president was aware of the situation and denied a request by commanders on the ground to proceed. Kerry wrote, [Secretary of Defense Donald] "Rumsfeld said at the time he was concerned that too many U.S. troops in Afghanistan would create an anti-American backlash and fuel a widespread insurgency."[81]

Gary Berntsen, a former C.I.A intelligence commander who was at Tora Bora, said that he and his team found bin Laden hiding near the shared border of Afghanistan and Pakistan. He begged CENTCOM for hundreds of reinforcements "to block a possible al Qaeda escape into Pakistan." Journalist Frank Rich wrote, "He was ignored by [General Tommy] Franks and the Pentagon, who inexplicably entrusted the job to Afghan warlords with agendas of their own. Bin Laden slipped away while Berntsen fumed.[82]

What does this have to do with the war in Iraq? Senator Kerry wrote, "When we went to war less than a month after the attacks of 9/11, the objective was to kill or capture its leader, Osama bin Laden, and other senior figures in the terrorist group, which had hosted them."[83] In essence, the president diverted the country's attention from what should have been the country's primary goal. Had he accomplished that goal, it could have weakened or eliminated completely one of his arguments and motivations to move against Iraq. If bin Laden was dead, the way forward would have been vastly different and an invasion of Iraq inherently more problematic. A watchful eye could have been kept on Iraq, but the rationale for a full-scale invasion would have been diminished.

The Congress did not do enough to insist that this mission be accomplished first before moving forward on any other military front. The late Senator Edward Kennedy, a Democrat from Massachusetts, was against the Iraq war from the very start. He wrote, "President Bush violated the trust that must exist between government and the people. If Congress and the American people had known the truth, America would never have gone to war in Iraq. No president who does that to our country deserves to be reelected."[84]

Meanwhile, the media had reported on some interesting stories, which got some attention but yielded little traction in terms of action. One example was a news story that emerged from CBS News, which reported the president had been directly forewarned of an impending attack on the United States by bin Laden using airplanes, and that the hijackers were being trained at American flight schools. This information came to the president by way of the President's Daily Brief (PDB), a top-secret document, while he was vacationing in August 2001. The intelligence brief was entitled "bin Laden Determined to Strike in US." According to the F.B.I. and other intelligence sources, "bin Laden wanted to hijack a U.S. aircraft." The information was reviewed by the president and his staff, but was dismissed.

The CBS news story was in direct contradiction to the administration's contention later that it had no "specific information" about an attack the summer before.[85] National Security Adviser Condoleezza Rice, said that neither she nor the president had such prior knowledge and said, "I don't think anybody could have predicted that these people would take an airplane into the World Trade Center."[86]

House Minority Leader Representative Richard Gephardt, a Democrat from Missouri, and Republican Senator Richard Shelby from Alabama wanted some answers. What did the president know and when did he know it? A swift rebuke of their questions came from the vice president who said their insinuations were "thoroughly irresponsible and totally unworthy of national leaders in a time of war."[87] A suggestion later by Senators John McCain (R-Arizona) and Joe Lieberman (D-Connecticut) for an independent inquiry into any pre-9/11 intelligence errors was also discouraged by the vice president.[88]

Congress does not need the permission of the executive branch to launch an inquiry. If some members had more questions they wanted answers to and increased oversight was in order, which was completely within their purview and control, then why didn't they act? Support to do so from the executive branch would have demonstrated good faith for more transparency in government and at least a desire to better explain decisions past and present. The vice president had great sway with the president and was one of his primary advisors on foreign policy and about military matters. Cheney had served as secretary of defense during his father's administration and was once a representative in the House, a former colleague in Congress of both McCain and Lieberman. Cheney may have believed that any semblance of support from the executive branch would have given credence to any inquiry, fuel to a fire that was, at the time, controlled.

By fall, public opinion poll numbers indicated support for the president was less fervent, but he maintained a healthy 70 percent "favorability" rating and a 64 percent "approval" rating. The Gallup pollsters also made an interesting observation noting, "Americans have a double standard" when it comes to a "first strike policy." By a 51 to 41 percent margin they believe the United States should not attack another country unless it has attacked us first, but when asked about Iraq, by two-thirds, 66 percent of those Americans polled believe the United States should be able to attack Iraq "out of concern for being attacked."[89]

Senator Byrd wrote, "Under our own U.S. Constitution, the president has inherent authority to repel an imminent attack, but beyond that only if there is a declaration of war or other authorization by Congress. Thus, a doctrine of preemption erodes Congress's role in declaring or authorizing conflict. The president on his own could order preemptive attacks simply by claiming intelligence information which threatened our country."[90] This is exactly what would happen. Based on intelligence information and with U.N. authorization, the president ordered the invasion of Iraq. We had been attacked by our enemies in Afghanistan, therefore, a military strike in that country was justified. However, there was no justification for any other military offensive on any other country.

White House Counsel Alberto Gonzalez had informed the president that he needn't consult Congress for authorization to launch a war, based on the nature of the attack on the United States. It was unprovoked. The president had legal standing to do what he wanted without it, according to Gonzalez.

Former Deputy Assistant General John Yoo, who worked in the Office of Legal Counsel of the Justice Department, said, "September 11, 2001 proved that war against al Qaeda cannot be won within the framework of the criminal law. They were acts of war."[91] So why was there no declaration of war?

Republican Representative Henry Hyde said, "There are things in the Constitution that have been overtaken by events, by time. Declaration of war is one of them. There are things no longer relevant to a modern society. We are saying to the president, use your judgment."[92]

There was also a secret Justice Department memo written by lawyer Yoo, who said there were "no limits" on presidential power when it came to waging the war on terrorism, that the president may "deploy force preemptively" against any terrorist group "or states that harbor them," regardless of whether "they can be linked to the specific terrorist incidents of September 11."[93]

South Carolina Republican Senator Lindsey Graham said, "The Bush administration came up with a pretty aggressive, bordering on bizarre, theory of inherent authority that had no boundaries." He added, "As they saw it, the other branches of government were basically neutered in the time of war."[94]

"Concerns were expressed by individual senators and representatives from both parties" about the realistic threat that Iraq may have posed, about the cost of another war, a post-war strategy, an exit strategy, and the political implications at home and around the world, but "these were lonely voices in a sea of silence. Republican leaders in Congress emphasized the importance of supporting the president and discouraged systematic hearings by committees that might raise embarrassing questions."[95] There was a mid-term election on the horizon in just another month. Campaign season was heating up. No senator would want to be on the wrong side of this issue come election day in November. Americans already believed Republicans were better at defending the homeland and her people.

In the fall of September 2002, the president invited eighteen senior members of Congress to the White House, specifically to talk about a war with Iraq. In the coming weeks the administration would launch a public relations blitz geared to persuade Americans to support another war in another part of the world. Bush wanted Congress to get behind the effort as well. The president asked those assembled for a quick vote within six weeks on a resolution giving him the authority to launch a military offensive against Iraq.[96] The president conveyed urgency about such a resolution. Many in the room wanted to wait until after the election. Senator Tom Daschle questioned the president about the speed with which he wanted this vote taken. The president applied some pressure. "We just have to do it now. This issue isn't going away. You can't let it linger," he said.[97]

House Majority Leader Dick Armey, a Republican from Texas, had been against this plan and was vocal about it previous to this meeting. He had called Saddam Hussein a "blowhard" and said, "We Americans don't make unprovoked attacks." He was consistent in this meeting cautioning the president, "If you go in there, you're likely to be stuck in a quagmire that will endanger your domestic agenda for the rest of your presidency." The vice president, also at this meeting, asked Armey to withhold public criticism until he had seen all the intelligence. Armey agreed, and when the legislators emerged from their audience with the president, they encountered the press and a bank of microphones and stood in support of the president.[98]

Senator McCain of Arizona said the president had "made a convincing case" for war. House Speaker Dennis Hastert promised that a resolution would come to a speedy vote "before the election." Congressman Richard Gephardt, a Democrat from Missouri, said he would help "convince Americans" about the danger Saddam Hussein posed to the world. Daschle wanted "more information and greater clarity."[99]

Some in Congress had serious concerns about what the president was asking for. West Virginia's Senator Robert C. Byrd deplored "the war fervor, the drums of war, the bugles of war, the clouds of war—this war hysteria has blown in like a hurricane."[100] But ultimately how members of Congress would vote on an authorization for war would be reduced to two very influential factors. Those were party line and political future.

Republicans were successful at reassuring the public about what party could best protect them. Senate and House leaders praised the president's efforts on working with Congress about Iraq. Press Secretary Ari Fleischer said, "Congress has an important role to play."[101]

Louis Fisher wrote, "Yet for Bush and his aides to merely 'consult' with Congress would not meet the needs of the Constitution. Consultation is not a substitute for receiving statutory authority to go to war. Congress is a legislative body that discharges its constitutional duties by passing statutes to authorize and define national policy. It exists to legislate and legitimate, particularly for military and financial commitments. Only congressional authorization of a war against Iraq would satisfy the Constitution."[102]

Many in Congress expressed concern about the intelligence on which the case for war was being built. Others said they were compelled to support their president because he knew better than any of them what was best because he, more than any of them, was privy to select information they were not. Democrats Senator Harry Reid, the Senate minority whip from Nevada, and Representative Nancy Pelosi, the House democratic whip from California, while giving the president kudos for coming to the congressional leadership for support of his plan, said they were skeptical until they were able to see better and more intelligence. Both hoped more information would be forthcoming:

> Reid: "I think everyone felt good about the fact he is going to build a case. I don't think anyone felt, after leaving that meeting, the case had been built. There's a lot of work to be done to make a case that hasn't been done yet. It's a start. I think it's a very important first start."

> Pelosi: "The president took a good first step today in saying that he would seek the approval of Congress. What he also had to do now is share the intelligence with Congress. Congress has at least as much right, if not more, because we have the power to declare war, to have that intelligence. The president needs to share it with us."[103]

Republicans struck a different tone. Both Congressman Duncan Hunter, Vice Chairman of the House Armed Services Committee from California, and Senator Richard Shelby, Vice Chairman of the Senate Intelligence Committee, expressed confidence in the information they had reviewed and connected Iraq's well-being to America's future and national security. Their sentiments had overtones of gravity and urgency.

> Hunter: "This is obviously a very dangerous world. A lot of things can happen. But the one thing we have to do is act in our supreme national interest. Our national interest right now is not giving to future generations an Iraq with nuclear systems. And that is what the president is concerned about."

> Shelby: "I think the question is going to be before the president, before the Congress, and before the world. Are we going to wait, are we going to defer it, or are we going to deal with this man five years from now, ten years from now? We know his record. He can't be trusted. I think it would be very foolish of us to believe that we can trust this man and this regime; it has to go." [104]

A draft of the Iraq war resolution came to Capitol Hill from the White House so that it could be discussed. Senators Ted Kennedy, Carl Levin, and Robert Byrd suggested improving the resolution because it wrongly bequeathed "the complete handing over of congressional war power to the president." [105] Some senators advocated tabling the issue, postponing any vote on the resolution until after the mid-term election in November.

Senator Byrd advocated taking more time to consider the consequences of a resolution. He wrote, "With an election staring one-third of the Senate, some Democrats would find it politically easier to give the president what he wanted. So simple to explain—terror threat, patriotism, support a popular president. Some senators were almost terrified at the prospect of being labeled 'unpatriotic'—just what Bush wanted. Also, I doubted that some members fully comprehended the magnitude of Bush's grab for power." [106]

Byrd was troubled by two other reports that had come to the attention of Congress from the White House. One was the thirty-three-page National Security Strategy (NSS), whose theme was "anticipatory action" as the United States would pledge to spread "democracy" to every "corner of the globe" by military supremacy. The other report was the administration's National Strategy to Combat Weapons of Mass Destruction, which said the United States reserved the right to use nuclear weapons as a deterrent should we learn that another nation was pursuing weapons of mass destruction. Byrd called the two reports "a witches brew" and was even more worried given the war powers resolution now before Congress. He decided to seek council from a former solicitor general who served under President Clinton. [107]

Walter Dillinger was asked to review the Iraq resolution and offer his reaction and advice. He met with Byrd and his staff and said: "If Congress passes this, you can just hang out a sign that says 'out of business.' It's a complete grant of authority for the foreseeable future. The administration can take military action in Iraq or anywhere else in the world that it chooses as long as there is some connection to Iraq." Dillinger advised Congress to at least insert a sunset clause, which is a date of expiration.[108]

Later, there were attempts to revise the resolution or, at least, to hinge any action on it to a preceding U.N. Security Council resolution vote. Six amendments to the bill were offered. There were three from the House, including a House Rules Amendment. There were three from the Senate. All were proposed by Democrats, excluding the House Rules Amendment, in order to slow momentum on the measure and to suggest conditions under which the president would have to operate before he could take up arms against Iraq. All failed, except the House Rules Amendment, which passed by a voice vote.

Many in Congress on both sides of the political aisle, who had once been reticent about war with Iraq, decided to stand with the president on the issue. Senator John Kerry, a Democrat from Massachusetts, said, "We are affirming a president's right and responsibility to keep the American people safe, and the president must take that grant of responsibility seriously." Senate Majority Leader Tom Daschle (D-SD) said, "We have got to support this effort. We have got to do it in an enthusiastic and bipartisan way." Daschle decided he would give "the president the benefit of the doubt."[109] But his Democratic colleague, Senator Byrd, angered by such a vote said, "I will not give the benefit of the doubt to the president. I will give the benefit of the doubt to the Constitution." Byrd believed the threat from Iraq was not "so great that we must be stampeded to provide such authority to this president just weeks before an election."[110]

Senator Bob Graham, a Democrat from Florida, said, "Unlike the George Bush who had purposefully put off the vote on the Persian Gulf War until after the elections of 1990—we voted in January of 1991—here they put the vote in October of 2002, three weeks before a congressional election. I think there were people who were up for election who didn't want, within a few weeks of meeting the voters, to be at such stark opposition with the president."[111]

Senator Byrd said never in his decades in the Senate had a situation pained him as much as this one. He harkened back to the 1964 Tonkin Gulf Resolution, which was purportedly designed to "prevent further aggression" in Vietnam and Southeast Asia. "This resolution," he wrote, "was worse than the Tonkin Gulf Resolution because it contained no sunset provision."[112] The Tonkin Gulf Resolution could be terminated by the president or by congressional resolution. This resolution was dangerous. However, the Authorization for Use of Military Force Against Iraq

Resolution of 2002 passed the House by a vote of 296 to 133 on October 10, 2002, and a day later passed the Senate 77 to 23.

A month later, the mid-term elections were a boon to the Bush administration and its agenda. The president had an approval rating that hovered at around 66 percent at the time of the election. He had traversed the country campaigning in some forty states for his agenda and in support of those running for election. He raised unprecedented amounts of money. Republicans took control of the Senate 51 to 46 seats and gained two seats in the House 226 to 204.

The *New York Times* reported the story this way: "Republicans swept to victory in the U.S. Senate last night, assuring Republicans control of the White House and Congress for the next two years, and thrusting President Bush into a commanding position for his legislative agenda. The results mean that a single party, the Republicans, will once again control both houses of Congress and the White House. The outcome [of the election] marked a break with historic patterns in which the party that controls the White House almost invariably lost, rather than gained, seats in mid-term congressional elections."[113]

White House Press Secretary Ari Fleischer said, "The president played a very constructive role in making history, historical trends are very hard to break. Not only have we kept the House, but we've gained seats." The two top Democrats in the Congress Senator Tom Daschle of South Dakota and Representative Richard Gephardt of Missouri attributed the president's success, in large measure, to his campaign for the war on terror, his popularity, and the post-9/11 environment. People, they said, wanted to unite behind their president.[114] The White House interpreted the results as an "across the board green light." One agency head from the Office of Faith-Based and Community Initiatives complained that "politics alone" would now drive the White House.[115]

By the time of the State of the Union address in January 2003, as a bolstered White House charged forward with its plan to attack Iraq, now appearing inevitable, the Democrats challenged the president's address with a rebuttal about domestic problems not being solved. Governor Gary Locke of Washington gave the official democratic response to the State of the Union address, declaring, "The country was headed in the wrong direction."[116] He discussed the burgeoning federal deficit, argued that cities and communities were being challenged by the growing lack of federal dollars to support services, and that the president and the Republicans offered few plans to remedy a country in distress. The response was also punctuated with a reaction to what the president revealed about Iraq. Locke encouraged the president to build a coalition of nations around the world before engaging Iraq in any military conflict. Other Democrats weighed in.

Senator Tom Daschle, a Democrat from South Dakota, said the president had the "right rhetoric, wrong policies" and was "out of touch" with

Americans. Congressman Charles Rangel, a Democrat from New York, said, "more evidence of a threat posed by Iraq" was needed. And Democratic Senator Ted Kennedy of Massachusetts, an early opponent of the war, said unequivocally that "no convincing case for war" with Iraq was made by the president. He also said Iran and North Korea posed more of a threat to the United States than Iraq. Kennedy said he would introduce a new resolution, which would require the president to inform Congress before or within forty-eight hours of a military strike against Iraq and would confirm that all diplomatic efforts through the United Nations had failed. It would assure Congress that a military offensive inside Iraq would not hamper efforts to capture bin Laden and would require the president to report to Congress every sixty days on the progress of the war.[117] The results of the mid-term election favoring the president's party, the president's healthy approval ratings, and a momentum for war that had been built since 9/11 would impede and did impede the success of such action.[118] Essentially, many Democrats in Congress would be too late to stop or slow the momentum toward war.

Senate Majority Leader Bill Frist, a Republican from Tennessee, said the president made a "very powerful" case against Iraq in his State of the Union address and that another vote brought to the Senate by Kennedy was "absolutely unnecessary. At the end of the day, the president will decide what is in the best interest of the American people and lead a coalition to disarm Saddam Hussein." John McCain, Arizona's veteran Republican Senator, said Kennedy "would have to give us a more concrete and compelling reason to revisit the resolution than just his own opposition to military action."[119]

The resolution required that the president inform Congress before or within forty-eight hours of a military strike against Iraq and that all diplomatic efforts through the United Nations had failed. It would assure Congress that a military offensive inside Iraq would not hamper efforts to capture bin Laden and would require the president to report to Congress every sixty days on the progress of the war.[120]

After Secretary Powell made the administration's final case for war in Iraq at the United Nations on February 5, 2003, he complained about the Congress and others who pinned the war on his testimony that day. "It's annoying me. Everybody focuses on my presentation. . . . Well the same goddamn case was presented to the U.S. Senate and the Congress and they voted for [Bush's Iraq] resolution. . . . Why aren't they outraged? They're the ones who are supposed to do oversight."[121]

Senator Byrd was disappointed in the behavior of Congress as well, for its timidity when it should have challenged information from the administration, including that from Powell. The senator called Powell's appearance convincing as a presentation, but also called it "courtroom theatrics" designed to appeal to the emotions of millions of viewers at home.[122] Byrd cited the fact that Powell was relying on old intelligence to make his case for a set of circumstances that had shifted since the 1990s. He also said the Bush administration was trying to belittle the inspections and discredit them while they were underway and working. [123]

"Congress took no for an answer" according to one journalist. [124] They asked many questions during a hearing of the Senate Foreign Relations Committee in February 2003, but "that was little more than a pose because it didn't object when it didn't get responses that spoke to the issue." Besides, Congress had already voted to give the president the power to engage Iraq militarily as he saw fit. This hearing appeared to be an exercise in futility as senators questioned Doug Feith, the Under Secretary of Defense Policy and General Anthony Zinni, a former Commander in Chief of U.S. Central Command (CENTCOM). Neither could be definitive about the war, the resources needed, the estimated length of the conflict, and an exit strategy. Senator Joe Biden, a Democrat from Delaware, had the last word that day: "The American people have no notion of what we are about to undertake." His reaction to that day's testimony may have typified the attitude of Congress at that point. "It was an important observation about a democracy about to launch a war in a distant land, alien culture, and hostile region. But it was made in a tone of passive resignation." [125]

One national security official said that the lack of congressional engagement on the impending war made it easier for the Bush administration to go to war. After the resolution from Congress, there was little standing in the way. "Rumsfeld and Wolfowitz are saying, 'we can't tell you how long it will take' or what it will cost. That's unknowable.' Why did Congress accept that?" [126] And further, why did Congress overlook the facts and new information as they emerged? In the weeks preceding the beginning of the war, Congress understood that Saddam was cooperating fully with the U.N. inspection team. It understood that information about uranium, supposedly being purchased by Iraq from Africa, which the president waved like a flag as hard evidence in the State of the Union address, was unfounded.

Senator Byrd said he felt "flattened" by a "freight train to war—a war open to so little discussion and public debate in Congress. We were following Bush like lambs to the slaughter, barely questioning the administration's claims or the certain consequences of war." The only hearing of much substance was the aforementioned Senate Foreign Relations Committee where the bulk of the discussion was about post Iraq war planning. The invasion was a foregone conclusion. There was no attempt to stop it.

It was clear by February 12, 2003, that inspections were working and turning up nothing. Senator Robert Byrd admonished Congress on the floor of the Senate. "This chamber is for the most part silent—ominously, dreadfully silent. There is no debate, no discussion, no attempt to lay out for the nation the pros and cons of this particular war. There is nothing.

We stand passively mute in the United States Senate, paralyzed by our own uncertainty, seemingly stunned by the sheer turmoil of events."[127] He decried the doctrine of preemption calling it "revolutionary."[128] He cited the failure of the administration to apprehend bin Laden. He charged that the Congress was "sleepwalking through history." He stressed that this war was not necessary at this time and implored his colleagues to "find a graceful way out of a box of our own making."[129]

Less than a month later, IAEA's ElBaradei would make an assertion that the documents the president had used as his trump card to go to war with Iraq were fraudulent. Twelve days later, U.S. bombs began to rain down on the capital of Baghdad, in what the Bush administration called a military campaign designed to instill "shock and awe" in the enemy.

Two veteran and opposing voices rose from the Senate floor to speak, one in response to the other. Senator Byrd noted the discredited documents on which the president hinged his case for war in his remarks.

> Today I weep for my country. I have watched the events of recent months with a heavy, heavy heart. No more is the image of America one of strong, yet benevolent peacekeeper. The image of America has changed. Around the globe, our friends mistrust us, our word is disputed, our intentions are questioned. We flaunt our superpower status with arrogance. We treat U.N. Security Council members like ingrates who offend our princely dignity by lifting their heads from the carpet. Valuable alliances are split. After war has ended, the United States will have to rebuild much more than the country of Iraq. We will have to rebuild America's image around the globe. The case this Administration tries to make to justify its fixation with war is tainted by charges of falsified documents and circumstantial evidence. We cannot convince the world of the necessity of this war for one simple reason. This is a war of choice. But this Administration has directed all of the anger, fear, and grief, which emerged from the ashes of the twin towers and the twisted metal of the Pentagon towards a tangible villain, one we can see and hate and attack. And villain he is. But he is the wrong villain. And this is the wrong war. What is happening to this country? When did we become a nation, which ignores and berates our friends? When did we decide to risk undermining international order by adopting a radical and doctrinaire approach to using our awesome military might? How can we abandon diplomatic efforts when the turmoil in the world cries out for diplomacy? War appears inevitable.[130]

Senator John McCain of Arizona:

> I observed the comments of the distinguished Senator from West Virginia concerning the events, which are about to transpire within the next hour or so, or days. I did not really look forward to coming to the floor and debating the issue. But to allege that somehow the United States of America has demeaned itself or tarnished its reputation by being involved in liberating the people of Iraq, to me, simply is neither factual nor fair. There is one thing I am sure of, that we will find the

Iraqi people have been the victims of an incredible level of brutaliza-
tion, terror, murder, and every other kind of disgraceful and distasteful
oppression on the part of Saddam Hussein's regime. And contrary to
the assertion of the Senator from West Virginia, when the people of
Iraq are liberated, we will again have written another chapter in the
glorious history of the United States of America, that we will fight for
the freedom of other citizens of the world. I am proud of the leadership
of the president of the United States. I respectfully disagree with the
remarks of the Senator from West Virginia. I believe the president of
the United States has done everything necessary and has exercised
every option short of war, which has led us to the point we are today. I
believe that, obviously, we will remove a threat to America's national
security because we will find there are still massive amounts of weapons of mass destruction in Iraq. Although Theodore Roosevelt is my
hero and role model, I also, in many ways, am Wilsonian in the respect
that America, this great nation of ours, will again contribute to the
freedom and liberty of an oppressed people who otherwise never
might enjoy those freedoms. So perhaps the Senator from West Virginia is right. I do not think so. Events will prove one of us correct in the
next few days. But I rely on history as my guide to the future, and
history shows us, unequivocally, that this nation has stood for freedom
and democracy, even at the risk and loss of American lives, so that all
might enjoy the same privileges or have the opportunity to someday
enjoy the same privileges as we do in this noble experiment called the
United States of America.[131]

In sum, the problems with Congress during the run-up to the Iraq war
were the following: It was timid in asserting its authority vested by the
Constitution before the resolution and after. It did not attempt to delay
the vote to authorize the Iraq War until after the mid-term elections.
Oversight by Congress has diminished over the years. The institution
itself has become increasingly polarized while its members have become
similarly partisan, dug-in, and steadfast in placing party above duty as
the country's and the people's elected stewards.

Congress abdicated its own power mandated by the Constitution
when it voted for the Iraq resolution giving the president broad, open-
ended authority to launch a military campaign in Iraq when he deemed it
appropriate. A definitive vote on that crucial resolution served as the
country's compass in Iraq and has, in large measure, influenced the integrity of our international political reputation and relationships going forward. Reverberations from that decision remain. The behavior of Congress at that particular juncture in history should serve as cautionary tale.
Congress voted to authorize war. It gave its consent. The decision about
when to launch war and the overall scope of the mission would be left to
the president's discretion. After this vote, the will of Congress was rendered peripheral to any decisions that would follow.

When perhaps it mattered most, from the time the vote was cast to the time of the Iraq war five months later, when no WMD were turning up anywhere and a fake document was used as evidence in the closing argument for war, "Congress had little role other than to offer words of encouragement and support to a president who already seemed to possess all the constitutional authority he needed to act single-handedly. Far from being a coequal branch, Congress was distinctly junior varsity. It no longer functioned as an authorizing body. Its task was simply to endorse what the president has already decided."[132] The Constitution's mandate for checks and balances was tossed aside while an executive branch took management and ownership of a foreign policy that had dangerous foundational cracks.

The role of Congress is to provide oversight—"making sure that the laws that it writes are faithfully executed and vetting the military and diplomatic activities of the executive. Vigorous oversight was the norm until the end of the twentieth century." Congressional oversight dropped from 782 [hearings] to 297 [hearings] from the first six months of 1983 to the first six months of 1997. In the Senate, during the same period of time, hearings dropped from 429 to an abysmal 175. Congressional oversight during the Bush II years had "virtually collapsed" on foreign and national security policy.[133]

When there were important hearings on Capitol Hill, particularly when the Iraq war resolution was being debated, there was just one reporter in the press gallery and "at the most intense points, the debates in both the House and Senate attracted fewer than ten percent of each body's members."[134] In all of 2003 to 2004, which included the crucial three months before the launch of the Iraq war, the Senate Armed Services Committee held only nine hearings about Iraq. That was less than ten percent of its total hearings. The House Armed Services Committee held 18, less than 14 percent of its total hearings.[135]

This might be tied to the increasing political and partisan rancor on Capitol Hill, but the fact remains that without proper oversight and accountability, Congress is no more than a perfunctory stop akin to merely getting a ticket punched. "The White House, the Defense Department, and a whole lot of other departments and agencies have no fear of Congress, because Congress has shown no appetite to do any serious or tough oversight, to use the power of the purse or the power of pointed public hearings to put the fear of God into them."[136] Why is this?

Thomas Mann and Norman Ornstein say that Congress has an institutional identity crisis, which has only deepened since the Bush II years. "Members of the majority party, including the leaders of Congress, see themselves as field lieutenants in the president's army far more than they of do as members of a separate and independent branch of government. Serious oversight almost inevitably means criticism of performance—and this Congress [the one at the helm during the George W. Bush years] has shied away from anything that would criticize its own administration."[137]

Another issue is raw politics, which has only deepened over the years and led to some venomous partisanship. This speaks to the future of Congress as an institution. The vote on the resolution took place before a crucial mid-term election. It turned out to be a referendum on national security and which party was perceived as the one to prevent another attack. This was political strategy. The Iraq War was a commodity, which had to be marketed and sold to an insecure public.

President Bush's chief of staff, Andy Card, told the *New York Times*, "From a marketing point of view, you don't introduce new products in August."[138] But initiatives are timed to bring the party in power a positive result. The pressure to vote for this resolution came after August 2002 and before the mid-term election three months later. Senator Patrick Leahy of Vermont said, "I think in a way, this administration set out to make the Republican Party an arm of the White House" and the necessity of a war was something to sell—a Republican product that would keep America and her citizens safe from future harm.[139]

The 9/11 attacks were a political game changer. The general discourse in the country had been about economic discontent, but the emphasis abruptly shifted to terrorism and national security. "In pre-election polls, most respondents thought the Democrats would do a better job dealing with health care, education, Social Security, prescription drug benefits, taxes, abortion, unemployment, the environment and corporate corruption. Most thought Republicans would do a better job of dealing with terrorism, the possibility of war with Iraq, the situation in the Middle East, and foreign affairs, generally."[140] Right or wrong, the polling and mood of the country was exploited for political gain. An impending war with Iraq was used as a political weapon in the mid-term elections of 2002.

President Bush used the attacks of 9/11 as a rallying cry, and the attention of Congress was squarely on homeland security and the vote to authorize the war with Iraq.[141] As he barnstormed the country campaigning for Republican candidates, he bullied some Democrat incumbents for not supporting homeland security, and political television ads reinforced the message. "Some of the ads juxtaposed pictures of the Democratic target (in Georgia, for example, Max Cleland) with those of Osama bin Laden and Saddam Hussein."[142]

"Several Republican nominees in congressional contests compared their 'strong stand' on Iraq to 'weak' positions by Democratic campaigners."[143] This rhetoric resonated with the American people. Democrats were struggling to turn the country's attention back to the gloomy economic outlook and a turbulent stock market, issues that were front and center prior to 9/11.

Democrats were furious and argued that the president and his party used the war as a tool for "leverage in the House and Senate races."[144] Politics were at play and divisive politics at that. There is little doubt the country would have been better served had they been placed aside. Questions about the war and any requests for deeper inquiry were successfully framed as weakness on national security.

This speaks to larger issues, which operate in tandem: politics, partisanship, and the polarization of the institution itself through its members. Members of Congress want to keep their jobs, and so their work is tempered by a watchful eye on the next election. Decisions are often influenced by a member's future electability and not as meaningfully on the merits of a particular piece of legislation. This sense may be heightened if legislation is particularly controversial.

One needn't look further for an example than the transformative health care reform bill of 2010, passed in March. Healthy debate was drowned out by partisan bickering and threats to members about future campaigns and the next election. The discourse, in several instances encouraged by each political party, became heated and ugly. One congressman was spat upon, and racial epithets were hurled at him and another African-American colleague as they walked to the chamber for debates on the bill. Another congressman was also verbally disparaged when, out of context, his sexual orientation was referenced. Some members even appeared with placards on the balcony of the U.S. Capitol egging on the protestors below. Voices of reason strained and struggled to be heard above the belabored din of acrimony coming from the Hill.

Representative John Larson, a Democrat from Connecticut, said, "It isn't about how many members are going to lose their seats. It's about this moment, it's about truth, it's every reason why you were elected to come and serve in Congress."[145] President Obama in his quest to ultimately sign the legislation into law also cautioned those in government not to use politics as a compass for governing. He spoke of doing the right thing for the country rather than for congressional careers and the next election. "I'd rather be a really good one-term president than a mediocre two-term president," he said.[146] Despite the divisiveness of the debate, the legislation passed and was subsequently signed into law, but without a single Republican vote in the Senate. The political and partisan divide in government had further widened.

An already altered climate in Washington has become more profound in its dysfunction. With electability as the cornerstone of a member's political life, he or she may have to spend even more time away from their offices as a result. Purpose as a lawmaker has given way to political survival. From the president, to members of the Senate and House, each position on the issues, and every vote they take are measured against the next election cycle. This has had an impact on the institution of Congress itself.

This collective mentality and behavior "has led to a sharp decline in the number of days Congress is in session and the number of committee hearings that are held. When Congress is in session, both the floor and the committees are sparsely and intermittently attended, as members rush away from Capitol Hill to make fundraising phone calls. During a typical week when Congress is in session, no votes occur before 6:30 p.m. on Tuesday or after noon on Thursday, leaving little time for extended oversight hearings or other related activities."[147] Abbreviated congressional sessions, hearings, and debates on any number of issues have a corrosive effect on the deliberative process that is the essence of the institution itself. Mistakes are made. Important issues are hastily debated, completely overlooked, or quickly glossed over for political gain. It becomes a travesty and begs larger questions and examination.

Scott McClellan wrote about a dangerous increase in partisanship and misguided loyalty in the executive and legislative branches. He blamed both the behavior of the president and the Congress, particularly during that time for blind loyalties, which divided starkly along party lines. Loyalty is essential, he said, but those in government should not "be shielded from responsibility" in their work as public servants. Presidents and the Congress were elected to their positions to serve the country and to enhance the lives of its citizens.

"Public servants must remember that they take an oath to the Constitution of the United States. Our first loyalty is to the nation and its people. When conflicts arise, loyalty to the nation must take precedence over party loyalty or personal loyalty. If this means blowing the whistle on misdeeds or insisting that wrongdoing in office be firmly and fully punished, so be it."[148]

McClellan called today's Zeitgeist on Capitol Hill, "the permanent campaign." He said, "Congress could help us move beyond partisan warfare and the culture of deception. Today, members are too consumed with raising money, appeasing special interests, and outmaneuvering the opposition to win the next election." He implored the leadership in both parties to trend away from partisanship toward statesmanship. "Leaders in both parties in both houses must lead by example in swimming against the tide of influences that neither enhance the institution nor serve the country."[149] And the country was far from well served from September 11, 2001, to the invasion of Iraq.

We cannot help but ask, if the Congress was more focused on doing its job than on engaging in the game of partisan politics, would better behavior have prevailed, preventing the Iraq war and the wave of consequences that it brought in its wake? Mann and Ornstein wrote that it was only after it was politically safe to oppose the invasion that Congress forcefully decided to do exactly that. "Months and years after the passage of the of the [Iraq War] resolution, Congress continued to play an episodic and inadequate role in overseeing the planning for and conduct of the

Iraq campaign. Not until after the fall of 2005, after the public had clearly soured on the war, did Congress begin to seriously challenge the president."[150] Those challenges came down along party lines as more information came to light and as people began to speak out.

Congressional Democrats began to stir due to a perfect storm of information that began to collect on the horizon. The toll of the war soberly clocked its 2000th U.S. death on the Iraqi battlefield. Emerging revelations about the failures of pre-war intelligence were slowly coming to light. The president's popularity was falling as the American public began to believe, in increasing numbers, that the war was a mistake. The 2006 mid-term elections were clearly in sight. That fall, Democrats would initiate debates, to the exclusion of other issues, about how to get out of Iraq. One representative, John Murtha (D-PA), called for the immediate return of all troops from Iraq, which would not happen in actuality until years later.

The next chapter will address the role of the press in the run-up to the war. What is the role of the press? Should it behave differently in times of crisis? Did it serve the public adequately enough by reporting the news, verifying information, and seeking out additional information to reveal the truth about the run-up to the war, without bending to corporate or political interests? Could better reporting and media coverage have helped prevent a misguided Iraq war?

NOTES

1. Mahler, Jonathan. "After the Imperial Presidency." *New York Times Magazine*, November 9, 2008, pg. 44.

2. Ricks, Thomas E. *Fiasco* (New York: The Penguin Press, 2006), 85–86.

3. Kaysen, Carl, Steven E. Miller, Martin B. Malin, William D. Nordhaus, and John D. Steinbruner. *War with Iraq: Costs, Consequences, and Alternatives* (Cambridge, MA: American Academy of Arts and Sciences, 2002), 7.

4. Fisher, Louis. "Deciding War against Iraq: Institutional Failures." *Political Science Quarterly* 118, no. 3 (2003): 389–90.

5. Steinhauser, Paul. "Poll: Bush's Popularity Hits a New Low," CNN, March 19, 2008.

6. Murphy, Cullen, and Todd S. Purdum. "Uncovering the Darkest Secrets of the Bush White House (An Oral History)." *Vanity Fair*, February 2009, pg. 100.

7. Mann, Thomas E., and Norman J. Ornstein. *The Broken Branch* (New York: Oxford University Press, Inc., 2006), 14.

8. Fisher, Louis. "Deciding War against Iraq: Institutional Failures." *Political Science Quarterly* 118, no. 3 (2003): 390.

9. Taylor, Stuart, Jr., and Evan Thomas. "Obama's Cheney Dilemma." *Newsweek*, January 19, 2009, pg. 26.

10. Byrd, Robert C. *Losing America: Confronting a Reckless and Arrogant Presidency* (New York: W. W. Norton & Company, 2005), 40.

11. Ibid., 21.

12. Ibid., 23.

13. Mahler, Jonathan. "After the Imperial Presidency." *New York Times Magazine*, November 9, 2008, pg. 47.

14. Byrd, Robert C. *Losing America: Confronting a Reckless and Arrogant Presidency* (New York: W. W. Norton & Company, Inc., 2005), 39.

15. Ibid., 39.

16. Ibid., 45.

17. Mann, Thomas E., and Norman J. Ornstein. *The Broken Branch* (New York: Oxford University Press, Inc., 2006), 17.

18. Baker, Ross K. *House and Senate* (New York: W. W. Norton & Company, Ltd., 2001), 41.

19. Fenno, Richard F., Jr. *The United States Senate: A Bicameral Perspective* (Washington, DC: American Enterprise Institute for Public Policy Research, 1982), 5.

20. Ornstein, Norman J., and Thomas E. Mann. "When Congress Checks Out." *Foreign Affairs* (November/December 2006): 1.

21. Wilson, James. *The Founders Constitution* (Chicago: The University of Chicago Press, 1987), chapter 7, Document 17, December 11, 1787, McMaster 414–18.

22. Mahler, Jonathan. "After the Imperial Presidency." *New York Times Magazine*, November 9, 2008, pg. 45.

23. Byrd, Robert C. *Losing America: Confronting a Reckless and Arrogant Presidency* (New York: W. W. Norton & Company, Inc., 2005), 45.

24. Hamilton, Lee. *Strengthening Congress* (Bloomington: Indiana University Press, 2009), 8.

25. Ibid., 9.

26. Schlesinger, Arthur M. *War and the American Presidency* (New York, London: W. W. Norton & Company, 2004), 46.

27. Ibid., 45.

28. Ibid., 46.

29. Graubard, Stephen. *Command of Office* (New York: Basic Books, 2004), 542.

30. Hamilton, Lee. *Strengthening Congress* (Bloomington: Indiana University Press, 2009), 5–6.

31. Woodward, Bob. *Bush at War* (New York: Simon & Schuster, 2002), 145–46.

32. Byrd, Robert C. *Losing America: Confronting a Reckless and Arrogant Presidency* (New York: W. W. Norton & Company, Inc., 2005), 21.

33. Ibid., 63.

34. Ibid.

35. Official Transcript, US President message to Congress, September 14, 2001, Doc. 27, No. 37.

36. Official transcript, Congressional Record, September 14, 2001.

37. Transcript. "War Made Easy: How Presidents and Pundits Keep Spinning Us to Death." Written and directed by Loretta Alper and Jeremy Earp. November 1, 2007.

38. Official White House transcript, September 14, 2001.

39. Lewis, Neil A. "A Nation Challenged: The Resolution; Measure Backing Bush's Use of Force Is as Broad as a Declaration of War, Experts Say." *The New York Times*, September 18, 2001.

40. Ibid.

41. Official White House transcript, October 7, 2001.

42. Official White House transcript, October 10, 2001.

43. Lancaster, John, and Jonathan Krim. "Ashcroft Presents Anti-Terrorism Plan to Congress." *Washington Post*, September 20, 2001.

44. Official Department of Justice transcript, September 24, 2001.

45. Lancaster, John. "Anti-Terrorism Bill Hits Snag on the Hill: Dispute between Senate Democrats, White House Threatens Committee Approval." *Washington Post*, October 3, 2001.

46. Gallup News Service, "Latest Summary: American Public Opinion on the War on Terrorism." December 21, 2001.

47. Byrd, Robert C. *Losing America: Confronting a Reckless and Arrogant Presidency* (New York: W. W. Norton & Company, Inc., 2005), 46.

48. Official Senate transcript, October 11, 2001.

49. Ibid.
50. Byrd, Robert C. *Losing America: Confronting a Reckless and Arrogant Presidency* (New York: W. W. Norton & Company, Inc., 2005), 47.
51. Schlesinger, Arthur M. *War and the American Presidency* (New York, London: W. W. Norton & Company, Inc., 2004), 58.
52. Hentoff, Nat. "Terrorizing the Bill of Rights." *Village Voice*, November 9, 2001.
53. Official website, Rep. Jerrold Nadler, 2003 press archives, February 9, 2003.
54. Official White House transcript, October 26, 2001.
55. Ibid.
56. Hentoff, Nat. "Terrorizing the Bill of Rights." *Village Voice*, November 9, 2001.
57. Grieve, Tim. "Climate of Intimidation." *Salon*, March 24, 2003.
58. Hentoff, Nat. "Terrorizing the Bill of Rights." *Village Voice*, November 9, 2001.
59. O'Meara, Kelly Patricia. "Police State." *Insight*, November 9, 2001.
60. Ibid.
61. Scher, Robert. "With Powers Like These, Can Repression Be Far Behind." *Los Angeles Times*, October 30, 2001.
62. Baird, Brian. "We Need to Read the Bills," *Washington* Post, November 27, 2004, A31.
63. Byrd, Robert C. *Losing America: Confronting a Reckless and Arrogant Presidency* (New York: W. W. Norton & Company, Inc., 2005), 45–46.
64. Graubard, Steven. *Command of Office* (New York: Basic Books, 2004), 544.
65. Schlesinger, Arthur M. *War and the American Presidency* (New York, London: W. W. Norton & Company, Inc., 2004), 51.
66. Ibid., 66.
67. Keen, Judy. "Strain of Iraq showing on Bush, those who know him say." *USA Today*, April 2, 2003.
68. Murphy, Cullen, and Todd S. Purdum. "Uncovering the Darkest Secrets of the Bush White House (An Oral History)." *Vanity Fair*, February 2009, pg. 100.
69. Ibid., 99.
70. Byrd, Robert C. *Losing America: Confronting a Reckless Arrogant Presidency* (New York: W. W. Norton & Company, Inc., 2005), 129.
71. Rich, Frank. *The Greatest Story Ever Sold* (New York: The Penguin Press, 2006), 234.
72. Byrd, Robert C. *Losing America: Confronting a Reckless Arrogant Presidency* (New York: W. W. Norton & Company, Inc., 2005), 123.
73. Rich, Frank. *The Greatest Story Ever Sold* (New York: The Penguin Press, 2006), 36.
74. Ibid.
75. Moore, David. "Speech Watchers Overwhelmingly Behind Bush." *Gallup News Service*, January 30, 2002.
76. Ibid.
77. Murphy, Cullen, and Todd S. Purdum. "Uncovering the Darkest Secrets of the Bush White House (An Oral History)." *Vanity Fair*, February 2009, pg. 100.
78. Byrd, Robert C. *Losing America: Confronting a Reckless Arrogant Presidency* (New York: W. W. Norton & Company, Inc., 2005), 126.
79. Ibid., 127.
80. Kerry, John F. "Tora Bora Revisited: How We Failed to Get bin Laden and Why It Matters Today." Report to the Senate Committee on Foreign Relations, November 30, 2009, pg. 1.
81. Ibid., 2.
82. Rich, Frank. *The Greatest Story Ever Sold* (New York: The Penguin Press, 2006), 46.
83. Kerry, John F. "Tora Bora Revisited: How We Failed to Get bin Laden and Why It Matters Today." Report to the Senate Committee on Foreign Relations, November 30, 2009, pg. v.
84. Kennedy, Edward M. "A Dishonest War." *Washington Post*, January 18, 2004.

85. Ibid., 47.
86. Ibid., 49.
87. Ibid., 48.
88. Ibid., 49.
89. Gallup News Service Presidential Approval Ratings, Fall 2002.
90. Byrd, Robert C. *Losing America: Confronting a Reckless and Arrogant Presidency* (New York: W. W. Norton & Company, Inc., 2005), 136.
91. Yoo, John. *UC Berkeley News*, January 4, 2005.
92. Official Congressional transcript, October 3, 2002.
93. Isikoff, Michael, and David Corn. *Hubris* (New York: Three Rivers Press, 2006), 22.
94. Mahler, Jonathan. "After the Imperial Presidency." *New York Times Magazine*, November 9, 2008, pg. 45.
95. Mann, Thomas E., and Norman J. Ornstein. *The Broken Branch* (Oxford: Oxford University Press, Inc., 2006), 222.
96. Isikoff, Michael, and David Corn. *Hubris* (New York: Three Rivers Press, 2006), 21–22.
97. Ibid., 22.
98. Ibid., 24.
99. Ibid., 25.
100. Fisher, Louis. "Deciding War against Iraq: Institutional Failures." *Political Science Quarterly* 118, no. 3 (2003): 396. (Congressional Record, 148: S8966; daily edition, September 20, 2002).
101. Fournier, Ron. "White House Lawyers Give Bush OK on Iraq." *Washington Times*, August 26, 2002.
102. Fisher, Louis. "Deciding War against Iraq: Institutional Failures." *Political Science Quarterly* 118, no. 3 (2003): 395.
103. Official transcript, *PBS NewsHour* with Jim Lehrer, September 4, 2002.
104. Ibid.
105. Byrd, Robert C. *Losing America: Confronting a Reckless and Arrogant Presidency* (New York: W. W. Norton & Company, Inc., 2005), 160.
106. Ibid.,163.
107. Ibid., 163–64.
108. Ibid., 165.
109. Dewar, Helen, and Juliet Eilperin. "Iraq Resolution Passes Test, Gains Support." *Washington Post*, October 10, 2002.
110. Byrd, Robert C. "Congress Must Resist the Rush to War." *New York Times*, October 10, 2002.
111. Murphy, Cullen, and Todd S. Purdum. "Uncovering the Darkest Secrets of the Bush White House (An Oral History)." *Vanity Fair*, February 2009, pg. 149.
112. Byrd, Robert C. *Losing America: Confronting a Reckless and Arrogant Presidency* (New York: W. W. Norton & Company, Inc., 2005), 171.
113. King, John. "White House: We've Made History." *CNN*, November 6, 2002.
114. Ibid.
115. Murphy, Cullen, and Todd S. Purdum. "Uncovering the Darkest Secrets of the Bush White House (An Oral History)." *Vanity Fair*, February 2009, pg. 100.
116. Hulse, Carl, and Sheryl Gay Stolberg, "State of the Union: Opposition Response; Democrats Say the Nation Heads in 'Wrong Direction,'" *New York Times*, January 29, 2003.
117. Karl, Jonathan. "Kennedy to Seek New Measure on War with Iraq," *CNN*, January 28, 2003.
118. Hulse, Carl, and Sheryl Gay Stolberg, "State of the Union: Opposition Response, Democrats Say the Nation Heads in 'Wrong Direction,'" *New York Times*, January 29, 2003.
119. Karl, Jonathan. "Kennedy to Seek New Measure on War with Iraq," *CNN*, January 28, 2003.

120. Ibid.

121. Isikoff, Michael, and David Corn. *Hubris* (New York: Three Rivers Press, 2006), 190.

122. Bryd, Robert C. *Losing America: Confronting a Reckless and Arrogant Presidency* (New York: W. W. Norton & Company, Inc., 2005), 183.

123. Ibid., 184.

124. Ricks, Thomas. *Fiasco* (New York: The Penguin Press, 2006), 86.

125. Ibid.

126. Ibid., 88.

127. Byrd, Robert C. *Losing America: Confronting a Reckless and Arrogant Presidency* (New York: W. W. Norton & Company, Inc., 2005), 277–78.

128. Ibid.

129. Ibid., 282.

130. Official transcript, United States Senate, March 19, 2003.

131. Ibid.

132. Fisher, Louis. "Deciding War against Iraq: Institutional Failures." *Political Science Quarterly* 118, no. 3 (2003): 406.

133. Ornstein, Norman J., and Thomas E. Mann. "When Congress Checks Out." *Foreign Affairs* (November/December 2006): 2.

134. Ricks, Thomas E. *Fiasco* (New York: The Penguin Press, 2006), 61.

135. Ornstein, Norman J., and Thomas E. Mann. "When Congress Checks Out." *Foreign Affairs* (November/December 2006): 2.

136. Mann, Thomas E., and Norman J. Ornstein. *The Broken Branch* (Oxford: Oxford University Press, 2006), 156.

137. Ibid., 155.

138. Dadge, David. *The War in Iraq and Why the Media Failed Us* (Westport, CT: Praeger, 2006), 15.

139. Mahler, Jonathan, "After the Imperial Presidency," *The New York Times Magazine*, November 9, 2008, pg. 45.

140. Jacobson, Gary C. "The Bush Presidency and the American Electorate." *Presidential Studies Quarterly* 33, no. 4 (2003): 707.

141. Mann, Thomas E., and Norman J. Ornstein. *The Broken Branch* (Oxford: Oxford University Press, 2006), 134.

142. Ibid.

143. Fisher, Louis. "Deciding War against Iraq: Institutional Failures." *Political Science Quarterly* 118, no. 3 (2003): 397.

144. Ibid., 398.

145. Official transcript, ABC *This Week*, March 21, 2010.

146. Official transcript, ABC *World News*, January 25, 2010.

147. Ornstein, Norman J., and Thomas E. Mann. "When Congress Checks Out." *Foreign Press Quarterly* (November/December 2006): 6.

148. McClellan, Scott. *What Happened* (New York: PublicAffairs, 2008), 318.

149. Ibid.

150. Mann, Thomas E., and Norman J. Ornstein. *The Broken Branch* (Oxford: Oxford University Press, 2006), 223–24.

FOUR

The News Media

Reporting and the Run-Up to War

A cantankerous press, an obstinate press,
a ubiquitous press, must be suffered by those in authority
in order to preserve the right of the people to know.
—Murray I. Gurfein, federal judge, U.S. Court of Appeals for the
Second Circuit

I think it's one of the most embarrassing chapters in American journalism and I think there was a sense of pressure from corporations who own where we work and from the government to really squash any kind of dissent or any kind of questioning of it. Our responsibility is to sometimes go against the mood of the country and ask the hard questions.
—Katie Couric, news anchor, CBS *Evening News*

INTRODUCTION

There was a confluence of factors, which in concert, created the perfect atmosphere for the Iraq war. The performance of the news media was one of those factors. It may have been what the news media *did not do* rather than what *they did do* that helped contribute to a collective American mind-set that was clouded about Iraq and what to do about it. There is little doubt that the news media helped clear the way for an imminent Iraq war.

The news media and those journalists for whom they work are the conduits between the gathering of the news itself from the source and the

151

distribution of that news to the public they serve. It is their role to make sense of what is happening and explain it to the people. The role of the journalist is to check those in authority and stand as a beacon for accuracy and the truth where it concerns both the public interest and the public good. A journalist's obligation to get at the truth is a basic and first tenet of the profession and is a critical premise for operation, the news media in relation to the people, their democracy, and their government.

In 1997, the Pew Research Project for Excellence in Journalism assembled a committee of journalists. For over four years the committee researched journalism history and launched a national conversation in twenty public forums across the country. The group identified nine principles of journalism, the first of which was about seeking the truth. It reads in part, "Democracy depends on citizens having reliable, accurate facts put in a meaningful context. Journalism does not pursue truth in a philosophical sense, but it can and must pursue it in a practical sense. This is a process that begins with the professional discipline of assembling and verifying facts."

The second principle is about the news media's first loyalty, which must be to their citizens, their audience, readers, listeners, and viewers. "While news organizations answer to many constituencies, including advertisers and shareholders, the journalists in those organizations must maintain allegiance to citizens and the larger public interest above any other if they are to provide the news without fear or favor."

The story of the Iraq war in 2003 may have been one of the most important political stories of modern times. It is important to examine how the reporting and how the news coverage of this story may have hurt, rather than served, the country during the time from the terrorist attacks on September 11, 2001, to the start of the Iraq war, March 19, 2003. It is in the context of getting at the truth and service to the public that will determine, to some extent, whether the performance of the news media served as a cautionary tale for the future of journalism. Or instead did the news media serve as shining example, a textbook example, of how to perform?

This chapter will discuss the confidence of the public in the press, provide information about the relationship of President Bush to the press, examine the corporate and commercial pressures on the press, and explain several key story points for the press that could have made a dramatic difference in the perception of the public about engaging Iraq in battle.

A discussion about the press and the war in Iraq may have more meaning with a brief understanding of what the founders had to say about the role of the press during the creation of the country when the constitution was being written and what the press itself has to say about its own governance and its role in American society. Therein may lie some of the conflicts, contradictions, and questions that remain today about the press, its purpose, and, indeed, its value.

WHAT HISTORY SAYS ABOUT THE PRESS

The framework under which the United States of America operates and was organized is its defining document, the United States Constitution. It was debated and drafted in Philadelphia at the Constitutional Convention between May and September of 1787. Many people at that time had much to say about the role of the press before and after the document was ratified.

Thomas Jefferson did not attend the Constitutional Convention, but he was a founding father of the United States and its third president. He wrote extensively to others about a free press. In a letter to Edward Carrington in 1787 he said if he had to choose between a government without newspapers or newspapers without a government, he would not hesitate to prefer the latter.[1]

Later in 1804, in a letter to John Tyler, he also wrote about the relationship of people to their new government and to the press. "No experiment can be more interesting than we are now trying, and which we trust will end in establishing the fact, that man may be governed by reason and truth. Our first object should, therefore be, to leave open to him all the avenues to truth. The most effectual hitherto found, is the freedom of the press. It is, therefore, the first shut up by those who fear the investigation of their actions."[2]

William Thomas Stead, a newspaper editor in England during the 1800s, called the press "the engine of social reform." He wrote, "The press is at once the eye and the ear and the tongue of the people. It is the visible speech, if not the voice of the democracy. It is the phonograph of the world."[3]

The notion of the press as the so-called fourth estate of government was thought to come from Edmund Burke, the Irish statesman, philosopher, and author in the late 1700s. He considered the press a fourth estate after "the three estates" of France during the French Revolution, which he said were the nobility, the commoners, and the clergy. These had great influence in the politics and governing of a country, as did the press, Burke surmised.

Thomas Carlyle, a British historian, recorded what Burke had to say about the press as fourth estate when he [Burke] spoke before [British] Parliament. Carlyle wrote:

> Burke said there were Three Estates in Parliament; but in the Reporter's Gallery yonder, there sat a Fourth Estate more important than they all. It is not a figure of speech, or a witty saying; it is a literal fact—very momentous to us in these times. Literature is our Parliament too. Print-

ing, which comes necessarily out of Writing, I say often, is equivalent to Democracy; invent Writing, Democracy is inevitable. . . . Whoever can speak, speaking now to the whole nation, becomes a power, a branch of government, with inalienable weight in lawmaking in all acts of authority. It matters not what rank he has, what revenues or garnitures: the requisite thing is that he have a tongue which others will listen to; this and nothing more is requisite. The nation is governed by all that has tongue in the nation. Democracy is virtually there.[4]

It is interesting that the First Amendment, a part of the Bill of Rights, only included a sparse few words about the press. Its inclusion in the Constitution was a rather contentious issue and could have derailed the document's path to adoption by the states. What would become the First Amendment was a basic prescription for the American people and their civil rights. It said the people of the United States should be able to worship as they wish. The people should be able to speak freely. The press should operate freely and openly. People can peaceably assemble to demonstrate their feelings and thoughts. They can petition the government, should they have grievances.

"Considered word for word, the First Amendment is almost everything a free press advocate might hope for, but most scholars doubt that the majority of the framers intended the First Amendment to be an absolute prohibition on any government actions that might curtail the freedom of the press."[5] The absence of a Bill of Rights stood in the way of a smooth transition to ratification of the constitution. Here is why.

Our two party system was already forming. The Federalists and Anti-Federalists had differing views about how the new country would take shape. "They had conflicting ideas—about government, about power."[6] The Federalists were supporters of the Constitution and wanted a strong national government. The Anti-Federalists, opponents of the Constitution, thought that, "as written, would create a centralized and potentially despotic government and, at the same time, give no guarantees for freedom of religion, speech, press, or assembly or any right to petition the government."[7] Federalists thought such language was unnecessary and that such concerns would be left to the states.

Men of the times had different points of references. Federalists "were men engaged, for the most part, in commerce, manufacturing and banking, property owners mostly, who were more interested in preserving and extending their economic advantages than in risking social experiments."[8] Anti-Federalists were "largely an agrarian class. They were small farmers and city wage earners, supported by intellectuals and political philosophers, who wanted to continue the social reforms that had brought on the American Revolution in the first place."[9]

The notion of a Bill of Rights to be included as part of the United States Constitution was first discussed at the Constitutional Convention of 1787 in Philadelphia where the Constitution itself was being debated.

Many demanded that a Bill of Rights be included in the new Constitution as a condition for its ratification.[10] High-profile framers weighed in, very concerned that a Bill of Rights be seriously considered. John Adams expressed his concern. Thomas Jefferson in a correspondence to James Madison wrote: "I do not like . . . the omission of a bill of rights providing clearly and without the aid of sophisms for freedom of religion, freedom of the press, protection against standing armies, restriction against monopolies, the external and unremitting force of the habeas corpus laws, and trials by jury in all matters of fact triable by the laws of the land and not by the law of nations."[11]

It wasn't until 1789, the same year the Constitution was ratified, that James Madison formally introduced the Bill of Rights to the first United States Congress as a series of articles. They would now be considered as amendments to the Constitution. Madison chaired the committee to draft the amendments. The first draft did not include anything about the press. The select committee, where the draft was referred, added the words "or of the press."[12] Its inclusion almost seems like an afterthought—tacked on. To be sure, "it is the cornerstone of our press liberty, but there is evidence that the authors of the Constitution spent little time discussing this issue. James Madison's careful minutes show only casual and infrequent mention of the press."[13]

The reason it may have been included at all is that precedent had been established in many of the states, which used British common law, calling for freedom of expression.[14] Those principles were also reflected in the Declaration of Rights written by John Dickinson when the first Continental Congress convened in 1774. Nine of the thirteen states provided for such constitutional protection by 1787. The Virginia Bill of Rights of 1776 stated "the freedom of the press is one of the great bulwarks of liberty, and can never be restrained, but by despotic governments." Article XVI of the Massachusetts Bill of Rights of 1780 expressed similar sentiments, and other states also used variations on this theme.[15]

The Bill of Rights became the first ten amendments to the Constitution in 1791, and the notion of a free press may have been reluctantly adopted to reflect public sentiment. Perhaps its brevity is in direct proportion to the weight those in Congress gave it, even though many of our founders and those who fought for independence from Great Britain believed in a free press as an imperative to protect the people's interests. No matter. Its inherent strength or limitation can only be left up to interpretation.

No one could know for certain what members of Congress had in mind when they drafted the First Amendment to the Constitution and, specifically, how broad a mandate it truly gives those in the news media. It seems at the time there were more pressing issues to be debated. The mention of the press may have been a simple add-on or meant as a tenacious few words, which knowingly packed muscle and wielded power. To be sure, the first amendment for a free press was a gift and precipitated the very thoughts about how the press came to regard itself.

THE PRESS ON ITS ROLE

The practice of journalism, the practice of reporting is not, nor ever was, an exact science. There were no, nor are there today, any laws requiring any strict adherence to any hard-and-fast standard rules of journalism. Journalists take no oath before they practice their craft of writing and reporting the news. There is no license required to practice journalism, to be a reporter or a producer or for those who manage newsrooms, publishers, and media owners, those who dictate the gathering of news and its dissemination.

Those people who regard themselves as journalists, however, operate under the mandate they believe was given to them by the United States Constitution, which specifies the broad freedoms we enjoy in this country, including a free press. The press has practiced self-governance over the years and has grown on its own to become, by itself, what it is today. In part, the news media are big business, self-interested with concerns far beyond the purity of the news. That notwithstanding, how does the press represent itself and what does it say about its modus operandi as a group?

The Society of Professional Journalists (SPJ) is probably the most prestigious organization representing the craft of journalism, its member journalists, and journalism educators. There are other smaller guilds that represent broadcasters and print journalists separately, but it is the SPJ, which seeks to include all who are journalists, no matter the distribution platform (print, radio, television, cable, web) or company.

The SPJ has been in existence since 1909. It was founded as a fraternity called Sigma Delta Chi in Greencastle, Indiana, at DePauw University. The university's daily newspaper "was looked upon dubiously by influential faculty and the student body and 'had failed to attain any great eminence or respectability.'"[16] The editor-in-chief, LeRoy H. Millikan, noticed with dismay that other undergraduates were drawn together by a "mutual expectancy of professional life in the same field." Journalism students of the day were not.[17]

Although not a social organization, it adopted Greek fraternity letters as its moniker and ascribed to these early, simple terms; "better journalism, both amateur and professional, a truthful, honorable press, one not dominated by commercialism and that by planting journalistic ideals in student newspapermen, they would make great strides toward these goals" later as working professionals. The founder of Sigma Delta Chi, Eugene Pulliam, said, "We didn't know what we were creating. We only knew what we believed."[18]

What Pulliam and the others ultimately created was what would become the oldest and largest journalism association in the United States. The organization estimates a fluctuating membership between 8,500 and 9,000 people—professional journalists and academics. It considers itself "broad-based" because it includes journalists of "any media, topic or background."[19]

SPJ publishes the following information about itself: "The Society of Professional Journalists is dedicated to the perpetuation of a free press as the cornerstone of our nation and our liberty. To ensure that the concept of self-government outlined by the U.S. Constitution remains a reality into future centuries, the American people must be well informed in order to make decisions regarding their lives and their local and national communities. It is the role of journalists to provide this information in an accurate, comprehensive, timely and understandable manner."[20]

The organization adopted a code of ethics, which it says has been embraced by "thousands of writers, editors and other news professionals" across the country. It was adapted from a code of ethics used by the American Society of Newspaper Editors in 1926. SPJ wrote its own code in 1973. It was subsequently revised several times, in 1984, 1987, and in 1996, to reflect emerging technologies and the rapidly changing face of the business. The code has broadly noted four areas of focus, which are to seek truth and report it, to minimize harm, to act independently, and to be accountable. In each of these areas, the organization enumerates very specific points.[21]

In the most exhaustive section about seeking truth and reporting it, the code says journalists should "test the accuracy of information" and be fair, honest, and courageous in gathering, reporting, and interpreting information. It also states that journalists "have a special obligation to ensure that the public's business is conducted in the open and that government records are open to inspection." In the section entitled "Act Independently," the code says journalists should be "free of obligation to any interest other than the public's right to know" and that journalists are only accountable to their "readers, listeners, viewers and each other."[22]

Despite this framework and a formal organization to help journalists be better at serving the public, not much has changed since post-revolutionary times. Journalists often express their own views or the views of their employers in their reporting. Reporters are often also pundits, giving opinions and offering judgments. If reporters also act as pundits, they should at least be an expert or authority on the subject about which they are writing or speaking. That is not always the case. The news media has been used as a tool to propagandize in varying degrees throughout American history. Much to the consternation of many news purists, the press often develops characteristics of its own and takes sides or advocates positions.

Many papers, magazines, websites, radio stations, and television networks have adopted specific political leanings. It is also fair to say that many journalists do their best to practice their craft under the auspices of the SPJ, the umbrella organization that best represents their interests. However, there is little doubt the quality of the reporting is, in large measure, dependent on the integrity of the owners, publishers, and editors of those media companies for whom the rank and file work. It is also largely dependent on the business, economic, and financial climate of the day.

Recently, news organizations across the country have been decimated with layoffs, especially for those who work in the print industry. Much of this is due to the decline in newspaper readership. This has impacted advertising dollars, the engine that keeps the presses running. Higher-priced, experienced journalists began their careers in print. That is where, in many instances, news stories originate and are later repurposed for other platforms. Those veterans of print journalism have been replaced by younger people who cost less to employ and are far less experienced. This contributes to the lack of quality, reliability, and credibility of the news and information we consume. How this might have directly affected news coverage between 9/11 and the start of the Iraq War is a factor to be considered.

The late Philip Graham, the iconic publisher of the *Washington Post*, has been widely credited with saying that the press writes "the first rough draft of history," but there is a 2007 study, which suggests that the news media go far beyond that. According to a researcher at the University of Missouri, the news media "significantly influence" the very shaping of history itself. Based on her study of nineteenth-century newspapers and magazine articles, the researcher, Dr. Betty Winfield, a professor of journalism, concluded that journalists create a particular national story by referencing certain people and events, creating a collective memory, which has inherent power and influence.[23]

The story, which emerged after 9/11 and led to the Iraq War, did just that. The press, as it repeatedly referenced certain people and certain events in a particular manner, developed a story line over time not much different from that of the Bush administration, which also referenced certain people and events. From those repeated narratives over days and weeks, a certain collective memory was burnished into the minds of the American people about why 9/11 happened and, subsequently, why the Iraq war was necessary.

President Bush did what President Roosevelt did after the attack on Pearl Harbor, which was to create a national narrative regarding the attacks. Both articulated the way forward for the United States. Both conveyed a sense of urgency.[24] Storytelling was shaped by the constant news coverage of the attacks, creating a collective identity. There was a "them," the enemy. There was an "us," Americans and victims of several horrible attacks. Journalism was part of the "us" and responded to the president's tone.[25] As it turned out, however, our collective memory was formed with help from the news media as it recorded and wrote that "first rough draft of history." In varying degree, an inaccurate portrait of the situation took shape. As valuable as the work of the news media can be on some stories, it can also be just as damaging for the work it does not do on other important stories.

The news media, both print and electronic, became so emotional and so entangled in our damaged national psyche, which the 9/11 event itself generated, that they in many ways failed to move beyond the story lines of the attacks themselves and how the United States and Americans were impacted to a new narrative, the next narrative. The story was evolving. The news media, as a group, needed to summon clearer heads and step back from the curtain of emotion to critically report the actions undertaken by the United States and the Bush administration that followed. That did not happen.

What was the Bush administration getting the country into and did it characterize the situation about Iraq accurately and fairly to the American people? Ultimately, it was an inaccurate portrait the news media painted for the American people, which was that the Iraq war was justified and that Saddam Hussein had an active weapons program, whose target was likely the United States. Also, not much coverage was given to the protests and marches of those in opposition to any action against Iraq. The lack of balanced coverage may have skewed poll numbers that showed overwhelming support of the president's plan to attack Iraq.

This is where the story of the news media and making a case for the Iraq war began. We must evaluate the performance of the news media by considering what the American people said about the news media during this time and what members of the press have said about the quality of their own reporting. Also considered will be what the Constitution and the founders provided regarding a free press, what the press believes its responsibility to be, and the contemporary challenges presented by so-called "new media." Today the press operates under a new set of economic and technological realities, which is critical in understanding the reporting of the Iraq war.

Considering this important story and others that will inevitably follow, expectations about the press may be both antiquated and unrealistic, given new modern variables, which never could have been anticipated. Or given this major story, like others before it, the news media may have gotten swept off course because it became swallowed up in the story, ultimately abandoning its role as objective observer.

THE BUSINESS OF THE PRESS VERSUS THE PRESS
AS PUBLIC SERVANT

Who and what is today's press? For purposes here "the press" and "the news media" will be used interchangeably and mean, collectively, journalists and the companies for whom they work. The news media are those who cover the news for traditional media—hard copy newspapers and magazines, radio, and television—and also for what is now commonly referred to as "new media," which refers to all digital content produced by journalists, much of it found on the World Wide Web, more commonly referred to as the "Web" or "Internet."

Today's journalism is in every sense a mass communication, completely global in scope, from which the news can now be distributed on a multitude of platforms around the planet in so-called "real time." Information can be circulated to mass populations almost instantaneously by the simple click of a computer mouse. All these platforms for which news content is produced are distributed for commercial gain by a few giant media outlets. For the most part, news is no longer primarily produced and distributed for the public good, but more for profit. Once the business of news was a money-losing enterprise. This was widely accepted as necessary to fulfill an important obligation to the people without conflict of interest. The public would be educated and informed. Today, news and profit do not mix well and often have competing interests.

Correspondent and CBS *Evening News* anchorman, Walter Cronkite, once regarded as the most trusted man in America, said that we must regard ourselves as simple, humble public servants who provide the public with a clear and honest record of the day's events and a deeper understanding of the continuing stories that affect our lives and the lives of others. He said that journalists would be doing their jobs better if they were able to relate at a more basic level to the average working American. He was critical of the business, in general, and the exorbitant salaries paid to both news anchors and reporters. Excessive salaries, when considering the actual work of journalists and the purpose of news reporting, tend to importantly remove them from truly understanding the people they cover.

He wrote, "There was a day not far distant, just before World War II, when nearly all of us news people, although white collar by profession, earned blue collar salaries. We were part of the 'common people.' We drank in our corner bars with our friends, the cops and the firemen, the political hacks from City Hall, the shoe salesmen and the ribbon clerks. We suffered the same budgetary restraints, the same bureaucratic indignities, waited in the same lines. We could identify with the average man because we were him."[26]

Journalists should be cautious about becoming celebrity news stars, hobnobbing, socializing with the powerful and rich and famous. They must not be of them but apart from them so as not to lose perspective and objectivity. The news media are charged with holding those in power and who have fame and money to account. It is part of the job. Members of the news media, and especially those on the anchor desk, Cronkite cautioned, must not move from observer to player.[27]

In government, the people support those in charge by electing them to important posts from the local school board to judges and to town boards and city halls to the chambers of Congress and to the White House. The people support those who govern and others in power—those who manage the country and our affairs—through our tax dollars and by participating in our communities. One way to participate is to vote. Another way is to debate issues and initiatives. We write to our elected officials with our gripes and concerns. We may protest in the streets and attend rallies. We attend community meetings.

Within that framework, we deserve to have an accurate and thorough accounting about how our tax dollars are spent and how those who run the country decide to manage our affairs locally, nationally, and internationally. The press is one vehicle by which people learn about their world, process the events of the day, ultimately come to understand it, and make judgments.

In this country, democracy's wheels have been spinning for over 230 years with the help of a press that has collected information, verified it, and disseminated it. The necessity of a free press is as fresh a concept today as it was at the forming of the republic. "The secret of our past success as a nation may be traced to the fact that we have been a free people, free to discuss ideas and alternatives, free to teach and learn, free to report and to hear, free to challenge the most venerable institutions without fear of reprisal."[28]

This is not some lofty, idealized, outdated mission, but a practical formula to attract and sustain an informed, educated citizenry if the people so choose to engage. For the benefit of the people, it is the job of the news media to collect the facts, verify those facts, and report them with balance, accuracy, and with a sense of fairness.

These are difficult times for the press, however. The quality of reporting has been threatened by economic pressures born of the so-called digital information age. The incredible speed at which information travels may be economically efficient, but it is not good for journalism, nor is it good for the consumer. Faster information, at least in the news business, is often not reliable information. It is, however, information that has come by more cheaply.

Teams of researchers in newsrooms come at a premium. Bureaus and reporters posted strategically across the country and in bureaus around the world are expensive. Because of harsh economic realities, the numbers of those bureaus and their reporters are dwindling. This is because the huge corporate conglomerates that own networks, programming, web sites, and all their content are under pressure to improve the bottom line and increase shareholder value. Information is easily and readily accessible from numerous sources; despite the fact that the information is not always the best scrutinized material. This often happens by any means necessary and at the expense of the product itself.

"Real reporting is expensive. Foreign bureaus can cost millions of dollars a year to maintain. Air travel and hotels are not cheap, television teams travel with hundreds of pounds of gear, and satellite costs for transmitting video from foreign countries were, until recently, a major expense."[29] The networks and all news organizations have cut back.

For example, networks used to send teams of people to cover presidential elections. On average, in television, four people would be assigned to each and every candidate until the candidate would either drop out of the race or prevail, in which case more people would be added, covering a multitude of story angles in numerous cities at once. Recently, the most important, prestigious corps of reporters in the country, those who travel with the president of the United States, the White House press corps, have been cut back or eliminated completely by some news organizations across the country.[30]

Without being there consistently, especially with the president, reporters will miss the nuance of important stories or be unable to recognize when the news has shifted. They will not be knowledgeable enough to ask the right questions. Reporters and producers need to be where the news is happening, not collecting it from behind a desk via a computer, based, in some cases, countries and continents away from where news is being made. Also, new organizations should not be purchasing news from other sources unless they can verify the accuracy of the information. And some news comes for free, from so-called "citizen journalists," whose identities and motives are unknown and whose "reports" cannot as easily be checked for accuracy. News organizations now solicit these reports from average viewers and readers. News and information that come both cheaply and quickly have dangerous ramifications, especially when involving big important stories such as the terrorist attacks of 9/11 and the Iraq war.

Tom Fenton, formerly of ABC News, who was based in London for years, claims that the networks are "outsourcing the news." Basically, he means that networks and other news organizations buy the news from other sources and tout it as their own. Sometimes the news networks will fly in their correspondent as a big story is breaking and use video and information shot and gathered by another source. "The network cannot vouch for the voracity of the report and in most cases has no idea who shot the video and whether the photographer avoided filming certain events or might even have staged them. It is remarkably easy to cheat when filming the news."[31]

Moreover, when reporters fly in to cover news about which they have no previous, detailed knowledge, the audience, dependent on the information they impart, suffers. "The correspondent has little local knowledge and few contacts."[32] He/she has not been able to gather facts by understanding the area, the politics, the culture. The information is not vetted thoroughly. "This whole idea of parachuting correspondents and camera crews into a place where there's a crisis, that's too late. When you parachute people in, the fire's already burning."[33] Tom Fenton calls these practices "deceptive." News organizations, he says, "have lost sight of their duty to the public."[34]

The use of the Internet as a source for news has complicated the business of news even more. To be sure, the use of the Internet by journalists and the companies for whom they work is an inexpensive way to distribute news and information. It is also a place where anyone can post material. That has cultivated the latest trends in journalism, called "blogging," or web logging. On the web, all of us can participate and can do so anonymously if we choose. All of us can get news and information from hundreds and thousands of sources. We can even be those sources. It has expanded and diversified just how and where people get their news and information, which has created a serious challenge for the news media.

Audience determines ratings and readership, which in turn determines earning potential for news organizations and publishers. But speed and the efficiency of modern distribution methods have not yielded sufficiently to accuracy, the proper vetting of information, and the luxury of digging for facts rather than relying on information based on conjecture. Some say this has weakened the craft and practice of journalism, which, in turn, has hurt the coverage of the political process and those who depend on it.

Others say the opposite—that new media and its home base, the Internet, have "democratized" access to information. Campaign manager to former presidential candidate Howard Dean, Joe Trippi, was among the first to change the nature of presidential campaigning by using the web to solicit small sums of money from all those who might support Dean's candidacy, not just relying on donations from a privileged, well-heeled few. He has discussed the old media versus the new by saying, "While television was a medium that rendered us dumb, disengaged, and disconnected, the Internet makes us smarter, more involved and better informed."[35] With more and more people having access to a computer, "the web's low barriers to entry expand access to innovative or even revolutionary ideas."[36]

These points help to provide more context for the discussion when examining the role of the press and the run-up to the war in Iraq as we now ask the larger question: Did the press miss the more important story? It covered the war itself, but while the Bush administration claimed it was a necessary war, did the news media pursue those claims independently of the administration? And was it even equipped to do so?

Tom Fenton says no. Most networks and other news organizations had cut so far back on coverage that they had no permanent presence in the Muslim world during the time of 9/11, except for CNN. Before the attacks, Fenton had been investigating "the trail of Islamic militants in Hamburg, Germany where they had plotted the 9/11 attacks, and visited a flight school near Cologne, where some of them trained."[37] He was close to meeting with a nuclear scientist who had been in contact with Osama bin Laden, but subsequent network cutbacks prevented more reporting. If Fenton had been allowed to continue to follow the story he had been investigating, who knows where that trail would have led with respect to bin Laden and the plot that was incubating to attack the United States.

At another time in history, what would have happened had the *Washington Post* suspended the investigative reporting of newspapermen Bob Woodward and Carl Bernstein? They were assigned to cover the seemingly insignificant story of a break-in at the Democratic National Committee headquarters at the Watergate complex in Washington, DC, in 1972. They reported the burglary at the headquarters of the DNC. They reported what the Nixon administration had to say about it. The administration had characterized the crime as a "third rate burglary." But the young reporters persisted, following up on bits of information, as the trail of impropriety grew exponentially larger, ultimately pointing to the president of the United States. Their editors, supported by the publisher, left their reporters on the story to follow it, investigating claims made by the Nixon administration and their own sources until the story reached its devastating and riveting conclusion.

Had those reporters and the newspaper for which they worked left it there, accepting the claim that it was an insignificant burglary with no relationship to anything beyond that, we never would have known nor understood the extent of the Watergate scandal, arguably the biggest political story of the twentieth century. While other news media dropped the story early on, believing also that there was nothing much to it, Woodward and Bernstein, with a reluctant but courageous newspaper and editor behind them, kept asking questions and pursuing sources to ascertain whether it was indeed just a petty burglary or a bigger story with serious ramifications.

The press stands between what the government is doing and the right of the people to know what it is doing. It is important that the people have access to the best and most reliable information. It is important that there is integrity in the news. It is important that the journalists who generate the news and produce it for public consumption are beyond reproach and operate according to high ethical and professional standards.

It is also true, however, that the press throughout history often has been controlled by those who want to advocate a point of view or encourage mass thinking for a certain issue or cause. As far back as colonial times, some publishers have used their newspapers this way and so, too, have many of today's broadcasters, magazines, and websites. Those in government have also used the news media to their advantage—to advocate a position or to reinforce a particular, sustained, and consistent message.

Public support for the Bush administration and the decisions to follow regarding Iraq were the consequence of 9/11. The news media was provided a captivated audience by virtue of the enormity of the story and its aftermath. The amount of coverage was overwhelming, sustained over many days, weeks, and months. It depicted and discussed the death of our people and the destruction of a recognizable symbol of affluence in the most iconic of American cities. The news media garnered a sustained, fully invested audience, and the Bush administration garnered the instantaneous support of a public, which reconsidered the way it would regard this president. Both the news media and the Bush administration each differently enlisted the tragedy of 9/11 to help them achieve their own long-term goals. One was political. The other, ultimately, was economic.

No matter what its motivations were, intentional or otherwise, what is undeniable is the power of the news media to bring the country together, to experience the stories of life, good and bad, as one people, creating a national community. Even in the thick of huge complex stories, those with major consequences and numerous story lines that can unfold over months and years, it is the responsibility of the press to deconstruct those stories, determine the facts, and verify them. It must report back to the people in a fashion that is as objective as possible without passion or bias and independent of a news organization's penchant for profit and the government's quest for unanimity. This is paramount.

THE NEWS MEDIA, 9/11, IRAQ, AND THE POLLS

"Journalism created a strong sense of community in the immediate aftermath of September 11, with headlines encouraging the nation to unite against the terrorists and never to allow another attack to take place."[38] Like other catastrophes that preceded this one, a collective American experience was born. Through the press—radio, television, and newspapers, and now the Internet with people reacting by "blogging" in real time, Americans experience news together when an event occurs, good and bad, large and small.

Mass media, the tools of which are radio, television, newspapers, and the web, help to create a national experience, a national conversation by virtue of their sheer power and reach. These stories were magnified by the news media which reported about them: World War II, the Vietnam war, the assassination of a president and later of his assassin on live television, the first moon walk, the collapse of the Berlin Wall, the violent protests at Tiananmen Square, the death of Princess Diana, the first space shuttle accident, Hurricane Katrina, the tsunami in Indonesia, the first Gulf War, the Iraq War, the inauguration of the first African American president of the United States, and 9/11. Americans watched, listened, read, and gave witness to history together. They felt together.

According to the Pew Research Center for People and the Press, at the time of 9/11, the people generally felt the media did a good job and overall had a good reputation. "These are the best of times and the worst of times for the news media when it comes to public support. By and large, Americans continue to praise the press for its coverage of the war on terrorism here and abroad so much so that the general image of the media has, at least temporarily, lost some of its tarnish. At the same time, however, the public shows strong support for government control of the news for the sake of national security."[39]

After 9/11, as Americans were digesting their news about 9/11, they were generally appreciative of the intimate portrait about what was happening at ground zero, the Pentagon, and in Pennsylvania, and who was responsible for the attacks as the story gradually unfolded. While they supported an unfettered news media to bring them this detailed coverage, they also understood, on some level, that there were limits to the coverage. News reporting might sometimes be compromised if it meant keeping America safe. It was after the war in Iraq began, as lives were being lost and no weapons of mass destruction were turning up, that Americans began to believe the news media had faltered.

Generally, there tends to be a love/hate relationship with the press, and the polling about the performance of the press appears, at times, to be in conflict. There seems to be an understanding about the need for the news media, perhaps especially in crisis or on big national stories, and the acknowledgment that it sometimes does a respectable job. At the same time, there is evidence that, overall, there is declining respect for the news media.

According to a poll taken by the Pew Center for the People and the Press, on November 28, 2001, on the question of whether the news media got its facts straight, 46- percent of respondents said yes, up ten points from early September, before 9/11. Sixty-nine percent of those participating in the survey said the news media stands up for America, 60 percent thought the news media was "protecting democracy," and 53 percent thought it was "moral."[40]

The traditional evening newscasts on CBS, NBC, and ABC historically have remained the newscasts of record and have had the largest audience share compared to the news on cable. The other cable networks tend to monitor their coverage. That was the case after the attacks of 9/11 and the wars that followed. But what resulted overall for all televised news was increased coverage of terrorism and international news. "The number of minutes devoted to coverage of foreign policy was up 102 percent. Coverage of armed conflict rose 69 percent and coverage of terrorism increased by 135 percent."[41] The same was also true in local news, but not nearly to as large a degree.

Overall, while the increase in international news coverage on television may be good news for some, "The American public continues to fault news organizations for a number of perceived failures, with solid majorities criticizing them for political bias, inaccuracy, and failing to acknowledge mistakes. Interestingly, some of the harshest indictments of the press now come from the growing segment that relies on the Internet as its main source for international and national news." That audience is roughly a quarter of all Americans and tends to be younger and better educated than the rest of the public as a whole.[42]

Polling numbers about how favorably the American people regard the press have faltered and fallen between 1985 and 2007. In its initial poll taken by Times Mirror in 1985, most people said most news organizations "try to cover up their mistakes" while "pluralities" said "they don't care about the people they report on" and were "politically biased." Also, in 1985, only 55 percent of Americans said news organizations "get the facts straight." Since the 1990s, "consistent majorities have expressed the belief that news stories are often inaccurate." The "believability rating" for individual news organizations is lower today than in the 1980s and 1990s.[43]

Despite these sentiments, Americans have more positive than negative impressions of local television news, network news, cable news, and the daily newspapers, which are the sources of news with which they are most familiar. Also, they have more positive than negative impressions of these news organizations and rate them higher than most political institutions, including Congress, the Supreme Court, and political parties. There remains a "broad and continuing support" for the news media as watchdog. Fifty-five percent said "that by criticizing political leaders, news organizations keep political leaders from doing things they should not be doing."[44]

Scott McClellan has said, "I welcome media that are skeptical and untrusting. The more so the better—as long as they are honest and fair. Those who are in positions of power should have to continually earn the trust of the governed. They should be constantly challenged to prove the policies are right, to prove they can be trusted, and to prove they are accountable. That is the way we are more likely to get to the important sometimes hard truths."[45]

President George W. Bush and the Press

Getting at the hard truth was more difficult during the Bush II years. One of the problems reporting about the run-up to the Iraq war after 9/11 was the disposition of the president toward the press. His White House closed ranks after 9/11 and was less than transparent after 9/11. Scott McClellan, who became White House press secretary a few months after the start of the Iraq war, said he "gradually came to understand, more troubling than the press secretary's access limitations, was the overall mind-set of secrecy within the administration, its negative attitude toward the national news media, and the limited support given to the press secretary as a result of such thinking."[46]

President Bush held the press in low esteem. Presidents before Bush had their problems with the press, some more than others, but "each accepted the role of the other."[47] Some presidents were quite skilled at working with the press and used it to their political advantage. Some enjoyed intellectually engaging members of the press. Other presidents had disdain for the press.

President Bush disregarded the role of the press as a "vital check and balance on government and, more importantly, that the media acts on behalf of the American people."[48] President Bush admitted that he rarely looked at the news or read news in newspapers. "I glance at the headlines, just to get kind of a flavor. I rarely read the stories," he told Fox News. "I get briefed by [White House Chief of Staff Card] Andy and Condi [National Security Adviser Rice] in the morning. The best way to get the news is from objective sources. And the most objective sources I have are people on my staff who tell me what's happening in the world," he said.[49]

How do you know what the public thinks if you don't watch or read the news, one journalist asked the president? The president replied, "You're making a powerful assumption—that you represent what the public thinks." The president's [White House] chief of staff said, "They [the media] don't represent the public any more than other people do. In our democracy, the people who represent the public stood for election. . . . I don't believe you have a check and balance function."[50]

David Dadge, editor of the International Press Institute in Vienna, called the Bush administration "perhaps the most disciplined administration to ever sit in the White House. Its constant desire to remain on message through the use of specific talking points, the rarity of unauthorized leaks from members of the administration, and the use of off-the-record background briefings and the lack of press conferences have made it extremely difficult for the media to carry out its normal function of holding the administration to account."[51]

According to the Pew Research Center, in the first term of his presidency, Bush held only seventeen solo press conferences (not counting brief joint appearances with visiting heads of state). That was the lowest total of any president in the television age."[52] This compares "unfavorably" with other presidents in their first terms. Dwight D. Eisenhower held seventy-four. John F. Kennedy held sixty-five. Lyndon B. Johnson conducted eighty. Richard Nixon held twenty-three. Bill Clinton stood before the press thirty-eight times.[53] More interesting was that the nation was most acutely in crisis during the first fourteen months President Bush was in office. Arguably, that was the most important time in his two terms combined, yet Bush stood before the press only twice; one month after September 11, 2001, and two weeks before the Iraq war in 2003.[54] Dan Bartlett, counselor to the president, said he doesn't do many press conferences because "at press conferences you can't control the message."[55]

During the lead-up to the Iraq war this was particularly important for the White House. Control was needed "for the public to have a greater understanding of the need for war; however, the media had numerous obstacles to obtaining this information and to a very large extent it failed in its attempts to give greater context about why the administration was seeking public approval for war."[56]

McClellan said, "If anything, the national press corps was probably too deferential to the White House and to the administration in regard to the most important decision facing the nation during my years in Washington, the choice over whether to go to war in Iraq. The collapse of the administration's rationale for war, which became apparent months after our invasion, should never have come as a surprise."[57] It was the duty of the press to explain about the historical context of such action, the lack of credible intelligence, and what the political and social ramifications of such an invasion might be. "Their [the press'] focus was elsewhere—on covering the march to war, instead of the necessity of war."[58]

David Dadge said the president's attitude and his administration's attitude toward the press perhaps had a more profound effect than policy on the march to war with Iraq. "Shorn of its watchdog duties, the media could be viewed as merely another obstacle to convincing the American people that the war was both correct and just. In consequence, the Bush administration could direct all its efforts to selling the war without having to justify it to the Fourth Estate."[59] The Bush administration did what it could to eliminate or minimize the filter of the news media by making its case more directly and straight to the American people.

The Iraq War and the Press

The press was stunned by the events of 9/11 and was initially docile in its deference to a commander in chief whose job it was to protect and defend the nation after a terrible attack. This was appropriate. Reporters are human beings first and, understandably, reacted as such with sympathetic, gut-wrenching coverage and images of the aftermath of 9/11 in New York, in Washington, DC, and in Pennsylvania. The reporting focused on the United States and the damage that was inflicted, the thousands of lives that were lost, and the pervasiveness of fear and sadness that had settled in the hearts of Americans.

But during retaliatory attacks against Afghanistan, and in the subsequent hunt for bin Laden, the news media was pressured to behave in a certain fashion. As time went on, the press became complicit as the administration waged war against Iraq, positioned successfully by the Bush administration as a country that had something directly to do with 9/11, and would in all likelihood attack again.

This must be said unequivocally. The war with Iraq simply could not have happened *without* the press. "The media failed on so many levels that they seemed to have suffered a systemic collapse. They were lapdogs that rolled over for the president. They were fearful of being accused of lack of patriotism and were easily bullied by Washington conservatives and right-wing talk show ranters. Many journalists were intimidated, but were also lazy."[60]

Executives at the television networks such as CNN were encouraged to tone down the coverage of the violence that was exacted on Afghanistan and to not at all be critical of the government during such operations. CNN, for one, is a twenty-four-hour news operation. It is compelled to fill and sell airtime around the clock. Images of destruction, war, and violence were constant during 9/11 and the subsequent invasion of Afghanistan. Also constant were sound bites from interviews with important military personnel, the president, and others who served in the administration. With interviews comes news analysis and questions regarding vision, performance, and the wisdom of the mission at hand.

Walter Isaacson, the president and chief operating officer of CNN, said he got calls from advertisers complaining that the network was being unpatriotic and un-American when it questioned something the president or a member of his administration might have said. CNN also received calls of criticism from the Bush administration that were similar in tone. Isaacson, said, "The administration used it [the patriotic fervor] so that if you challenged anything you were made to feel that there was something wrong with that."[61] He gave into the pressure by issuing a memo to his staff, which eventually leaked to the *Washington Post*. It said in part, "It seems perverse to focus too much on the casualties or hardship in Afghanistan."[62] Balance the coverage, he requested, with images from the attacks of 9/11.

According to one former London-based CNN correspondent, Richard Blystone, "CNN fell into the trap that ensnares everyone before and during wars. Patriotism. Executives, managers, editors, whatever their personal views may be, are put under pressure to not offend the government and even more worried about offending public opinion. Sadly, CNN and

CNN International looked and sounded like a pep rally for war. All adopted Washington-produced buzzwords, such as 'WMD' and 'shock and awe' without attribution and qualification."[63] It was as much a media-induced war as it was war encouraged by other factors.

Many newspapers were also asked by their publishers to censor some information. "One in Florida told its editors 'do not use photos on page 1A showing civilian casualties . . . our sister paper . . . has done so and received hundreds and hundreds of threatening e-mails.'"[64] There is no evidence to suggest the e-mail campaign was orchestrated by the Bush administration.

Many reporters knew that this administration had its sights on Iraq even before there was open discussion about it in the media. According to former CBS News anchorman Dan Rather, "I knew before 9/11 that many of the people who came into the administration were committed to toppling Saddam Hussein. And doing it with force if necessary."[65] This had more resonance after the president's State of the Union address in January 2002 when the president identified Iraq and Hussein as part of the world's "Axis of Evil," which launched the global war on terrorism by targeting specific regions of the world.

Bob Simon, a foreign correspondent with CBS News, had been captured as a prisoner during the first Gulf War. He had crossed the border from Kuwait into Iraq and was taken by Iraqi soldiers behind enemy lines for forty days, an experience he chronicled in a book, *Forty Days*. He describes Washington, DC, as an echo chamber and marks an important distinction—reporting "inside the bubble" of the nation's capital and reporting outside of it. Those inside it were more likely to miss the story and/or get it wrong. Those reporting outside the bubble did better reporting, were closer to the truth, and challenged the claims made by the Bush administration in Washington, but with little or no consequence. Those stories were buried deep in the newspaper or did not make the day's news at all.

"That certainly was the case at the *Washington Post*," according to journalist Peter Eisner, a deputy editor at the *Post* and former foreign editor at *Newsday*. "Reporters such as Walter Pincus and Joby Warrick were casting doubt on some versions of the Iraq story about WMD and alleged connections to 9/11, but those stories were buried deeper in the publication. The editor of the *Post*, Len Downie, apologized for not giving prominence to good stories that could have made a difference, but the damage was done, to historic proportions."[66]

The Washington press corps is assigned to cover events in Washington, which emanate from the Hill, from government departments and agencies, and the Supreme Court. White House reporters cover anything that happens there and travel with the president, where presidential events and appearances are carefully staged and comments are scripted and orchestrated. Theirs is an insular existence. The information they receive, for the most part, is what government officials want to tell them. They are dependent on those government sources and others they cultivate for news, so they are careful about challenging them to the degree that would prevent their access to newsmakers. They are hesitant to bite the hand that feeds them.

Bob Simon of CBS News said, "From overseas we had a clearer view. We knew things that perhaps the Washington press corps could not suspect. We who've spent weeks just walking the streets of Baghdad just were scratching our heads. Saddam was a total control freak. He wanted total control of the country. And to introduce a wild card like al Qaeda in any sense was just something he would not do. I didn't believe it for an instant." [67]

Outside the bubble of Washington, DC, Simon also said there were "running arguments, as there are today about Gaddafi, about what, if anything, the U.S. should do about him [Saddam]." Simon was as skeptical about WMD as he was about Saddam's link to al Qaeda. He reported as much in a *60 Minutes* report, "Selling the Iraq War to the U.S.," in December 2002. [68] It had no long-term impact.

Inside the bubble of Washington, ABC's Tom Fenton said, the media "failed to check and question the government's assertions even when they made no sense. Most of the media accepted the president's claim that Saddam Hussein and al Qaeda were somehow connected—the Big Assertion that legitimized the war on Iraq as part of the global war on terror." [69]

"Just repeat it and repeat it and repeat it and repeat it. Repeat al Qaeda, Iraq. Al Qaeda, Iraq. Al Qaeda, Iraq. Just keep it going. Keep that drumbeat going. And it was effective," said CBS's Bob Simon. Long after we knew there was no established link between al Qaeda and Iraq, the American people still believed Saddam Hussein was also responsible for 9/11. [70] A reporter for the Knight Ridder News Service, Jonathan Landay, said, "Most people actually believed and accepted that Saddam Hussein had weapons of mass destruction. I have to admit that until we really started burrowing into the story, I believed it, too." [71]

Landay represented a news service [Knight Ridder] that fed smaller, local newspapers across the country. While it operated in Washington, it was not *of* the culture in Washington as the other larger news organizations were. John Walcott, the bureau chief said, "Our readers aren't here in Washington. They aren't up in New York. They aren't the people who send other people's kids to war. They're the ones who get sent to war, and we felt an obligation to them to explain why that might happen. We were determined to scrutinize the administration's case for war as closely as we possibly could. Some of things that were said about Iraq, many of things that were said about Iraq, didn't make sense." [72]

Knight Ridder News Service and other smaller news networks, which feed smaller papers across the country, are David compared to the Goliaths in journalism—the national newspapers, cable, and broadcast networks. Those publications are automatically regarded by consumers as better sources for news because of their size and national reputations. They also operate differently. Smaller news services are accustomed to the tedium of actual reporting, finding sources, meeting with people, making calls, practicing shoe leather journalism, which meant straying away from the official line and independently digging for facts.

A reporter for Knight Ridder, Warren Strobel, who worked with Jonathan Landay said they knew two weeks after 9/11 from intelligence officials that the Bush administration "was stretching 'little bits and pieces of information' to connect Saddam to al Qaeda 'with no hard evidence.'"[73] Strobel said, "There was a lot of skepticism among our editors because what we were writing was so at odds with what most of the rest of the Washington press corps was reporting, and some papers, frankly, just didn't run the stories. They had access to the *New York Times* wire and the *Washington Post* wires, and they chose those stories instead."[74]

Another factor was the reticence among reporters and news media organizations to challenge a popular president even when the facts showed information emanating from the White House was flawed. A case in point was when the Bush administration was trying to link Saddam Hussein to al Qaeda by insisting there was a meeting in Prague between an Iraqi operative and Mohamed Atta, the lead hijacker in the 9/11 attacks. There was no meeting. Bob Simon of *60 Minutes* sought to prove it by interviewing a source from the C.I.A. Other news organizations claimed this particular agent was difficult to find, elusive, and, if found, would refuse to be interviewed. Simon said he was easily found and quite willing to talk.

In a December 8, 2002, report, Simon interviewed Bob Baer, a former undercover officer who spent sixteen years with the C.I.A. in the Middle East. Baer was sent by the Bush administration to confirm the meeting in Prague and verify the al Qaeda-Iraq link. He came up empty-handed. Simon said Baer would have been a hero had he delivered the information the administration was looking for. Simon admitted he didn't follow up on his own reporting and, in fact, backed away from the story. "We did not know that there were no weapons of mass destruction in Iraq. We only knew that the connection the administration was making between Saddam and al Qaeda was very tenuous at best, and the argument it was making over the aluminum tubes was highly dubious."[75] According to Bill Moyers of PBS, "What the White House was marketing as fact would go virtually unchallenged."[76]

The *American Journalism Review* reported that many journalists—those from mainstream, reputable, large media organizations—CNN, the *New York Times*, the *Washington Post*, CBS, and others—"reported in lockstep with White House statements about Iraq's weapons of mass destruction, Saddam Hussein's ties to al Qaeda and his involvement in the 9/11 terrorist attacks."[77] It is not enough to simply report what those in authority said is true, but to verify the information with independent, enterprise reporting.

These bigger, well-endowed news organizations needed to make more of an investment in investigative reporting. Reporters needed to spend more time working the good sources they had, cultivating other, better sources, independent of the administration and the military— working more closely with U. N. weapons inspectors, who had been in country, former C.I.A. agents, and others who knew the history of Iraq and understood its politics and culture. There were evidence and sources available, which would cast aspersions on the claims being made by the Bush administration. However, efforts to cull that information were only made after the fact.

Also, the burden of proof, especially about WMD, and claims about Saddam being an accomplice in the 9/11 attacks was squarely on the Bush administration, but few reporters held it to account. The news media were errant in taking that information at face value and reporting it as fact without verification. It should have been more suspicious of the information until the Bush administration could provide tangible evidence.

Consequently, much of the reporting by many of those journalists was wrong. They didn't challenge the administration, and the public was misinformed. Leading up to the Iraq war, given all the claims made, more journalists got the story wrong than right. Even respected giants, the *New York Times* and the *Washington Post*, "published mea culpas about their deficient coverage, admitting mistakes were made."[78]

"When the full history of the Iraq war is written, one of its most scandalous chapters will be about how American journalists so easily allowed themselves to be manipulated by both dubious sources and untrustworthy White House officials into running stories that misled the nation about Saddam Hussein's weapons of mass destruction," wrote reporter James Moore.[79]

Some mistakes by the news media are particularly noteworthy. Big organizations, given their power, influence, and weight of their reputations, had both the strength and credibility to persuade masses of people across the country. Not only did they convince their audiences of certain realities about the threat of Saddam Hussein's Iraq, but their competition was swayed by it as well. In the echo chamber of Washington, the press corps fed off each other's information, attributing it to other sources, which compounded the problem.

Peter Eisner agrees. He says what was being fed to journalists by the Bush administration was "garbage" in the first place, but that was only part of the problem. Information was first published by "The *New York Times* and then repeated unchecked about Saddam Hussein and nuclear weapons. The resulting weak, untested Washington reporting had a great impact on other news organizations such as the *Washington Post* and the

Associated Press. The same was true of television news. The reports and assumed scoops about his [Saddam] attempts to obtain nuclear weapons led to a predisposition to look for stories to prove that it must be true. That's an important matter. Once the Washington press corps and editors assume that their sources are telling the truth, they often march lockstep in the same direction to the same tune. The *New York Times* was hoodwinked by its own reporter."[80] So were CBS and *Vanity Fair* [magazine], both respected for the quality of their journalism and the excellence of their reporters.

Ahmad Chalabi, the Iraqi Defectors, and the New York Times

The most infamous example of the shoddiest reporting, which also had the most powerful effect, was the stage the *New York Times* gave to Ahmad Chalabi and the defectors he helped make available to the press. The story was important precisely *because* it came from the prestigious *New York Times*, for years regarded as the newspaper of record. Eric Boehlert, Senior Fellow at Media Matters for America, said, "Those sorts of stories when they appear on the front page of the so called liberal *New York Times*, it absolutely comes with a stamp of approval. I mean if the *New York Times* thinks Saddam is on the precipice of mushroom clouds, then, there's really no debate."[81]

Ahmad Chalabi represented the Iraqi National Congress (INC), an opposition group that operated in exile. It wanted to overthrow the regime of Saddam Hussein. Chalabi and his team partnered with many in the Bush administration to accomplish such a goal. He was paid some thirty-nine million in American taxpayer dollars—between the State Department and Defense Intelligence Agency (DIA)—to bring other defectors forward to testify about claims of weapons of mass destruction and burgeoning nuclear weapons programs inside Iraq. In exchange for his loyalty and the information he provided, the administration promised Chalabi a position of influence in the new Iraq. He was the one who encouraged the administration to believe, as it already did, that Iraq was an imminent threat to the Untied States.[82]

It was Chalabi who produced a source called "Curveball" who described the building of Saddam's mobile bioweapons labs. It was Chalabi who verified information about the alleged clandestine meeting in Prague between an Iraqi defector and the ringleader of the 9/11 attacks, Mohamed Atta. It was Chalabi who produced one defector who claimed there were bioweapons labs hidden all over Baghdad, one even underneath a hospital in the center of city. It was Chalabi who produced another defector who claimed Iraqis were being trained inside Iraq to hijack passenger planes. It was Chalabi who insisted the Americans would be greeted as liberators if they were successful in toppling the regime and was subsequently a special guest of the president, seated behind First

Lady Laura Bush, at the 2004 State of the Union address—a place of honor for an exemplary individual.[83]

Even though the Bush administration understood that much of what Chalabi peddled was suspect, he proved useful—a tool to help bolster the case for war, which would ultimately enhance his own standing upon his return to Iraq, once Saddam had fallen from power. "If the CIA and other spy services weren't going to come up with the goods on Saddam, then Chalabi would. He found a receptive audience in the office of the vice president, and at the Pentagon. I. Lewis "Scooter" Libby, the veep's chief of staff, and [Paul] Wolfowitz were eagerly looking for links between Saddam and Al Qaeda."[84]

It does not take much digging to analyze the motivations of Ahmad Chalabi. In their reporting journalists should have been made aware of Chalabi's relationships while he was being touted as a friend to America during the run-up to the Iraq war. Chalabi has been described by some as a con man, a charlatan, the quintessential political operative, a self-serving opportunist. He recognized that "the neocons, while ruthless, realistic and effective in bureaucratic politics, were remarkably ignorant about the situation in Iraq and willing to buy a fantasy of how the country worked. So he sold it to them."[85]

Born a wealthy Shia Muslim and reared in Kut, a town in southern Iraq, Chalabi had a checkered past, the details of which were completely accessible. Dr. Chalabi was educated in America at the Massachusetts Institute of Technology (MIT) and the University of Chicago where he earned his PhD. On the surface he appeared erudite, well connected, and was both charismatic and persuasive. He lived much of his adult life in London and the United States. For a period in 1990, he returned to Iraq and attempted to organize an uprising of Iraqi Kurds, who were often terrorized by Saddam. The uprising failed. Hundreds were killed. Many in Chalabi's Iraqi National Congress were executed. He fled the country.[86]

"In 1992, he [Chalabi] was sentenced in absentia by a Jordanian court to twenty-two years in prison with hard labour for bank fraud after the 1990 collapse of Petra Bank [in Jordan], which he had founded in 1977."[87] The self-interested Chalabi and his INC proved useful to U.S. intelligence and the Pentagon particularly during the run-up to the Iraq war. They were helpful in mustering up opposition to Saddam as the United States planned the overthrow of his government. While the United States funneled millions to Chalabi, he spoon-fed the *New York Times* and CBS information, through defectors, who erroneously made claims about weapons of mass destruction.

At the prestigious *New York Times* it was the once celebrated and respected reporter, Judith Miller, who has now left a stain on the newspaper, arguably regarded as the nation's best and most respected newspaper, one that competitors follow and attribute in their own stories. It "sets the news agenda for the press and the nation" and certainly did so during the run-up to the Iraq war.[88] Even her fellow journalists distanced themselves from Miller and turned on her for her zealous, aggressive style, her race for a "scoop" at the expense of accuracy.

Jack Shafer of *Slate* wrote, "Miller, more than any other reporter, showcased the WMD administration and the Iraqi defector/dissidents. Our WMD expectations, such as they were, grew largely out of Miller's stories."[89] He continued, "In the eighteen-month run-to war on Iraq, Miller grew incredibly close to Iraqi sources, both identified as anonymous, who gave her detailed interviews about Saddam Hussein's weapons of mass destruction. Yet one hundred days after the fall of Baghdad, none of the sensational allegations about chemical, biological or nuclear weapons given to Miller have panned out, despite the furious crisscrossing of Iraq by U.S. weapons hunters."[90] Miller simply blamed the sources. "If your sources are wrong, you are wrong," Miller told NPR's *On the Media*.[91]

Her colleague at the *New York Times*, Maureen Dowd, says Miller's attitude is bunk. "Investigative reporting is not stenography." Dowd wrote in her weekly column, "Judy's stories about WMD fit perfectly with the White House's case for war. She was close to Ahmed Chalabi, the con man, who was conning the neocons to knock out Saddam so he could get his hands on Iraq, and I worried that she was playing a leading role in the dangerous echo chamber that Senator Bob Graham, now retired, dubbed 'incestuous amplification.' Using Iraqi defectors and exiles, Mr. Chalabi planted bogus stories with Judy and other credulous journalists."[92]

Perhaps the most insidious reporting by Miller was a story that appeared in the *Times* on Sunday, September 8, 2003. It was positioned at A1, a front-page story about how Saddam was shopping for aluminum tubes, a building block in the construction of nuclear weapons. The same morning Bush administration officials blanketed the morning talk shows—Vice President Cheney on NBC's *Meet the Press*, who pointedly mentioned the *Times* story, National Security Advisor Condoleezza Rice on CNN, Colin Powell on FOX *News Sunday*, Defense Secretary Donald Rumsfeld on CBS's *Face the Nation*, and Richard Meyers, Chairman of the Joint Chiefs, on ABC's *This Week*—all "raised the specter of a nuked up Saddam."[93] Miller got the story directly from the vice president's office, citing high-level, unnamed sources. Cheney credited the *Times* for its crack reporting and pointed to it as an independent source, which just happened to back up the administration's case.

MSNBC's Chris Mathews on his program *Hardball* explained to viewers that the vice president used the press while the press appeared as if it had done some thorough reporting, saying that the vice president "leaked to the *New York Times* the story that there were aluminum tubes; there was, in fact, a case for a nuclear weapons program by Saddam

Hussein. And three major figures in the administration, the vice president, secretaries of state and defense went on Sunday television, all pointed to that story that had been planted there by Scooter Libby [the vice president's chief of staff]."[94]

Judith Miller had reported a great story, and great stories can be compelling and convincing. They are "more important than memos, mission statements, newsletters speeches, and policy manuals," says Howard Gardner, professor of education at Harvard. Stories "constitute the single most powerful weapon in the leader's literary arsenal."[95] President Bush's key administration officials made their case by pointing to a compelling story in the newspaper. CBS's Bob Simon said, "I thought it was remarkable. You leak a story, and then you quote the story. I mean that's a remarkable thing to do."[96] Because of the stellar, enduring reputation of the *New York Times*, because it is a high-profile, world-renowned source for news and analysis, its error in judgment naturally was magnified. The *Times* was not the only news organization by any means that was errant and also picked up or retold the same basic story.

The venerable CBS news magazine program *60 Minutes* and its correspondent, Leslie Stahl, profiled Admad Chalabi and interviewed an unnamed Iraqi dissident during its March 3, 2002, Sunday broadcast. Chalabi told Stahl the defector was a former major in the Iraqi military. The defector told Stahl's audience "how Saddam Hussein evaded weapons inspectors by placing mobile biological-weapons laboratories in seven trucks that he, the defector, personally purchased from Renault." This same information had been included in Secretary of State Colin Powell's testimony before the United Nations Security Council.[97]

The news magazine *60 Minutes*, a program that has remained among the most watched programs on television for more than twenty-five years, gave a source like Chalabi a national stage and millions of viewers. Chalabi was a shady figure, and his sordid history should have been vetted. *Vanity Fair* made the same mistake in its May 2002 feature story by David Rose entitled, "Iraq's Arsenal of Terror." According to Bill Moyers of PBS, other news organizations went after the same Chalabi-fed defector story, including *The New Yorker, USA Today,* the *Washington Post,* the *New York Daily News,* and PBS.

CBS retracted the Leslie Stahl story a year after the Iraqi invasion. David Rose at *Vanity Fair* said his story was confirmed by high-level government sources, but those were the same sources that had depended on Chalabi to help sell the war. Warren Strobel, foreign affairs correspondent for the McClatchey Newspapers, said, "The first rule of being an intelligence agent, or a journalist, and they're not that different, is you're skeptical of defectors because they have a reason to exaggerate. They want to increase their value to you." John Walcott, Washington bureau chief for the McClatchy Newspapers said, "Everything had to be looked at in that light and scrutinized in that light. Why anyone would give him

[Chalabi] a free pass, or anyone else a free pass for that matter as important as going to war, is beyond me."[98]

The Italian Letter

The so-called Italian Letter was the document the Bush administration held up as the smoking gun to justify the war with Iraq. It was proof, the president proclaimed, that Hussein was purchasing uranium from Niger in Africa. The information was neither properly vetted nor did it have any basis in fact, which was common knowledge in the intelligence community.

Elisabetta Burba, currently the foreign editor of the Milan-based Italian right-wing magazine, *Panorama*, was the first and only journalist recipient of those documents. They came to her by way of one Rocco Martino. Martino was a former agent of SISMI, the Military Intelligence and Security Service of Italy, who now sold information around the world to people and organizations who would pay. Although he had been an inconsistent source, he sometimes would have something worthy of further investigation.

Martino came to Burba again in 2002 and asked her to meet him at a restaurant in Rome on October 7. He told her he had some papers, which she might find of great interest. Even though she knew to regard any information Martino provided with some suspicion, it was worth it for Burba to at least examine what he had to share. She understood fully that she would have to check the authenticity of the information.

"Martino showed Burba a folder filled with documents, most of them in French. One of them was purportedly sent by the president of Niger to Iraqi President Saddam Hussein, confirming a deal to sell 500 tons of uranium to Iraq annually. This was the smoking gun in the package, claiming to show the formal approval of Niger's president to supply Iraq with a commodity that would in all likelihood only be used for a nuclear weapons program: Iraq had no nuclear power plants."[99]

Martino wanted payment for the documents, but Burba refused, saying she would consider payment only if they proved to be authentic. Payment for stories is common is Italy. Martino, she acknowledged, was nothing more than a "merchant of information."[100] For a good story, based on credible information that would eventually check out, her magazine would pay. The magazine routinely verified information that would come from a plethora of sources on a variety of stories.

She took the folder back to her editors at *Panorama* in Milan knowing, if authentic, she would have a major story to develop and later publish. She asked her editor in chief, Carlo Rossella, for permission to travel to Niger to determine the authenticity of the documents. He agreed, but also suggested a two-pronged approach to the potential story. He suggested she also take the documents to the American Embassy because the

Americans, he said, were trying to prove that Saddam was hiding evidence of weapons of mass destruction. Documents like these might prove crucial to them.

Burba returned to Rome on October 9 and met U.S. Embassy press spokesman, Ian Kelly, who called in a colleague to also view the documents. Both told her they would look into the matter. She handed them a copy of the dossier and left. On October 17 she was on a plane to Niamey, the capital of Niger, and would investigate the story. Her path and findings would be similar to the one of former U.S. Ambassador to Gabon, Joseph Wilson.

According to Wilson, "In February 2002, I was informed by officials at the Central Intelligence Agency that Vice President Dick Cheney's office had questions about a particular intelligence report. While I never saw the report, I was told that it referred to a memorandum of agreement that documented the sale of uranium yellowcake, a form of lightly processed ore, by Niger to Iraq in the late 1990s. The agency officials asked if I would travel to Niger to check out the story so they could provide a response to the vice president's office."[101] Later that same month, Wilson traveled to Niger where he had been a diplomat in the 1970s and visited as an official on the National Security Council years later. For eight days, he investigated the report the vice president was curious about.

In an op-ed article for the *New York Times* on July 6, 2003, Wilson wrote, "Before I left Niger, I briefed the Ambassador [Barbro Owens-Kirkpatrick] on my findings, which were consistent with her own. I also shared my conclusions with members of her staff. In early March, I arrived in Washington and promptly provided a detailed briefing to the C.I.A. I later shared my conclusions with the State Department African Affairs Bureau. There was nothing secret or earth-shattering in my report, just as there was nothing secret about my trip." Given the size of Niger, the weak structure of the government, and the convoluted manner in which such a transaction would occur, he clearly discounted the story of a sale of uranium by Iraq from Niger.

Twice now, this story would be carefully vetted and proven false, once by Wilson on a mission assigned by the C.I.A., and then by Burba, an Italian journalist who independently followed up on material a source gave to her. A sale and shipment of uranium to Iraq would have been impossible to conceal and "daunting" to execute. "They would have needed hundreds of trucks." In such a small country, those trucks would have been conspicuously suspect. She had been in the country for a week meeting with "officials, diplomats, and members of non-governmental organizations," and there was no evidence of any shipment to Iraq.[102]

There was also the problem with the documents themselves, which Burba initially had been suspicious of. They were sloppy and unprofessional. There were corrections on the documents, and the names of the people were wrong. Burba returned to editor Rosella and told him the story was no good. She also contacted Rocco Martino to inform him of her analysis. The documents he provided were clearly fraudulent. That was the end of the story as far as Burba was concerned, until she heard President's Bush's State of the Union address on January 28, 2003, and the following sixteen words: "The British government has learned that Saddam Hussein recently purchased significant quantities of uranium from Africa."

Burba did not watch the address live on television. In Italy, it was three in the morning. Instead, she read the newspapers later in the day and watched a replay of the address on television. She said she became sick to her stomach. She also could not believe what she was reading. "I was shocked, you know. The documents were not good, and the president of the United States was directly referring to the papers I had in my possession." She had confirmed herself that the documents were not authentic. How did the information make its way into a celebrated, annual address by the leader of the free world? Burba said she knew immediately the president was making his case for war with Iraq after months of saber rattling and threats. "You know I feel bad about it. The fact is the documents I brought to them, they justified the war."[103]

In the months that followed, after the start of the Iraq war, Burba realized the story of the forged documents was now a better one. She returned to her editor to request that she be put on the story permanently until she could learn who forged the documents and to investigate why the administration used them at all. Carlo Rosella refused her request. They argued as she tried to convince him to her put her on the story permanently. Burba began to regret having shared the dossier with the Americans at the U.S. Embassy in Rome. She began to realize she was staring in the face of a political blockade and was also confronted with a personal and professional dilemma.

Panorama was owned by the powerful Italian Prime Minister Sylvio Berlusconi. Italy and the United States were allies. Berlusconi was "President George Walker Bush's best friend on the European mainland; he had made his fortune in the news business and was the preeminent owner of publications and radio and television networks throughout Italy. Berlusconi had shown that he was not interested in journalistic independence. He used the news media to build his fortune—he was the richest man in Italy—and as a political force. *Panorama* was part of the system, and its editor, Carlo Rosella, was aligned politically with Berlusconi."[104]

It was now September 2003. With the Iraq war now months old and fully underway, Burba was preoccupied by the story and bothered that the war was based on false pretense. It was a big story, she believed. She returned to editor Rosella and requested that she be put back on the Niger story permanently until she could trace the documents to the one who forged them and to others who may have ordered them forged.

"Forget Niger," Rosella told her. "I don't want to know any more about that." He was really in a fury about it, Burba said. "I told him that all the journalists of the world, in particular American journalists, wanted to know who forged those documents. He told me to think about my baby, who was due in February, and he told me to think about other stories I could develop. I was in a corner, but I wanted to know what happened, so I went to my lawyer. My lawyer [Giovanni Brambilla Pisoni] said I could pursue the story for my own personal interest, but not for publication anywhere in the world." Burba could have been taken to court in Italy or summarily fired.[105]

Burba said she was feeling both frightened and conflicted. She was building a family, but her career was still very important to her. She was being threatened with her job at a time when she could least afford to lose it. Burba had built a reputation for being an excellent and well-respected journalist. Known throughout Italy for her reporting, she was well paid, and she would be well cared for in the benefits-rich country with its generous vacation scheme, retirement package, and other perks. To pursue the story on her own meant also going against her editor and, beyond him, a well-oiled political machine, loyal to the Americans and George W. Bush.[106]

On a brief vacation with American journalist friends in Liguria, she was distressed about the suppression of her story and conflicted about what to do. She asked them for their advice, and both suggested talking to American news organizations—feeding them the information to get the story out—including CNN and CBS News. One told her that CBS would stand up to any government interference with her story. The company had a long-standing reputation for being both tough and fair. She never called CBS or CNN, but spoke to some other American journalists such as *The New Yorker*'s Seymour Hersh, who told her the Niger story was an important story to tell and that if traced, in any way, to the Bush administration, "could ultimately bring it down."[107]

Hersh later published his own story about Niger in *The New Yorker* dated March 31, 2003, titled "Who Lied to Whom." He did not mention Burba, but he did chronicle how the information about the alleged sale of uranium by Niger to Iraq made its way through intelligence and diplomatic circles as it made its way to the State of Union address.

He wrote that in 2002 C.I.A. Director George Tenet had briefed the Senate Foreign Relations Committee about the alleged sale while Tony Blair's government in London was making the same Niger dossier public. Two days later, Secretary of State Colin Powell cited the information in a closed meeting of the Senate Foreign Relations Committee and two months later the same information was present in the President's Daily Brief (PDB), which was to have been carefully "scrubbed," meaning that the information was carefully vetted. Director Tenet had advised against touting such a claim, but the following month, the president announced the sale to a joint session of Congress and the American people.[108]

Hersh said any warnings from the intelligence community about the integrity of the Niger documents were not heeded by the White House. "Was the message—the threat posed by Iraq—more important than the integrity of the intelligence-vetting process? Was the administration lying to itself? Or did it deliberately give Congress and the public what it knew to be bad information?"[109] In subsequent hearings held in Great Britain about the Niger documents, some witnesses testified that they were not reliable.

Senator Jay Rockefeller of West Virginia and the senior Democrat on the Senate Intelligence Committee said, "There is a possibility that the fabrication of these documents may be part of a larger deception campaign aimed at manipulating public opinion and foreign policy regarding Iraq."[110] Rockefeller requested that the F.B.I. investigate. The agency did, and in 2005 CBS News reported that the F.B.I. "determined that financial gain [for Martino], not an effort to influence U.S. policy, was behind the forged documents that the Bush administration used to bolster its pre-war claim that Iraq sought uranium ore in Africa."[111]

CBS News and the Italian Letter: A Postscript

A year after the Iraq war, in March 2004, Burba was contacted by producers Anna Matranga, based in Italy, and David Gelber of the CBS news magazine program *60 Minutes II*, the Wednesday night (extra) edition of the popular series. Veteran correspondent Ed Bradley was assigned to the story. They wanted to interview Burba's source, Rocco Martino, and they wanted to interview Burba. Martino may have had knowledge about who forged the documents, and it would be the first time Burba would speak on the record about the story beyond the realm of her own publication.

Burba was on maternity leave from *Panorama* and on the advice of her lawyer, Pisoni, she worked out a deal with CBS. She would appear as an interview subject for the larger story, the focus of which was Martino, the documents he was trying to peddle, and, most importantly, who might have forged them. She would not discuss the conflict she was having with her magazine, *Panorama*, over the story, nor would she mention the role of her editors as she was developing the story. This would presumably keep her out of trouble.

"I was donating the scoop of my life" to CBS, she said, but her lawyer assured her that handling the story this way would keep her out of legal trouble at home. She was also elated that finally the story would come to light. The CBS news piece would likely prod more news organizations to pursue the story, and the truth, she believed, eventually would be revealed. "A team of *60 Minutes'* correspondents and consulting reporters spent more than six months investigating the Niger uranium documents fraud."[112] A camera crew spent hours interviewing Burba in Grado, Italy, where she was on holiday with her husband and young son. The network flew Martino to New York City where it would conduct his interview. But, to date, the story has never seen the light of day.

"Just hours before the story was set to air on the evening of September 8 [2004], the reporters and producers on the CBS team were stunned to learn the story was being scrapped to make room for a seemingly sensational story about new documents showing that Bush ignored a direct order to take a flight physical while serving in the National Guard more than 30 years ago."[113] The documents used for this story, however, were soon proven to have been provided by a disgruntled former National Guard official and "democratic partisan, who lied about where he got the material."[114] Anchorman Dan Rather was forced to retract the story and apologize for the faulty reporting.

Joshua Micah Marshall, who had collaborated on the *60 Minutes* Niger story, said, "Here we had a very important, well-reported story about forged documents that helped lead the country to war. And then it gets bumped by another story that relied on forged documents."[115] The National Guard story implicated the president, citing his lack of military service, his efforts to often avoid reporting for duty, and the most damaging charge, that the president was given preferential treatment, avoiding the battlefield in Vietnam because his family was both influential and powerful.

The program *60 Minutes* had intended to broadcast the Niger story at a later date after it had been "bumped," which is common when making way for a breaking news story or a big story with serious consequence. But the Niger story would not be merely postponed to a later date. It would be permanently dumped. Many thought CBS never resurrected the Niger story because it was afraid of retribution from the Bush White House after the network fudged the handling of the National Guard story.

In the Niger story, which has never been publicly viewed, correspondent Ed Bradley explained, "How fiercely the White House had fought the story being broadcast. Administration officials and Republicans in Congress turned down *60 Minutes'* requests for interviews. So did former Representative Porter Goss, the Florida Republican whom Bush had appointed as the new director of the C.I.A."[116] This was before the National Guard story was aired.

One online magazine called CBS the "Cowardly Broadcasting System" and contended that the report should have been broadcast despite the National Guard story. "Millions of viewers will not see a hard-hitting report making a powerful case that in trying to build support for the Iraq war, the Bush administration either knowingly deceived the American people about Saddam Hussein's nuclear capabilities or was grossly credulous."[117]

As for Burba, she remains the Foreign Editor at *Panorama*. She steadfastly claims she has more important information about this story, which people have never heard about and would want to know about. Despite efforts to interview her about what more information she has, she is reluctant to share it until she is no longer employed by *Panorama*, where she says there still exists a menacing atmosphere.

The Final (Scripted) Press Conference

On March 6, 2003, just thirteen days prior to the start of the Iraq war, President Bush called a prime time news conference. It was important for several reasons. First, the president was known for his infrequency in meeting the press in such a forum. (This was only his eighth since taking office.) Second, it was conducted before a controversial and costly military initiative, an unusual "pre-emptive war." (The president wanted to make a final case for it.) And third, it was a tightly managed press conference. (Most presidential press conferences are organized with a prescribed protocol, but none to this extent.)

First, reporters were ushered to their seats in the East Room of the White House two by two, "like school children being led onto the stage for the holiday pageant."[118] After the president made his opening remarks, he had a list of reporters on whom he would call for questions. But unlike other press conferences, he called on reporters based on a list preselected by White House Press Secretary Ari Fleischer, leaving out media organizations with the largest audiences, including *USA Today*, *Time*, *Newsweek*, and the *Washington Post*. Usually, they are the first called on. No follow-up questions were allowed, which is customary. And Helen Thomas, formerly of United Press International (UPI) and then Hearst, who traditionally had been called upon to ask the first question at presidential press conferences since President Kennedy, was completely ignored. What was also striking was that the reporters who were called on did not challenge the president on the claims he was making and had been making for months. They were claims that had holes in them.

The president's opening statement was a reminder to Americans about Iraq's president. He said, "Saddam Hussein has a long history of aggression and terrible crimes. He possesses weapons of terror. He provides funding and training and safe haven to terrorists—terrorists who would willingly use weapons of mass destruction against America and other peace loving countries. Saddam Hussein is a direct threat to our country, our people, and to all free people."[119] A live television audience and ninety-six reporters in the room heard the president's closing argument. It was surprising that reporters did not ask pointed questions about the case the president was making for war.

Journalist Eric Boehlert said the press conference "remains an indus-
try-wide embarrassment."[120] The president mentioned al Qaeda thirteen
times in less than an hour. "Not a single journalist challenged the presumed connection Bush was making between al Qaeda and Iraq, despite
the fact that intelligence sources had publicly questioned any such association. And during the Q&A session, nobody bothered to ask Bush about
the elusive bin Laden, the terrorist mastermind who Bush had vowed to
capture. Follow-up questions were non-existent, which only encouraged
Bush to give answers to questions he was not asked."[121]

Reporters, instead, threw what are referred to in the business as "soft-
ball" questions. One such question came from reporter April Ryan of the
Urban Radio Networks, who was on the president's list. She asked,
"How is your faith guiding you?" The president responded, "I appreciate
that question a lot. My faith sustains me because I pray daily. I pray for
guidance and wisdom and strength. One thing that's great about our
country, April, is that there are thousands of people who will pray for me
that I will never see and be able to thank."

At one point, as the president was shuffling through his papers, look-
ing through the list so he would know who next to call on, he quipped,
"This is scripted." All in the room nervously laughed. Then he said,
"King. John King." The president called on CNN's reporter who asked
whether going after Saddam was personal. In his question, King quoted
Senator Ted Kennedy, who had said that the president's fixation with
Saddam Hussein is actually making the world a more dangerous place.

The president answered and said what he had been repeating for
months, "People can describe all kinds of intentions. I believe Saddam
Hussein is a threat to the American people. I believe he's a threat to the
neighborhood in which he lives. He has weapons of mass destruction and
he has used weapons of mass destruction in his neighborhood and on his
people. He's invaded countries in his neighborhood. He tortures his own
people. He's a murderer. He's trained and financed al Qaeda-type organizations before—al Qaeda and other terrorist organizations."[122]

The news conference was palpably uncomfortable. *USA Today* White
House reporter Larry McQuillan, who sat in the front row, stopped raising his hand when he realized he was not going to be called on. He said
the press conference was "demeaning" to the press and to the president.
"He's a smart man who knows how to answer questions. It created an
image in the press corps that some were favored and some were not.
Does it mean that I am being punished and others are being rewarded?"[123]

Boehlert said, "I don't know if it was out of embarrassment for him or
embarrassment for them because they still continued to play along after
his question was done. They all shot up their hands and pretended they
had a chance to be called on. I think it just crystallized what was wrong
with the press coverage during the run-up to the war. I think like they felt

the war was going to happen, and the best thing to do was get out of the way."[124]

Elisabeth Bumiller, a reporter for the *New York Times*, said, "I think we were very deferential because it's live, it's very intense, it's frightening to stand up there. Think about it. You're standing up there on prime time live TV asking the president of the United States a question when the country's about to go to war. There was a serious, very somber tone that evening, and no one wanted to get into an argument with the president at this very serious time."[125]

Eric Boehlert wrote, "The entire press conference performance was a farce—the staging, the seating, the questions, the order, and the answers. Nothing about it was real or truly informative. It was, nonetheless, unintentionally revealing. Not revealing about the war. Instead, the calculated kabuki press conference, stage-managed by the White House employing the nation's most elite reporters as high-profile extras, did reveal what people needed to know about the mindset of the MSM (main stream media) on the eve of the war."[126]

Harold Myerson, a contributor to *The American Prospect* [magazine] and a columnist for the *Washington Post*, noted a distinction between a conflict such as Pearl Harbor and a "preemptive war," such as Iraq, where it concerns the press. "When America has been attacked—at Pearl Harbor, or as on September 11—the government needed merely to tell the people that it was our duty to respond, and the people rightly confirmed their authority. But a war of choice is a different matter entirely. In that circumstance, the people will ask why. The people will need to be convinced that their sons and daughters and husbands and wives should go halfway around the world to fight a nemesis that they didn't know was a nemesis."[127]

In the case of Saddam, he was not at fault for 9/11 nor was he poised to attack America with weapons of mass destruction. These realities could have been vetted by a press corps that was tenacious in its work and faithful to its mission. Instead, a case counter to the facts was made by the administration that night and was echoed and indeed underscored by the news media in not challenging the president.

This issue is not about dogging a president and an administration, anticipating that they are not truthful in every policy or pronouncement. The exercise of the news media checking those in power and an administration expecting to be monitored is designed to ensure integrity in those who serve the American people. It also ensures that Americans can depend on their news media for accurate, factual, fair, and balanced information regarding the work of elected officials serving on their behalf and who should be safeguarding their interests.

When the American people see or read a story enough times and when the same story is repeated from other sources, it is reasonable to expect that they will begin to believe and trust what they hear and what they see. What reason did any American have to doubt a president in such dire times? But in this case, when the slightest doubt was cast on the president's information, there was great effort to discredit both the messenger and the message.

In the best-case scenario, the only way to have known what the facts were and what the real story was, as they emerged over time, was through a news media that made a concerted effort to do their job without fear of retribution from the White House or any other organization. Eric Boehlert wrote, "In truth, Bush never could have ordered the invasion of Iraq—never could have sold the idea at home—if it weren't for the help he received from the MSM (mainstream media)." He reported that the *Washington Post* editorialized for war twenty-six times between February 2002 and 2003 and nine times in February 2003. In articles and columns, *The New Yorker*, *Newsweek*, *Time*, the *New York Times*, and the *New Republic* all supported a pre-emptive war against Iraq.[128]

Howard Kurtz is the media critic for the *Washington Post*. He said, "The *Washington Post* or any newspaper is a billboard of what the editors are telling you. These are the most important stories of the day. And stories that don't run on the front page, the reader sort of gets that, well, these are of secondary importance." Kurtz reported that from August 2002 until the war was launched in March 2003, there were approximately 140 front-page pieces in the *Washington Post* making the administration's case for war. Most of those stories were based only on what White House and cabinet officials had to say. Conversely, there were only a handful of stories in the same period of time that attempted to make the opposite case questioning the official line from those in authority by going to other reputable sources.[129]

Norm Solomen, another nationally known media critic, says journalists want to be ahead of the curve, but not out on a limb. "If you took seriously the warning flags that were profuse before the invasion of Iraq, the administration's story was a bunch of nonsense about WMDs, you would not just be ahead of the curve a little, you would have been way out on a limb."[130] Journalists did not want to risk their reputations and the wrath of their employers to swim against the conventional wisdom.

Michael Messing, a contributing editor for the *Columbia Journalism Review*, agrees. "I think that what happened in the months leading up to the war is that there was sort of acceptable mainstream opinion that got set. And I think that people who were seen as outside that mainstream were viewed as sort of fringe and they were marginalized."[131]

In years immediately following the Watergate scandal, journalists were proud of reporters Woodward and Bernstein, the men who broke that story. The success of the Watergate story encouraged other journalists to be more aggressive, more thorough in their work. It also prompted increased enrollment at schools of journalism across the country.

News departments used as profit centers in media and entertainment organizations have altered the profession itself. Journalism has become more business than public service. Journalists today are beholden to their companies for salaries and health benefits and vacations. Their work must generate profits, increase shareholder value, and so they generally exhibit a lack of courage and a hesitancy to practice crusade journalism.

Like Watergate, the Iraq war story called for a bolder press, a crusading press. Instead, a group-think mentality set in. Also called pack journalism, it means reporters cover the same stories in the same manner, which produces the same information. Senator Bob Graham called it "incestuous amplification."[132] Media organizations are independent of one another only in name and character, but not in content. In the run-up to the Iraq war this practice was at its worst.

Journalists of the day between 9/11 and the Iraq war were timid. They were in some cases lazy. They were remiss and absent. Eric Boehlert called the press compliant and said, "Being meek and timid and dictating administration spin amidst a wartime culture is one thing, but to be actively engaged in the spin and to give it a louder and more hysterical voice, is something else all together." The press repeated the claims the Bush administration made about WMD and aluminum tubes from Africa. All were patently false, and that "added to the media's malpractice."

Many prominent journalists agreed, including Ted Koppel of ABC's *Nightline*, who said journalists were criticized for being timid and justifiably so. Dan Rather said journalists did not do their jobs and didn't ask the right questions often enough. The ombudsman of the *Washington Post*, Michael Getler, said that the performance of the news media in 2002 and 2003 was the "most crucial newsroom failing in half a century."[133] He wrote, "How did a country on the leading edge of the information age get this so wrong and express so little skepticism and challenge? How did an entire system of government and a free press set out on a search for something and fail to notice, or even warn us in a timely or prominent way, that it wasn't or might not be there?"[134]

Americans eventually were reflective about the failings of the news media. Even though Americans may have wanted the news media to exhibit some degree of patriotism in the confusing days following the attacks, they also wanted them to be vigilant in keeping them informed as the story began to take shape over the days and months that followed. According to a poll conducted by Chicago's McCormick Tribune Foundation in 2005, a majority of the American people they surveyed said they wished the news media had done a better job of informing the public about a war with Iraq and what might likely be at stake in a war against Iraq.[135]

The news media is by no means perfect on its best days and has its faults, which are often exacerbated by economic and corporate pressures. But it has an important function to fulfill on which democracy, in part, is dependent. As Thomas Jefferson said, if we had to choose between a government in which a free press plays a vital role and a government in which it does not play a vital role, we would choose the former. With no accountability and with no questions asked by an external "watchdog" in the news media, government and those elected to administer it would operate in a vacuum, potentially making decisions at their own peril and at the peril of the American people.

NOTES

1. "Letter to Edward Carrington (January 16, 1787)," *The Writings of Thomas Jefferson* (19 vols., 1905), edited by Andrew A. Lipscomb and Albert Ellery Bergh, 6:57.
2. "Letter to John Tyler, 1804," University of Virginia, Thomas Jefferson on Politics and Government, ME 11:33.
3. W. T. Stead (The Contemporary Review, vol. 50, Nov. 1886, pp. 663–79.)
4. Carlyle, Thomas. "The Hero as Man of Letters. Johnson, Rousseau, Burns." Lecture V, May 19, 1840."
5. Fellow, Anthony R. *American Media History* (Belmont, CA: Wadsworth Group, 2005), 69.
6. Emery, Michael, Edwin Emery, and Nancy L. Roberts. *The Press and America* (Boston: Allyn and Bacon, 2000), 61.
7. Ibid.
8. Fellow, Anthony R. *American Media History* (Belmont, CA: Wadsworth Group, 2005), 69.
9. Ibid.
10. Ibid., 68.
11. Ibid., 69.
12. Emery, Michael, Edwin Emery, and Nancy L. Roberts. *The Press and America* (Boston: Allyn and Bacon, 2000), 63.
13. Ibid., 62.
14. Ibid.
15. Ibid.
16. The Society of Professional Journalists, http://www.spj.org/.
17. Ibid.
18. Ibid.
19. Ibid
20. Ibid.
21. Ibid.
22. Ibid.
23. Dr. Betty Winfield. E-mail exchange, July 20, 2009.
24. Dunkin, Andrea. "Journalism After 9/11." *The Newark Metro*, September 2006.
25. Ibid.
26. Cronkite, Walter. *A Reporter's Life* (New York: Alfred A. Knopf, 1996), 352.
27. Ibid., 354.
28. Ibid., 380.
29. Fenton, Tom. *Junk News: The Failure of the News Media in the 21st Century* (Golden CO: Fulcrum Publishing, 2009), 33.
30. Stelter, Brian. "When the President Travels, It's Cheaper for Reporters to Stay Home." *New York Times*, May 23, 2010.
31. Ibid., 35.
32. Ibid., 36.
33. Ibid., 36.
34. Ibid., 37.

35. Jenkins, Henry. *Convergence Culture* (New York: New York University Press, 2006), 220.

36. Ibid.

37. Fenton, Tom. *Junk News: The Failure of the Media in the 21st Century* (Golden, CO: Fulcrum Publishing, 2009), 46.

38. Dunkin, Andrea. "Journalism After 9/11." *The Newark Metro*, September 2006.

39. Pew Center for People and the Press. November 28, 2001, poll analysis.

40. Pew Center for People and the Press. September 11, 2006, poll analysis.

41. Ibid.

42. Ibid.

43. Pew Center for People and the Press. September 13, 2009, poll analysis.

44. Ibid.

45. McClellan, Scott. *What Happened* (New York: PublicAffairs, 2008), 157.

46. Ibid., 154.

47. Dadge, David. *The War in Iraq and Why the Media Failed Us* (Westport, CT: Praeger Publishers, 2006), 12.

48. Ibid., 13.

49. Kinsley, Michael. "Filter Tips." *Slate*, October 16, 2003.

50. Auletta, Ken. *Fortress Bush* (New York: Penguin, Inc., 2003), 308.

51. Dadge, David. *The War in Iraq and Why the Media Failed Us* (Westport, CT: Praeger Publishers, 2006), 33.

52. Pew Research Center's Project for Excellence in Journalism, "All the President's Pressers," October 16, 2006.

53. Ibid., 29.

54. Ibid.

55. Ibid.

56. Ibid., 31.

57. McClellan, Scott. *What Happened* (New York: Public Affairs, 2008), 156–57.

58. Ibid., 157.

59. Dadge, David. *The War in Iraq and Why the Media Failed Us* (Westport, CT: Praeger Publishers, 2006), 33.

60. Fenton, Tom. *Junk News: The Failure of the News Media in the 21st Century* (Golden, CO: Fulcrum Publishers, 2009), 55.

61. Moyers, Bill. "Buying the War." *Bill Moyer's Journal* (PBS), Washington, DC, April 25, 2007.

62. Ibid.

63. Blystone, Richard. E-mail exchange. April 29, 2010.

64. Ibid.

65. Ibid.

66. Eisner, Peter. E-mail exchange. May 10, 2010.

67. Moyers, Bill. "Buying the War." *Bill Moyer's Journal* (PBS), Washington, DC, April 25, 2007.

68. Simon, Bob. E-mail exchange. March 2, 2011.

69. Fenton, Tom. *Junk News: The Failure of the News Media in the 21st Century* (Golden, CO: Fulcrum Publishers, 2009), 55.

70. Moyers, Bill. "Buying the War." *Bill Moyer's Journal* (PBS), Washington, DC, April 25, 2007.

71. Ibid.

72. Ibid.

73. Ibid.

74. Ibid.

75. Ibid.

76. Ibid.

77. Ricchiardi, Sherry. "Second Time Around." *American Journalism Review* (February/March 2008).

78. Ibid.

79. Moore, James C. "Not Fit to Print." *Salon*, May 27, 2004.

80. Eisner, Peter. E-mail. May 10, 2010.

81. Moyers, Bill. "Buying the War." *Bill Moyer's Journal* (PBS), Washington, DC, April 25, 2007.

82. BBC News. "Profile: Ahmed Chalabi." October 3, 2002.

83. Ibid.

84. Thomas, Evan, and Mark Hosenball. "The Rise and Fall of Chalabi: Bush's Mr. Wrong." *Newsweek*, May 31, 2004.

85. Dizard, John. "How Ahmed Chalabi Conned the Neocons." *Salon*, May 4, 2004.

86. BBC News. "Profile: Ahmed Chalabi." October 3, 2002.

87. Ibid.

88. Shafer, Jack. "The *Times* Scoop That Melted." *Slate*, July 25 2003.

89. Ibid.

90. Ibid.

91. "Former *New York Times* Staffer Judith Miller." *On the Media* (PPB-WNYC), New York City, November 11, 2005.

92. Dowd, Maureen. "Woman of Mass Destruction." *New York Times*, October 22, 2005.

93. Huffington, Arianna. "Chris Mathews and the Power of Repetition." *Huffington Post*, November 2, 2005.

94. Mathews, Chris. "CIA Leak Story." *Hardball* with Chris Mathews (MSNBC), October 10, 2005.

95. Stewart, Thomas A. "The Cunning Plot of Leadership." *Fortune*, September 7, 1998.

96. Moyers, Bill. "Buying the War." *Bill Moyer's Journal* (PBS), Washington, DC, April 25, 2007.

97. Shafer, Jack. "Dealing with Defective Defectors." *Slate*, April 13, 2004.

98. Moyers, Bill. "Buying the War." *Bill Moyer's Journal* (PBS), Washington, DC, April 25, 2007.

99. Eisner, Peter. "How Bogus Letter Became a Case for War." *Washington Post*, April 3, 2007.

100. Eisner, Peter, and Knut Royce. *The Italian Letter* (New York: Rodale, 2007), 19.

101. Wilson, Joseph C. "What I Didn't Find in Africa." *New York Times*, July 6, 2003.

102. Eisner, Peter, and Knut Royce. *The Italian Letter* (New York: Rodale, 2007), 41–42.

103. Ibid., 15.

104. Ibid., 19.

105. Burba, Elisabetta. E-mail exchange. May 17, 2010.

106. Ibid.

107. Ibid.

108. Hersh, Seymour M. "Who Lied to Whom?" *The New Yorker*, March 31, 2003.

109. Ibid.

110. Ibid.

111. Alfano, Sean. "FBI: Niger Documents Fraudulent." CBS News, November 5, 2005.

112. Isikoff, Michael, and Mark Hosenball, "The 60 Minutes Story That Didn't Run." *Newsweek*, September 23, 2004.

113. Ibid.

114. Ibid.

115. Ibid.

116. Jacoby, Mary. "The Cowardly Broadcasting System." *Salon*, September 29, 2004.

117. Ibid.

118. Boehlert, Eric. "Lapdogs." *Salon*, May 6, 2006.

119. White House official transcript, March 6, 2003.

120. Boehlert, Eric. *Lapdogs: How the Press Rolled Over for Bush* (New York: Free Press, 2006), 205.

121. Ibid., 205–6.

122. CBS News, full text of White House press conference, March 6, 2003.

123. Johnson, Peter. "Bush Has Media Walking a Fine Line." *USA Today*, March 10, 2003.

124. Moyers, Bill. "Buying the War." *Bill Moyer's Journal* (PBS), Washington, DC, April 25, 2007.

125. Boehlert, Eric. Salon.com, May 4, 2006.

126. Boehlert, Eric. *Lapdogs: How the Press Rolled Over for Bush* (New York: Free Press, 2006), 207.

127. Ibid.

128. Ibid., 208.

129. Moyers, Bill. "Buying the War." *Bill Moyer's Journal* (PBS), Washington, DC, April 25, 2007.

130. Ibid.

131. Ibid.

132. Boehlert, Eric. *Lapdogs: How the Press Rolled Over for Bush* (New York: Free Press, 2006), 207.

133. Ibid., 209.

134. Ibid.

135. Ibid., 210.

FIVE

The Iraq War

Reflections, Repercussions, and Resolution

Men, it has been well said, think in herds; it will be seen that they go
mad in herds, while they only recover their senses slowly, one by one.
—Charles Mackay, Scottish journalist/poet

INTRODUCTION

His code name was "Geronimo," and he had been under surveillance by
U.S. intelligence agents for nine months. On May 1, 2011, after decades
on the run, global terrorist and mastermind of the 9/11 attacks, Osama
bin Laden, was shot and killed by an elite team of Navy Seals in Abbottabad, Pakistan.

Some in the intelligence community believed bin Laden had been living in the affluent suburb for at least five years. He was tucked away,
hiding in a spacious walled compound under the nose of and just a mile
from Pakistan's version of "West Point," an elite training academy for the
Pakistani military. U.S. intelligence had been confident, but was not certain, that bin Laden was there. President Obama was informed that the
intelligence was by no means ironclad, but was, at the very least, promis-
ing after the trail on bin Laden had reportedly gone cold for years.

After months of deliberation and remarkably preventing any leak of
the best kept secret in Washington, even from the most senior staff in the
Obama administration, the president finally gave the order to storm the
compound. In a raid that lasted just forty minutes, bin Laden was killed
and his body was immediately ferreted to Afghanistan where a DNA test
was conducted to verify his identity. According to the Obama administration, in accordance with Islamic law, bin Laden's body was appropri-

ately prepared for a Muslim burial and was swiftly and summarily dropped in the Arabian Sea at an undisclosed location.

On the news magazine program, *60 Minutes*, Defense Secretary Robert Gates praised President Obama. He said, "I worked for a lot of these guys and this is one of the most courageous calls, decisions that I think I've ever seen a president make . . . for all the reasons I've been talking about. The uncertainty of the intelligence. The consequences of it going bad. The risk to lives of the Americans involved. It was a very gutsy call."[1]

It is too early to tell what long-term ramifications bin Laden's death will have on the geopolitical stage. Many experts have surmised that his influence had diminished long before he was killed. Meanwhile, the Arab world has been experiencing dramatic changes, which have not been associated with the radical extremism of al Qaeda and bin Laden. On May 19, 2011, President Obama delivered a speech at the State Department about U.S. foreign policy relating to the Middle East. He said, "By the time we found bin Laden, al Qaeda's agenda had come to be seen by the vast majority of the region as a dead end, and the people of the Middle East and North Africa had taken their future into their own hands."[2]

Countries across the northern tier of Africa, in the Middle East and on the Arabian Peninsula, in Tunisia, Egypt, Libya, Jordan, Syria, Yemen, and Bahrain thousands of people took to the streets in pro-democracy demonstrations in early 2011. Ordinary people, who were unhappy with their oppressive governments, crushing unemployment, low wages, inadequate living conditions, and inferior public services, rose up to protest by the hundreds of thousands. It has been an unprecedented public display of discontent in that part of the world and has been called "The Arab Spring."

In Tunisia, President Zine al-Abidine Ben Ali, in power for twenty-three years, fled the country. In Yemen, President Ali Abdullah Saleh first announced he would not seek re-election and left for Saudi Arabia where he underwent "urgent medical treatment." According to a June 5, 2011, report in the *New York Times*, "The Saudis are likely to make sure Mr. Saleh, who has been in power for thirty-three years, does not return as president, analysts said—a goal they and other regional Arab leaders tried unsuccessfully to arrange for weeks." However, Saleh did return to Sanaa in late September 2011 and called for a "truce and ceasefire." The country now risks a civil war. In Jordan, King Abdullah abruptly reorganized his government in response to civil unrest. In Egypt, President Hosni Mubarek, in office for three decades, was forced to relinquish power. He stood trial and was found guilty for "complicity in the deaths of protestors during the uprising, which led to his ouster," according to the Associated Press. Egypt has a newly elected president and the military's role in government is being diminished. In Syria, a bloodbath, which has lasted for months, continues as President Bashar al Assad attacks his own people with military might and firepower no match for the ragtag band of rebels who oppose the regime and demand democracy. Hundreds have been killed. Smaller protests also sprang up in Bahrain, Morocco, and even in Iran.

Before Moammar Gaddafi was killed in a violent gun battle on October 20, 2011, the situation in Libya was troubling because the United States once again elected to involve American military forces. Protesters, referred to in the media as "rebel forces," struggled to oust their president, who had been in power since a bloodless military coup in 1969. In response, he attacked his own people killing and wounding hundreds.

On March 17, 2011, the United Nations Security Council adopted resolution 1973, which demanded "an immediate cease fire in Libya, including an end to the current attacks on civilians, which it said might constitute 'crimes against humanity.' The Security Council imposed a ban on all flights in the country's airspace—a no fly zone and tightened sanctions on the Qadhafi regime and its supporters."[3] The vote was ten in favor of the resolution, which included the United States, and five abstentions.

Two days later President Obama authorized limited military support to Libyan rebel forces. Six days later he asked Congress for a bipartisan resolution to support the mission and on March 28 addressed the nation to explain his motivations. He said:

> The United States and the world faced a choice. Qaddafi declared he would show 'no mercy' to his own people. He compared them to rats, and threatened to go door to door to inflict punishment. In the past, we have seen him hang civilians in the streets, and kill over a thousand people in a single day. Now we saw regime forces on the outskirts of the city. We knew that if we waited—if we waited one more day, Benghazi, a city nearly the size of Charlotte, could suffer a massacre that would have reverberated across the region and stained the conscience of the world. It was not in our national interest to let that happen. I refused to let that happen. And so nine days ago, after consulting the bipartisan leadership of Congress, I authorized military action to stop the killing and enforce U.N. Security Council Resolution 1973.[4]

With those words, the United States would now be involved in its third military conflict in eleven years. The Libyan situation was dangerously familiar, given the ill-fated Iraq war against a similar dictator who also at one time had attacked his own people and threatened American interests. Some of the same ingredients that led to the Iraq war are present in Libya, which include an empowered executive branch, a Congress unwilling to be decisive about challenging the president, a looming election year, and a news media hampered by a host of issues, which may be again preventing a clear and honest portrait of American involvement in a complex international situation.

What is perplexing is the Obama administration's seeming duplicity in its willingness to involve the United States in Libya, while avoiding a similar situation in Syria where President Assad, like Colonel Gaddafi, refused to give up power and whose military had been ordered to fire into crowds that have included children. Also confusing is the attitude of the United States toward Bahrain. While Mr. Obama characterized Bahrain as a "longer-term partner," he also noted that the Bahraini government has engaged in "mass arrests" of those opposed to the ruling class and "brute force" by the police in trying to quell the protests. There has been no U.S. military engagement there either. President Obama said of Libya that we cannot stand by with "the imminent prospect of a massacre."[5] Doesn't the same "prospect" exist in both Syria and Bahrain?

Most mainstream media have insufficiently answered this question. Some have not addressed it at all. The mainstream media (MSM) are repeating many mistakes it made during the time of the Iraq war. On June 1, 2011, in an episode of *The Daily Show*, PBS journalist Bill Moyers told host Jon Stewart that journalists continue to be "declarative" rather than "comparative."[6] Many report the obvious, which is news as it breaks, but do not ask the questions they should to challenge decisions that are in the making by a president and his administration. This was the case when Obama ordered military involvement in Libya and as he has refrained from doing the same in Syria and Bahrain.

Without asking pertinent questions, the MSM have accepted the stated intentions of the administration at face value, much as it did during the run-up to the Iraq war. They report information as released by the administration, but continue to lack both the necessary independence in coverage and investment of resources where the news is happening. Where the news is happening is in the countries where these political conflicts have blossomed. Those conflicts are similar in that they include brutal dictatorial regimes that are wounding and killing their own people, most of whom are innocent civilians. However, it must be noted that the media today and the media during the Iraq war are dissimilar in one important way.

A distinction must be made between the MSM that covered the news between 9/11 and the Iraq war and today's media. Today's media now include a new contingent. New media, social media now compete directly with the MSM. These new media purveyors have created alternative sources for news and information. Social media existed during the Iraq war, but not nearly to the degree that they do today. Those alternative voices today have played a significant role in the uprisings across the Middle East and North Africa. They changed the dynamic of coverage.

The MSM now compete with professional bloggers [web loggers] and other citizen journalists who effectively use all the social media at their disposal, including Facebook, Google, and Twitter, and operate independently of the ties, corporate and otherwise, that often bind the traditional

MSM. In fact, the MSM now often follow the coverage that social media entrepreneurs are generating. While the MSM employ social media as they covers stories, citizen reporters, activists, digital journalists, and others use social media exclusively and independent of any parent company. They break stories, set the pace of news coverage, and also bring to light stories the MSM has missed, ignored, or can't afford to cover. Social media journalists in many ways are beating the MSM at their own game.

The MSM can be completely bypassed as a means to tell Americans what is happening in other parts of the world. For example, it was an Egyptian Google executive organizing people on Facebook who brought the protests in Cairo's Tahrir Square to prominence. In 2009 in Iran, academics, students, and others on Twitter were "tweeting" messages of no more than 140 characters that organized and sustained mass protests in the streets of Tehran. In fact, the U.S. State Department asked executives at Twitter to delay a network upgrade in order "to protect the interests of Iranians using the service to protest the presidential elections that took place on June 12." *Time* magazine called Twitter "the medium of the movement" because it's "free, highly mobile, very personal and very quick. It's also built to spread and fast."[7] It was also a "Twitterer" who unassumingly covered the raid on Osama bin Laden's compound as it was happening, tweeting his frustration because of all the commotion in his otherwise peaceful Abbottabad neighborhood.

Even the Obama administration understands the powerful trend in alternative media sources. Beginning in Afghanistan, it is "leading a global effort" to finance Internet systems so that dissidents can communicate to the outside world, "subverting repressive Taliban censors." The *New York Times* reported, "The State Department, for example, is financing the creation of stealth wireless networks that would enable activists to communicate outside the reach of governments in countries like Iran, Syria, and Libya, according to participants in the project."[8] The accompanying photograph in the newspaper speaks volumes. It depicts an Afghani citizen sitting outdoors amid the rubble of a damaged village next to a new silver Apple computer, which is connected with a single cord to a crude tower of tangled wire.

The MSM are more expensive to operate, clunky, cumbersome, difficult to maneuver, and burdened with layers of bureaucracy and special interests that govern their news coverage. This was the case as the Iraq war took shape. Those constraining conditions hampered their independence then and continue to do the same now.

By their very nature social media journalists are independent. Information is collected and managed by those who create and publish it. Social media and their users, professional and otherwise, are agile and quick, unburdened by many of the limitations and rules that govern the performance of MSM organizations. Social media and their users also can easily report from where the news is being made and can quickly access those sources that are involved and important. In the case of the Middle East, they set the tone for news coverage, had a sustained presence, and told stories that were underreported or ignored by the MSM.

Like coverage of the run-up to the Iraq war, the MSM continues to have a limited presence in the Middle East due to sweeping layoffs and budget restraints. Also, it is either difficult or impossible to enter some countries that have sealed off their borders to foreigners. Since the "Arab Spring" began, the MSM covered breaking news, those punctuated events, which included the protests across the Middle East and the decisions of the leaders in those countries in response to them. However, breaking news tends to be "news light," and coverage in Libya was no exception.

Sustained news coverage of a country, its politics, and its people is vastly different than swooping in for a big story and stepping back out of the country. Sustained coverage would give audiences a truer picture of events including important background information, historical context about the Middle East, and information about what led to the protests, and who the protesters are, especially in Libya. Whom was the United States really supporting in Libya? It was unclear, and the MSM did not clarify this to any satisfaction.

Gaddafi had been regarded as persona non grata for years, but it was not long ago that the news media portrayed Libya as having been accepted back into the global community of nations. In fact, in July 2009, President Gaddafi appeared at the G8 Summit in L'Aquila, Italy, stood with other leaders for the traditional group photo, sat at the table as a negotiating partner, and shook hands with President Obama.

The MSM is, in fact, enamored of these kinds of moments, but generally is reticent to delve deeper and stay with a story over time. The behavior of the news media is akin to someone who reads only the first and last page of a book and tells other people about it. Under this circumstance, the portrayal of the book would be totally skewed and inaccurate. This is the mistake the MSM make over and over again.

One can only wonder what would have happened in Iraq had Saddam been left in power and been subject to the antigovernment wave that swept the region. Ironically, Egypt's Mubarek had advised President Bush not to interfere in Iraq by removing its president from power, later saying it was the "biggest mistake ever committed."[9]

Richard Haass, president of the Council on Foreign Relations, interviewed by *New York Times* columnist Maureen Dowd for her February 1, 2011, column said, "In many ways you can argue that the Iraq war set back the cause of democracy in the Middle East. It's more legitimate in Arab eyes when it happens from within than when it's externally driven."[10]

Haass had been privy to information about invading Iraq when he worked for the State Department during the second Bush administration.

Haass said he knew early in July 2002 that the president planned to wage war with Iraq. Both Secretary of State Colin Powell and National Security Adviser Condoleezza Rice told him the president had decided not whether to go to war with Iraq, but how and that there had been no collective, formal, definitive meeting to decide about invading. It was a foregone conclusion.[11]

The latest reflective, tell-all book from those who served in the Bush White House was from former Secretary of Defense Donald Rumsfeld. In it, Rumsfeld did much finger pointing, including taking aim at former Secretary of State Colin Powell. He wrote, "Over time, a narrative developed that Powell was somehow innocently misled into making a false declaration to the Security Council and the world."[12] Powell was not innocently led into supporting the Iraq war as he might have some believe. "Powell was not duped or misled by anyone," Rumsfeld wrote, "nor did he lie about Saddam's suspected WMD stockpiles."[13]

The administration has blamed the intelligence community for most, if not all, the faulty information about WMD. Colin Powell was no exception. He said, "There were some people in the intelligence community who knew at the time that some of those sources were not good [about WMD], and shouldn't be relied upon, and they didn't speak up. I can't answer why [they didn't speak up.]"[14] But some in the intelligence community have challenged Powell claiming that they had spoken up, including Tyler Drumheller.

Drumheller was the former head of the C.I.A. in Europe. He said he had warned the administration away from a man whose codename was "Curveball." He reported that "Curveball" was likely "a liar" and not to use the information he had provided.[15] Drumheller said he felt vindicated when "Curveball" gave an exclusive interview with *The Guardian* of London on February 15, 2011. "Curveball," whose real name is Rafid Ahmed Alwan al Janabi, said he made it all up [claims about Saddam Hussein and WMD] to hasten regime change.[16]

After Janabi's interview appeared in the newspaper, Powell called for an explanation from both the C.I.A. and the Pentagon.[17] Powell argued that he was never warned away from the information provided by this source.[18] He had used the information provided by "Curveball" in his crucial testimony to the U.N. Security Council. Also, George Tenet on his website issued a statement, which said, "The handling of this matter is certainly a textbook example of how not to handle defector provided material." He also said he does not understand why the warnings about "Curveball" did not travel up the chain of command to his desk.

Powell had deep reservations about the war and told President Bush so as late as the year of the invasion. President Bush said, "In a one on one meeting he [Powell] had told me he believed we could manage the threat of Iraq diplomatically. He also told me he was not comfortable with the war plans."[19] Even as Powell disagreed with the decision to invade Iraq, he would ever be the loyal soldier. In his own 1995 memoir, Powell wrote, "When we are debating an issue, loyalty means giving me your honest opinion whether you think I'll like it or not. From that point on, loyalty means executing the decision as if it were your own."[20] Even though Powell told the president the invasion of Iraq was ill advised, he ultimately accepted the president's decision and publically supported it.

Corroborating other similar stories, Secretary Rumsfeld has written that although Afghanistan was the immediate target after 9/11, the president was focused on Iraq just fifteen days after the attacks. "The President asked me to join him in the Oval Office alone. The president leaned back in the black leather chair behind his desk. He asked that I take a look at the shape of our military plans on Iraq. He wanted the options to be 'creative,' which I took to mean that he wanted something different from the massive land force assembled during the 1991 Gulf War."[21]

Rumsfeld asserted that no one lied about the reasons for going to war, particularly regarding weapons of mass destruction. However, on Rumsfeld's own website, rumsfeld.com, he published papers and memos, including one previously classified as "secret" from September 9, 2002, that admit the evidence about WMD was not substantive enough.

Rumsfeld sent a report to General Richard Myers with a note from him, which read, "Please take a look at this material as to what we don't know about WMD. It is big. Our assessments rely heavily on analytic assumptions and judgment rather than on hard evidence. Our knowledge of the Iraqi nuclear weapons program is based largely—perhaps 90 percent—on analysis of imprecise intelligence." Basically, he noted, the same was true for chemical and biological weapons—"little missile specific data" and "knowledge about 90 percent incomplete."[22]

Those weapons programs had been dismantled and destroyed long before 9/11, and there were reports at the time to substantiate that claim. The administration either put the claim aside or ignored it altogether. After the fact, in 2004, U.S. weapons inspector Charles Duelfer issued a report confirming what had been well-established before the invasion of Iraq: "Saddam Hussein ended the nuclear program in 1991 following the Gulf War." The same was true for any chemical weapons stockpile. The report also stated, "There were no credible indicators that Baghdad resumed production."[23] In his book, President Bush cited the same report this way: "Saddam wanted to re-create Iraq's WMD capability . . . after sanctions were removed and Iraq's economy stabilized."[24]

The president insisted there were WMD somewhere in Iraq and that U.S. forces would eventually find them. He had built a case for war or would find a case to fit his preconceived notion about Iraq as dangerous and uncontainable, its leader as evil, and its very existence under those conditions as inconceivable, intolerable, and irresponsible. Paul Pillar, a former national intelligence officer, said, "The administration used the intelligence not to inform decision-making, but to justify a decision already made."[25] This is, in part, what makes the handling of this war different from others in history.

There was inattention to some very public signs that a war with Iraq was a probability, should the governor of Texas be elected president and should he be able to convince the Congress, the people, and the news media that such action was warranted. George W. Bush was serious about invading Iraq before the events of 9/11, before he was elected the 43rd president of the United States, and even before he was a candidate for president two years prior to 9/11.

Reflections

George W. Bush appeared in a debate on December 2, 1999. He was one in a field of six G.O.P. hopefuls for the Republican nomination for president. The debate was held in Manchester, New Hampshire, at the studios of WMUR-TV. Bush told the audience that if elected he would overthrow Saddam Hussein. "No one envisioned him still standing. It's time to finish the task. And if I found in any way shape or form that he was developing weapons of mass destruction, I'd take them out. I'm surprised he's still there. I think a lot of people are as well," he said.[26] Bush also said he would not negotiate with Hussein or consider lifting U.S. sanctions against Iraq.

A reporter raised a question about whether Bush understood the stridency of his own position on Iraq. The following day, David Nyhan, a political columnist at the *Boston Globe*, wrote: "It was a gaffe-free evening for the rookie front-runner, till he was asked about Saddam's weapons stash. It remains to be seen if that offhand declaration of war was just Texas talk, a sort of locker room braggadocio, or whether it was Bush's first big clinker."[27]

Bush persisted about Iraq now as the G.O.P.'s presidential candidate. He appeared on *NewsHour* with host Jim Lehrer on February 16, 2000. He said, "I'm just as frustrated as many Americans are that he still lives. I think we ought to keep the pressure on him. I will tell you this: If we catch him developing weapons of mass destruction in any way, shape or form, I'll deal with that in a way he won't like." Lehrer pressed Bush by asking, "Like what, bomb him?" That is one option, Bush responded, but backed off another question by Lehrer who asked if he would consider assassinating the Iraqi president. Bush responded by saying he thought it was against the law for an American president to order the assassination of another world leader, but said the United States must keep the pressure on him [Hussein].[28]

Governor Bush pushed his position about Iraq once again, this time at a presidential debate a month before the election. Moderated by PBS's Jim Lehrer, it was held at Wake Forest University in North Carolina on October 11, 2000, where he faced off with his Democratic rival Vice President Al Gore. Bush told the audience, "I could handle the Iraqi situation better." Lehrer responded by asking, "Saddam Hussein, you mean get him out of there?" Bush said, "I would like to. He is a danger. We don't want him fishing in troubled waters in the Middle East."[29]

Even earlier, in spring of 1999, Governor Bush was explicit about the way in which he thought his father had mishandled Iraq and Hussein. He said he believed his father had an opportunity during the Gulf War not only to push Hussein out of Kuwait, but to force him out of his own country.

This was contrary to the policy of both his father, President George H. W. Bush, and Brent Scowcroft, who was the elder president's national security advisor. They strongly believed that it was irresponsible to remove Hussein and that it would further destabilize the region at a time when it least needed the instability. In time, they believed, the Iraqi people would rise up and depose Saddam on their own.

The younger Bush was clear in his opposition to that set of beliefs. He was also clear about the benefits of starting a war, which he believed would help ensure the success of a presidency. In fact, Bush shared those sentiments with a journalist during the writing of a book. Later, those musings would manifest themselves in the decisions he would make as president.

Mickey Herskowitz was the journalist to whom Governor Bush spoke. Herskowitz was a columnist for the *Houston Chronicle* and author and co-author of more than forty books. At the suggestion of his agent, Herskowitz approached the Bush campaign about a book "to introduce the candidate to the American public." The campaign agreed to such a book, which was later entitled *A Charge to Keep*. In 1999, Herskowitz interviewed Bush some twenty times and "had completed and submitted ten chapters of the book, with a remaining four to six on his computer."[30]

In part of the manuscript, Herskowitz described Bush's business dealings in the oil industry as "floundering." The Bush campaign was not happy about the negative characterization and abruptly told Herskowitz he was being pulled off the project. Russ Baker, a journalist who later interviewed Herskowitz for his own book, wrote, "A campaign official arrived at his home and took his notes and computer files. 'They took it, and rewrote it.'"[31]

In fact, the book was published in 1999 by William Morrow and noted only one author, Karen Hughes. She later became special counselor to Bush when he was elected president in 2000. One reviewer characterized the book as "light and breezy." Herskowitz said he has often thought about "what might have happened if the public had learned how W. really thinks."[32]

Herskowitz said he and Bush had discussed the qualities necessary to become a successful leader. Hershkowitz said, "He [Bush] told me that as a leader, you can never admit to a mistake. That was one of the keys to being a leader." He also told the reporter that what also makes a success-ful leader is being able to understand the political benefit of starting a war.[33]

Bush was thinking about invading Iraq in 1999, Herskowitz told Bak-er. "It was on his mind." It meant political capital, which he said he would never waste like his father did after pushing Iraq out of Kuwait nearly a decade earlier in 1991.[34] "He [George W.] thought of himself as a superior, more modern politician than his father and [the elder Bush's close friend and adviser] Jim Baker. He told me, '[My father] could have done anything [during the Gulf War]. He could have invaded Switzer-land. If I had the political capital, I would have taken Iraq," Bush told Herskowitz during one of their interview sessions.[35]

In his exhaustive 579-page book about the Bush family, Baker wrote, "While W. seemed somewhat hazy on specifics, on one point he was clear: the many benefits that would accrue if he were to overthrow Sad-dam. Herskowitz recalled that Bush and his advisers were sold on the idea that it was difficult for a president to realize his legislative agenda without the high approval numbers that accompany successful—even if modest—wars."[36]

The will, the plan, indeed the forethought to attack Iraq—these senti-ments were later cited by former Secretary of the Treasury Paul O'Neill. In addition to writing his own book about his experiences in the George W. Bush White House, O'Neill told news magazine *60 Minutes* it was all about finding a way to topple Saddam Hussein. "These things were laid and sealed, but for me the notion of pre-emption, that the U.S. has the unilateral right to do whatever it is we decide to do, is a huge leap," O'Neill told CBS correspondent Leslie Stahl. According to O'Neill, no cabinet member ever asked "Why Saddam, why now?"[37]

Campaigning *for* president is very different from governing *as* presi-dent. The American public and the news media expect a certain amount of bravado from candidates on the campaign trail about what direction they would take the country if elected. Some of it is a theoretical exercise to demonstrate strength and will. Some of it is to test ideas. Some of it comes from deeply held beliefs and/or from experience as governors and as members of Congress. Some of it changes over time as a candidate sharpens his/her message and as events in the world often dictate.

In this case, with this president, there is evidence to suggest he had an ax to grind from early on. Perhaps someday a psychological portrait of the 43rd president will emerge to reveal a deeper explanation. But for now and for this president, he felt compelled to move against Hussein if given the opportunity. Was it to prove something? Was it to take his place in history as a courageous leader? More might be gleaned by comb-ing through the Bush presidential papers once the George W. Bush Presi-dential Center in Dallas, Texas, opens in 2013.

In his book, President Bush did not personalize his disdain for Saddam Hussein nor did he mention Hussein's plot to assassinate his father during the Clinton administration. Instead Bush wrote a litany of descriptions about Hussein's nefarious deeds over the years. Those included his sympathizing with terrorists, the invasions of Iran and Kuwait, his brutal dictatorship, and the torturing of the Kurds.[38]

Paul O'Neill, who as treasury secretary, was a permanent member of the president's national security team, said the president "did not make decisions in a methodical way: there was no free-flow of ideas or open debate. At cabinet meetings the president was like a blind man in a room full of deaf people. There is no discernable connection."[39]

Details from those conversations that journalist Herskowitz collected during his interview sessions with Bush did not come to light until long after the Iraq war was underway. Even then, according to Russ Baker, whose book was by then published and who was interviewed numerous times about his findings, the story was "totally underreported, basically ignored by MSM [main stream media], which is shocking and yet unsurprising."

REPERCUSSIONS

In evaluating the wisdom of the invasion of Iraq and the justifications that were offered for such action, the tragic results of that decision must be noted. The Iraq war began on March 19, 2003. The mission was called "Operation Iraqi Freedom," although it was never initially intended to free anyone.

The invasion of Iraq was first presented as an operation that would bring Saddam Hussein to justice. The administration alleged he had a hand in the attacks of 9/11 and was developing weapons of mass destruction, which he was planning to use against the United States. At the time Hussein was sufficiently contained and so was prevented from doing any real harm before the war was launched. Freeing the Iraqi people and helping to create a democratic Iraq increasingly became the mantra of the Bush administration over time after 9/11 and even more so as the invasion drew near.

The bombing of Iraq from the air was an impressive show of military might and precision. Former Secretary of Defense Donald Rumsfeld promised and delivered a spectacle of "shock and awe." The initial attacks were swift and sharp, which began at 9:30 p.m. EST on March 19, 2003. The capital city of Baghdad was blanketed by firepower from the air. It was severely damaged, and so were the palaces and residences of President Hussein. He was on the run. His notorious army, The Republican Guard, began to crumble and surrendered in increasing numbers.

Less than two months later President Bush declared the mission in Iraq a success. On May 1, 2003, President Bush co-piloting a fighter jet and dressed in a flight suit, landed on the U.S.S. *Abraham Lincoln* to personally bring this message to the troops on board. The president was confident as he strode across the deck of the aircraft carrier, wading through a sea of adoring military personnel. He addressed the crowd in front of a huge banner that was strategically stretched across the flight deck. In red, white, and blue, it read "Mission Accomplished." The president said definitively, "Major combat operations in Iraq have ended. The United States and our allies have prevailed. And now our coalition is engaged in securing and reconstructing that country."[40]

Once again, the president linked Iraq to the attacks of 9/11. "Our actions have been focused, and deliberate, and proportionate to the offense. We have not forgotten the victims of 9/11—the last phone calls, the cold murder of children, the searches in the rubble. With those attacks, the terrorists and their supporters declared war on the United States. And war is what they got."[41]

A deadly insurgency ignited in Iraq just months after those assertive proclamations. Members of al Qaeda had recruited soldiers from other Arab countries. They began to descend on Iraq, waging Jihad, a Holy War proclaimed and managed by Osama bin Laden from afar, still in hiding, but believed to be somewhere in Pakistan near the rugged border of Afghanistan. He sent numerous cryptic messages on videotapes delivered to the doorsteps of key media organizations, which broadcast them for the world to see and hear.

Al Qaeda guerrilla fighters began to attack U.S. and coalition forces with snipers hidden away in destroyed villages and with deadly contraptions we have now come to know as Improvised Explosive Devices or I.E.D's. The country, already ravaged by the U.S.-led bombing campaign, came further undone as civil war broke out between warring factions, Kurd against Sunni against Shia. Thousands of Iraqis were killed in the ensuing violence and by suicide bomb, another unconventional, hideous weapon of choice used by guerrilla fighters and those recruited to join them.

Saddam Hussein was finally captured on December 15, 2003. He had been hiding in a grave-sized "spider hole" in the ground, which was camouflaged. It was on the property of a farmhouse near the leader's hometown of Tikrit. He emerged to face the barrel of a rifle aimed at his head by a United States soldier. He declared, as he emerged dirty and wearing a thick, long beard, "I am the President of Iraq." The soldier replied, "President Bush sends his regards." Some news organizations reported that President Hussein was "captured like a rat."[42] He was later accused of war crimes against humanity and brought to trial in Iraq by a special tribunal established by an interim Iraqi government, the Coalition Provisional Authority. He was found guilty and sentenced to death by hanging on November 6, 2006. The sentence was carried out on December 30, 2006.

In January 2005, Iraqis began to draft their first constitution and were represented by a coalition of leaders from the three major factions in the country. Their first election under a new constitution was held later that year in December. In January 2006, Nouri al Malaki, a Shia, emerged as prime minister after a national assembly was voted into office. The new government struggled as it attempted to rebuild its ruined country and control the violence that persisted.

In 2007, the United States launched a concentrated military offensive known as "the surge." It was designed to quell the increasing violence that took coalition forces and the Bush administration by surprise after President Bush declared the mission a success. The administration committed more troops, more military weaponry, more resources, and more dollars to the battlefield. Although controversial, it was effective. Violence began to diminish, but it was not until after four years of bloodshed. According to the U.S. Department of Defense, more than four thousand American soldiers have been killed and more than one hundred thousand Iraqi civilians also have lost their lives, caught in the crossfire of combat or as targets of suicide bombers and I.E.D.s.

Barack Obama was elected president in 2008. While still a United States senator and a candidate for president, he had opposed the surge but later supported the controversial, much-debated effort as commander-in-chief. He also promised that combat operations in Iraq would cease by the conclusion of summer in 2010.

Meanwhile, a second Iraqi election was held in March 2010. No government had emerged six months later after a "wafer thin victory" by a former interim prime minister, Ayad Allawi. The results were challenged by Prime Minister Nouri al-Malaki, who charged that there was widespread fraud. Both sides attempted to form a government. As a result, the threat of more violence loomed. Finally, some eight months later, in November 2010, Malaki was asked to form a new government and has since announced he will not run for re-election.

Combat operations were declared over in Iraq, as promised, by President Obama on August 31, 2010. He announced that "Operation Iraqi Freedom" would be replaced by "Operation New Dawn." The new orders were to bolster the fragile new democracy by supporting its new government and army. This was presumably different from active nation building and taking the lead in military operations, as had been the case previously.

President Obama said during a nationally televised address from the Oval Office, "I am announcing that the combat mission in Iraq has ended. Operation Iraqi Freedom is over, and the Iraqi people now have the lead responsibility for the security of their country." Fifty thousand troops would be left to support Iraqi security forces. Thousands more would be deployed or redeployed to Afghanistan "to break the Taliban's momentum."[43]

On another dangerous front in Afghanistan, the Taliban had gained strength well before the attacks of September 11, 2001. When United States forces invaded Afghanistan in hot pursuit of bin Laden in October 2001, they had broken the Taliban, restoring some measure of order and security and left room for the return of a proper, albeit fledgling, new government.

To this day, the war in Afghanistan festers and, according to Defense Department numbers, has claimed the lives of over thirteen hundred American soldiers. It now has the unfortunate distinction of being the longest war in American history. At this writing, American troops by the thousands have been in Iraq for seven years, a decade after 9/11. No weapons of mass destruction have been discovered. But President Bush insisted that even without finding WMD, Saddam had the infrastructure to create them and the desire to produce them. He wrote, "As a result of our actions in Iraq, one of America's most committed and dangerous enemies stopped threatening us forever."[44]

On September 1, 2010, Defense Secretary Robert Gates was in Iraq to mark the conclusion of combat operations. He said to reporters, "The problem with this war for, I think, many Americans is that the premise on which we justified going to war proved not to be valid. That is Saddam having weapons of mass destruction. It [the Iraq war] will be always clouded by how it began."[45]

Just days after combat operations officially ended in Iraq, "insurgents mounted coordinated attacks on one of the main military commands in Baghdad" in which Americans briefly became involved in the firefight. At least twelve people were killed. Thirty-six others were wounded. The truth is there is no real end in sight to the violence in Iraq, and the country remains fragile, at best, for the foreseeable future.[46]

What was different about the war in Iraq? It was launched preemptively despite warnings from many political and diplomatic circles in the United States and abroad to avoid any such invasion. The war in Iraq revealed that none of the previously held notions about the country and its leader were true, which were the justifications for going to war in the first place. No weapons of mass destruction. No viable weapons program. No uranium purchased from Africa. No involvement in 9/11. All this was known before a single shot was fired in March 2003. Never had so much gone so wrong at once.

Saddam was brutal and a tyrant. He had the capacity for evil and heinous atrocities against other human beings. But he was contained, and it was a serious mistake to launch an unprovoked, preemptive attack on his country. This, too, was well understood before the invasion of Iraq. Also understood was that deposing Saddam in Iraq would upset the delicate balance of power in the region, especially where it involved Iran.

No one will ever know what political situation would have emerged vis-à-vis Iran had Saddam been left in power to be overthrown by his own people in a revolution, similar to the ones which occurred across the Middle East early in 2011. If conservative President Mahmoud Ahmadinejad were in office as he is today, would he support a revolution next door? It would depend on who was attempting to force a change in regime. If a revolution was influenced and supported by Islamists, Iran might be inclined to quietly support such changes. However, if those changes were secular in nature and democratic, the regime in Iran might feel threatened. In fact, protestors in Iran, inspired by the 2011 events across North Africa, were quickly suppressed by force under orders from Ahmadinejad.

In the case of Iraq's government being overthrown by external forces, such as it was by the United States, President Bush wrote that others warned him about creating instability in the region. Donald Rumsfeld said a war with Iraq could "destabilize" Jordan and Saudi Arabia. George Tenet specifically expressed concern about a "broader regional war" where Iran could foment instability.[47] Iran already posed a threat.

According to Carpenter and Malou, "Even before the US-led 2003 invasion of Iraq, Iran possessed a budding nuclear programme, the region's largest population, an expansive ballistic-missile arsenal and, through sponsorship, influence over the Lebanese Shia group Hizbullah. The George W. Bush administration and neo-conservative proponents of the war overlooked these assets, and America's removal of Saddam Hussein as the principal strategic counterweight to Iran paved the way for an expansion of Iran's influence. The United States now faces the question of how it can mitigate potential threats to its interests if Iran succeeds in consolidating its new position as the leading power in the region."[48]

Israel, an ally of the United States, would also be threatened by a resurgent Iran. Professor Efraim Inbar said that Israel's biggest threat is a nuclear Iran. Iran would be able to destroy the tiny country before it could defend itself.[49] In his book, Bush did not specifically discuss a vulnerable Israel with respect to Iraq or Iran. However, he did write that he consulted with many scholars as he debated whether to invade Iraq. They included Holocaust survivor and Nobel laureate, Elie Wiesel. The president wrote that Wiesel told him he had "a moral obligation to act against evil."[50] Wiesel also wrote in a *Los Angeles Times* commentary that he supported "President Bush's policy of intervention" in the case against Iraq.

What also must be noted is that in the 1980s Saddam served the national interests of the United States. During the Iraq-Iran war, the United States favored Iraq during the crisis because of the Iranian hostage crisis. Francis Boyle wrote that there were American efforts to "punish, isolate, and weaken the Khomeini regime because of the [Iranian] hostage crisis" when U.S. citizens were taken hostage in the U.S. Embassy and held by Islamic students and militants for 444 days from November 4, 1979, to January 20, 1981. Although American foreign policy officially professed to be neutral concerning the conflict between Iran and Iraq, "a substantial body of diplomatic opinion believes that the American government has consistently 'tilted' in favor of Iraq throughout the [Iraq-Iran] war, despite its public proclamation of 'neutrality.'"[51]

Iraq was considered an ally. Many would say its president Hussein was an American-sponsored dictator. From President Ronald Reagan to George H.W. Bush, "The White House had been an eager backer of Saddam. The two administrations had provided millions of dollars in aid and had permitted the export of U.S. technology that Iraq used to build a massive arsenal of chemical, biological, and possibly nuclear weapons."[52]

Author Russ Baker wrote that the senior George Bush expressed "outrage" about Saddam's brutality against the Kurdish population and others, but the United States continued to do business with him.[53] This continued even after the infamous gassing of Kurds in 1988 when between 3,200 and 5,000 villagers were killed in the town of Halabja after Saddam ordered bombs filled with poisonous mustard gas dropped on the town. Baker wrote, "In a paradoxical twist, when W. sought to justify the invasion of Iraq in 2003, he cited those same weapons—without mentioning that his own father had helped to provide them. He also failed to mention what many proliferation experts correctly believed: that most or all the weapons had been destroyed as part of Saddam's scale-down after the imposition of the no fly zones and President Clinton's own threats to invade."[54]

George W. Bush's tenure as commander-in-chief ended precisely at noon on January 20, 2009, with the inauguration of Barack Obama. Since his departure from the biggest political stage in the world, Bush has maintained a low profile spending time at his beloved ranch in Crawford, Texas, and in north Dallas where he has a second home.

On November 9, 2010, the much-anticipated memoir by the former president was released amid much hype and media exposure. He appeared on Oprah and numerous morning talk shows touting his book *Decision Points*. He told Oprah Winfrey on her program November 10, 2010, that it still makes him "sick to his stomach" when he thinks about the absence of weapons of mass destruction in Iraq, given that was one of the main premises on which the war was built.

In the book the former president stated that "no one was more shocked or angry than I was when we didn't find the weapons."[55] He continued, "When Saddam didn't use WMD on our troops, I was relieved. When we didn't discover the stockpile soon after the fall of Baghdad, I was surprised. When the whole summer passed without finding any, I was alarmed. The press corps constantly raised the question, 'Where are the WMD?' I was asking the same thing."[56]

President Bush wrote that he firmly believes the world is a safer place without Saddam, but noted two major errors he made with regard to Iraq. The first, he wrote, was after Saddam fell that "we did not respond more quickly and aggressively when the security situation started to deteriorate."[57] The second was the "intelligence failure on Iraq's WMD."[58] His decisions were only as good as the intelligence he received, he said. "The reality was that I had sent American troops into combat based in large part on intelligence that proved false. That was a massive blow to our credibility—my credibility—that would shake the confidence of the American people," he said.[59]

Former C.I.A. Director George Tenet has written that there was absolutely nothing conclusive about WMD in much of the intelligence that was provided by the C.I.A to the president. While taking responsibility for any failures of intelligence at the time, he has stated that he was made the fall guy, a way for the administration "to deflect blame." Tenet wrote that the president's staff had different priorities. For them, preserving the president's reputation—particularly with an election coming up and a war plan coming apart—was job one. Perhaps I was just collateral damage."[60]

President Bush contemplates how history will judge him. There is little doubt it will be the Iraq war that will dominate in that assessment. Recalling Harry Truman, the 33rd president of the United States, Mr. Bush wrote, "I admired Truman's toughness principle, and strategic vision. 'I felt like the moon, the stars, and all the planets had fallen on me,' Truman said when he took office suddenly in the final months of World War II. Yet the man from Missouri knew how to make a hard decision and stick by it. He did what he thought was right and didn't care much what the critics said. When he left office in 1953, his approval ratings were in the twenties. Today he is viewed as one of America's great presidents."[61] Obviously, former President Bush hopes the same will happen for him in time.

Mr. Bush said he is resolved to let history be the final judge of his presidency, but said there can be no debate about one fact. He wrote, "After the nightmare of September 11, America went seven and half years without another successful terrorist attack on our soil. If I had to summarize my most meaningful accomplishment as president in one sentence, that would be it."[62]

RESOLUTIONS

In all these years, the country seems to have accepted the truth about the Iraq war and how it came to be, but it has been a long, difficult road to that truth. Scottish journalist and poet Charles Mackay said, "People are more prone to believe the 'wondrously false' than the 'wondrously true.'

Of all the offspring of time, Error is the most ancient and is so old and familiar an acquaintance, that Truth, when discovered, comes upon most of us like an intruder, and meets the intruder's welcome."[63]

There is a story of lore about the Pharaoh in Egypt. One of his subjects was curious and asked him, how did you get to be Pharaoh? The Pharaoh answered, "Well, nobody stopped me." That is precisely the way we must view the reality that became the invasion of Iraq. Nobody stopped it, and many mistakes of the past were repeated.

Defense Secretary Robert Gates, who served under President Bush three years after the invasion and who also served as President Obama's defense secretary, was extremely candid about the United States and war in a recent speech. He was speaking to cadets at the West Point Military Academy on February 25, 2011, and said, "When it comes to predicting the nature and location of our next military engagements since Vietnam, our record has been perfect. We have never once gotten it right, from the Mayaguez, to Grenada, Panama, Somalia, the Balkans, Haiti, Kuwait, Iraq, and more. We had no idea before these missions that we would be so engaged."[64] He continued, "In my opinion, any future defense secretary who advises the president to again send a big American land force into Asia or into the Middle East should 'have his head examined,' as General MacArthur so delicately put it."[65]

About learning the lessons the past has provided, Gates said, "The Army's vice chief of staff, General Pete Chiarelli, once said, it is important that the hard fought lessons of Iraq and Afghanistan are not merely 'observed' but truly 'learned'—incorporated into the service's [Army's] DNA and institutional memory."[66] It should also be incorporated into our memory as a nation to the extent that we all have a responsibility in preventing errors in judgment. This includes the president, the Congress, the news media, and we the people.

There is plenty of blame to go around regarding the Iraq war. Decisions made in the run-up to the war amounted to a collective foreign policy blunder of historic proportion, the effects of which have been reverberating and will continue to reverberate for years to come. How was this crisis different from others that the United States has faced? When the nation is faced again with a crisis of similar consequence, what can help prevent the same kind of reaction? In describing what was not accomplished, inherently what will emerge is what should happen in future decisions.

The attacks of September 11, 2001, spawned President Bush's "War on Terror," which was linked to Iraq and Saddam Hussein. It is not that the American homeland had never been attacked, but it was the first time a series of attacks had been waged on the continent. It was also an attack not waged by any leader of any sovereign nation. It was waged by a band of rogue terrorists, hiding in a faraway land, not their own, who had contempt for America.

This was a devastating attack, which came by way of an orchestrated, premeditated campaign specifically designed to destroy property and kill as many Americans as possible. More people were killed and injured in 9/11 than lost their lives at Pearl Harbor, which was launched during wartime. The 9/11 attacks were strategically invoked to expand the "War on Terror" to include Iraq. This new theater of conflict was constructed on false pretense. The extent to which a collection of selected facts, circumstance, and intelligence were hobbled together in building a case to invade another country was something the country had never experienced.

The road to this particular war was different because there was a failure on so many levels at once. Those few who may have attempted to change the course of events in Iraq would have done so at their own political peril. They either did not have the courage of their convictions to speak out or the opposing voices were speaking so much louder that they were overwhelmed and silenced into submission. The power and influence of the presidency coupled with the certitude of the president, privately and publically, however wrong he was, intimidated many of those who served in the cabinet, in Congress, in the intelligence community, and in the news media.

There was an arc of mistrust that developed over time as we examine the tenure of President Bush, congressional approval ratings, and the regard for the news media by the public, which is chief among the many methods people get their news and information. From 9/11 to the start of the Iraq war, politics seemed to have trumped good policy making. Partisanship widened preventing a willingness to work together for the public good. Many politicians were increasingly preoccupied with campaigning, raising money, and keeping their jobs. Money has more and more influenced the political process. It also has influenced how the news media cover that process and influenced the news coverage of the run-up to the Iraq war and those politicians who supported it, no matter how reluctant some were.

It has been convenient for most pundits, historians, critics, educators, political scientists, and journalists to place the lion share of responsibility at the feet of President George W. Bush. It is true. If anyone should be the most culpable for the errors, miscalculations, fabrications, and embellishment of the truth, it is the president.

The president went into the Iraq war with a set of beliefs, many of which he held before he took office. Over time, the president and his administration were simply proven wrong.

Leadership meant that the president should have mustered the fortitude to simply state the obvious. Evidence had come to light that refuted the claims he had previously repeated and reinforced. Instead, the president decided to cherry-pick the intelligence that would ultimately persuade the American people and the Congress to support the war anyway.

He failed to give the people of our country a full and accurate picture in all its contradictions and complexities.

Also, the relationship of President Bush to his father, a former president, and their relationship to a common political nemesis, Saddam Hussein, is an interesting aspect of the Iraq war story. Perhaps, at its core, the president's issue with Hussein was indeed deep-seated and personal, which may have distorted and clouded his reality.

But the problem never was President Bush's so-called "War on Terror," following 9/11, which began in Afghanistan hunting Osama bin Laden. The problem was to involve Iraq to the extent that it detracted from the primary mission in Afghanistan. We had failed to kill or capture Osama bin Laden when bin Laden was the rightful foe. The Bush administration employed a realigned focus when he also made Hussein a target. According to a CBS News poll taken in August 2010, 59 percent said the Iraq war was a mistake, and only 25 percent said they thought it made the United States safer from terrorism.

President Bush enjoyed a very high approval rating following the attacks of 9/11. That has dramatically changed over time. In Bush's second term, people began to learn that the premises on which the Iraq war was built were false, and the president was taken to task as reflected in polling numbers. According to a 2008 CNN/Opinion Research Corp. survey, George W. Bush left office with an approval rating of 28 percent, the third lowest approval rating of any president in history. That is slightly higher than Harry Truman, who had the lowest in history at 22 percent and Richard Nixon, who had the second lowest at 24 percent. [67]

President Bush also topped the charts with his disapproval ratings. CNN's polling director, Keating Holland, reported, "No president has ever had a higher disapproval rating in any CNN or Gallup poll. In fact, this is the first time that any president's disapproval rating has cracked the 70 percent mark." The second president Bush had a disapproval rating of 71 percent. He was more unpopular than was Richard Nixon at 66 percent, who was the first and only American president to resign his office in disgrace in 1974. This was a quite a fall for George W. Bush from the 90 percent approval rating immediately following the attacks of 9/11. [68]

So far the former president also is rated among the worst presidents in history. According to the Siena Research Institute (SRI) of Siena College in Loudonville, New York, in its fifth Presidential Expert Poll in July 2010, George W. Bush was rated one of the five worst American presidents in history, rating thirty-nine of forty-three. Two hundred thirty-eight presidential scholars rated the presidents on "six personal attributes, five forms of ability, and eight areas of accomplishment." The poll determined that just a year after leaving office, President George W. Bush "rated poorly in handling the economy, communication, ability to compromise, foreign policy accomplishments and intelligence." [69]

President Bush could not have proceeded as swiftly as he did were it not for the "support" and "encouragement" in varying degree from those partners in governing. Congress was complicit in managing the journey to Iraq. At the time, Republicans dominated Congress. The Republican Party was the political party of the president and as a cohort made decisions in unison and postured on defense and national security when the country did not need partisanship, but independence of thought and leadership from both branches of government. Many Democrats were also guilty of weighing personal political futures against the concerns of the party, which had historically been perceived as weak on defense and national security. Barbs flew back and forth between members in each party about whom and which party was more patriotic.

Politics and party loyalty interfered with making the best and right decisions for the country and the American people. When should the office of the presidency transcend politics? When should partisanship be put aside among the members of Congress?

The late Senator Edward M. Kennedy said that trust in government by the people is paramount. In a speech to The Center for American Progress in 2004, he said, "In these uncertain times, it is imperative that our leaders hold true to those founding ideals and protect the fundamental trust between the government and the people. Nowhere is this trust more important than between the people and the president of the United States. As the leader of our country and the voice of America to the world, our president has the obligation to lead and speak with truth and integrity if this nation is to continue to reap the blessings of liberty for ourselves and our posterity."[70] In the same speech he said that "election politics" prevailed over sound "foreign policy and national security."

Kennedy also said that, particularly in times of war, loyalty to political party must be subjugated by love of country. In another important speech in 2002 to the Johns Hopkins School of International Study he said, "The life and death issue of war and peace is too important to be left to politics. And I disagree with those who suggest that this fateful issue cannot or should not be contested vigorously, publicly, and all across America. When it is the people's sons and daughters who will risk and even lose their lives, then the people should hear and be heard, speak and be listened to. But there is a difference between honest public dialogue and partisan appeals. There is a difference between questioning policy and questioning motives. It is possible to love America while concluding that it is not wise to go to war. The standard that should guide us is especially clear when lives are on the line: we must ask what is right for country, not party."

President Bush wrote that he tried to remove Saddam from power without war. He also said that he invaded Iraq because Saddam was a dangerous presence in the region and because he believed he had weapons of mass destruction. The president, other advisors, and some members of Congress also spoke about the spread of democracy once Saddam fell. However, the president, his advisors, and many in Congress were also confined by the day's political forces. Political forces helped shift the country to neutral, moving nothing of major consequence forward, doing little good for anyone. It also plunged the country recklessly to war, which was a stain on both branches.

Politics and party loyalty in the case of Iraq influenced unwise decisions and irresponsible actions. These have help generate two bloody conflicts in two different countries, thousands of dead and wounded, and have left a fragile Middle East even more vulnerable, not to mention the cost of the wars to the American taxpayer, which has contributed to the national deficit now in the trillions of dollars. It was politics and policy at its worst, for the president and Congress, which clouded judgment and compromised greater, higher principles. The attacks of 9/11 and the wars that followed were politicized, costing the president, the United States Congress, and later the news media credibility with the American people.

The partisan divide in Congress became wider and deeper since the attacks of 9/11. Because Republicans have always been regarded as tougher on defense, Democrats weaker, this was capitalized on during the run-up to war in Iraq. Republicans were in charge and had the better reputation for managing national security. A vote authorizing the war with Iraq should have been postponed until after the midterm election. Because it was not, that fateful vote was naturally politicized. Even though that important vote was a bipartisan effort, Congress should have decided that America would have been better served by waiting to vote until after the election.

The late Senator Edward Kennedy lamented the role Congress played in the Iraq war. In a much-celebrated memoire published just days before his death he wrote, "The 'legitimate authority,' the Congress, indeed approved authorization for the use of force in Iraq in October, 2002, but it acted in haste and under pressure from the White House, which intentionally politicized the vote by scheduling it before a mid-term election. By contrast, in 1991, the administration of the first President Bush timed the vote on the use of military force against Iraq to occur after midterm elections, in order to depoliticize the decision."[71]

On the floor of the Senate in 2004 Senator Kennedy said the war in Iraq was "a fraud, cooked up in Texas to advance the president's political standing." He also said the administration had "told lie after lie to trigger and perpetuate one of the worst blunders in the history of U.S foreign policy." In his book, the senator wrote that there was no just cause for the invasion of Iraq.

The senator wrote that he arrived at this conclusion based on guiding principles he drew from St. Augustine and Saint Thomas Aquinas: 1) A war must confront danger that is beyond question; 2) It must be declared by a legitimate authority acting on behalf of the people; 3) It must be driven by the right intention, not by selfish motives; 4) It must be a last resort; 5) It must be proportional, so that the harm inflicted does not outweigh the good that it sets out to achieve; and finally 6) It must have a reasonable chance of success.[72]

Kennedy said the case against Iraq simply did not meet these standards. A litany of respected military leaders, who testified before the Armed Services Committee to which Kennedy belonged, all seemed to agree. The former chairman of the Joint Chiefs of Staff, General John Shalikashvili, former Supreme Allied Commander in Europe, General Wesley Clark, and Marine General Joseph Hoar, former commander in chief of Central Command—all were in opposition to the war and advised the committee so. Kennedy wrote that the administration and the Congress ultimately justified the war in Iraq by "departing from reality."[73]

Further, more scrutinized authorization for appropriations should have been insisted upon, and more oversight should have prevailed during the run-up to war. Unfortunately, neither was the case. Congress abdicated much of its responsibility as many members had an eye focused far beyond the present to the future and the next election cycle rather than what was in the best interest of the American people and our country.

In many cases, electability influenced voting and sentiments when principles should have trumped political motivation. This situation was underscored by the political ambitions of two recent presidential candidates. Former Senators Hillary Rodham Clinton and John Kerry both had an eye cast toward political future as they deliberated about war with Iraq. Their votes on Iraq, each supporting the war, may have been politically expedient, but from a policy standpoint, questionable.

Clinton and Kerry as candidates for president were asked numerous times to defend that one single vote authorizing the Iraq war in 2002. Kerry would later say that based on what he knew at the time, his vote to authorize war with Iraq was the right thing to do. Clinton said the same thing as senator, but as presidential candidate later said her vote to authorize the war was a mistake.

Another prominent Democratic leader in Congress, close associate and friend of Senator Kennedy, and also an adamant critic of the war in Iraq was the late Senator Robert Byrd of West Virginia. With the vote to authorize war, Byrd said, "We were giving Bush sole discretion to employ the full military might of the United States whenever he pleased." He called the president "callow and reckless" and said America had never been led "by such a dangerous head of state" who viewed Congress with contempt.[74]

About Congress, he also had some harsh sentiments. He said that it went basically "out of business" because of its behavior during the run-up to the war, handing the president a blank check to fund the effort.

"Congress hurled its sword in the sand and left the field, relegating itself to the sidelines—indefinitely—and gone a long way toward creating a truly imperial presidency."[75]

It was not only Senator Byrd who harbored hard feelings about a governing body he loved and in which he worked for decades. Americans also lost faith and trust in Congress. This is evident in polling numbers. Overall, the credibility of Congress in the eyes of the public has been in steady decline.

According to one Gallup poll, congressional approval ratings went from 84 percent in April 2002, when the Iraq war was being debated, to just 18 percent in 2007, after the war had persisted for four long years. In December 2010, Gallup announced the worst performance of Congress "in more than 30 years of tracking Congressional performance."[76] The report stated, "The 83 percent disapproval rating is the worst Gallup has measured. Americans' assessment of Congress hit a new low, with 13 percent of people saying they approve the way Congress is handling its job." A Rasmussen poll indicated only eleven percent of all voters polled think Congress has done an excellent or good job. In April 2010, 57 percent of those Americans polled think Congress has done a poor job. This is seven points down from March (the same year) and fourteen points down from February (the same year) at 71 percent, which was the highest negative rating in forty months.[77]

The news media must be allowed by their parent corporations to follow the tenets of responsible journalism, which are to report the news with fairness, balance, truth, accuracy, and passion, and to avoid bias. They must, as the Reverend Jesse Jackson once said, shine a much-needed light in dark places. News stories of particular magnitude must be sufficiently financed. When these conditions operate in concert, the news media serve the public in immeasurable ways. Sometimes, strong, highly principled, and independent publishers and editors also often make a difference.

It is true that historically the news media have not always had a stellar reputation. They often have been partisan, untruthful, sensationalist, and irresponsible. There have been many instances in American history when the media have overlooked some glaring mistakes by presidents and their administrations, essentially giving them free passes either by not being as critical in their reporting or by underreporting a story. This was the case in the reporting about the internment of the Japanese during World War II. But this has not always been the case. There have been some myths that have grown and been accepted as fact simply by being repeated over the years.

One such myth is that the *New York Times* bowed to pressure by the Kennedy administration and "suppressed" its reporting about the impending Bay of Pigs invasion of Cuba to topple Fidel Castro. W. Joseph Campbell wrote, "The *Times* did not suppress its reports about the impending Bay of Pigs. It did not censor itself. In fact, the *Times'* reports about preparations for the invasion were fairly detailed, not to mention prominently displayed on the front page in the days before the Bay of Pigs invasion was launched."[78] In fact, President Kennedy told his press secretary Pierre Salinger days before the invasion, "I can't believe what I'm reading. Castro doesn't need agents over here. All he has to do is read our papers. It's all laid out for him."[79]

Another example is from the Spanish-American War. That conflict was not a "newspaper made war." William Randolph Hearst, the powerful publisher and father of yellow journalism, never vowed in a series of telegraph exchanges with artist Frederic Remington that he would "furnish the war" if Remington furnished the pictures. This anecdote has now become folkloric.

The power of yellow journalism has been overstated in some cases. Hearst repeatedly denied he made any such request to Remington, and there was never any evidence of any telegram supporting such a claim. Campbell wrote, "The notion that the Yellow Press brought about the Spanish-American war can be rejected. American newspapers, including the yellow press, quite simply did not beat the drums for war in the months before April 1898." Coverage of the rebellion by the Cubans was "intermittent" and "sporadic," and sometimes weeks would go by with no coverage of the story at all.[80]

Hearst did not advocate for war, nor was the news published in the Hearst paper picked up by other newspapers. Campbell wrote, "There is no evidence that the newspapers of Hearst and Pulitzer exerted much agenda setting influencing at all for other newspapers. Few newspapers were inclined to follow the lead of Hearst and Pulitzer. Nor is there evidence that the yellow press influenced the thinking or action of American policymakers." There is also no evidence in the diaries and personal correspondence between McKinley administration officials that they gave the press much credence during the conflict.[81]

President McKinley went to war reluctantly. During his inaugural address on March 4, 1897, he said, "We want no wars of conquest. We must avoid the temptation of territorial aggression. Wars should never be entertained upon until every agency of peace has failed; peace is preferred to war in almost every contingency." McKinley and Congress were pressured into war after the mysterious sinking of the U.S.S. *Maine* in February 1898 in Havana's harbor and as Americans increasingly sympathized with the plight of the Cuban revolutionaries fighting for their freedom from Spain.

In contrast, President Bush and his administration instigated the Iraq war. The media developed their stories around specific bits of information the administration provided. The venerable *New York Times* was the newspaper of record, the principal agenda-setter in the coverage of the Iraq war. In fact, the administration was leaking information directly to the *Times*. The newspaper carried "exclusive reports," which other news-papers, magazines, and television and cable news networks subsequently picked up. The administration pointed to the "reputable" *New York Times* as an "independent" source of information substantiating some of the claims made by the administration. In essence, the news media was sup-porting the administration's claims by exploiting the leads to which the administration explicitly directed them. This became an endless cycle. The media did not want to get the story wrong as defined by the adminis-tration or miss the story entirely. For the most part much of the media were nervous about departing from the herd and a prescribed story line.

There is no question the press has struggled with its reputation as evidenced in some interesting polling data. The data accounts for the public's regard for the news media and also the politicians' regard for it. According to the Pew Research Center for the People & the Press, at the time of the Iraq war in 2003, the proportion of Republicans saying the news media is "too critical of America" was 47 percent and in 2005 that number jumped to 65 percent. The data revealed, "The partisan gap on this issue nearly tripled from 15 points to 43 points."[82] Overall the news media have been held increasingly in low esteem from 1985 to 2009 on questions of getting the facts straight to being inaccurate and lack of professionalism. There was an exception in 2001 "when coverage of 9/11 and terrorism, boosted the press's positive ratings," but the numbers steadily began declining again in 2003, 2005, and 2009 when "63 percent of the people polled said news reports were often inaccurate."[83]

The news media have had a sporadic record over the years and in the case of Iraq did not perform as responsibly as it could and should have. They could have brought more historical perspective to its reporting as the story of the war with Iraq was evolving in the months following 9/11. The coverage tended to be simplistic and focused more on the day-to-day news items, much of it fed to reporters by the White House. The report-ing was timid in challenging the president and his administration about the claims it was making immediately following 9/11 and in the months to follow. Admittedly, the news media were also overwhelmed and in-timidated by the sheer magnitude and implications of the 9/11 story and beyond as the "War on Terror" evolved.

Moreover, the media have been under increasing pressure to perform like a business rather than merely providing a public service. In fact, newspapers and television networks have begun running ads on their websites. The *New York Times* and *Wall Street Journal* now charge fees to read online content and more are considering doing the same, including Fox News chief Rupert Murdoch. Resources are severely limited, which has constrained reporters, especially those who work in foreign bureaus. The news cannot be covered from a desk in Washington or New York or outsourced to another agency from which content is often suspect. Cred-ible news with reliable sources can more likely be found where the stories are evolving on the ground and in the field. Those sources and stories must be cultivated over time.

Those who manage news organizations must decide what their priorities will be. The news media will not serve the public if they become a mouthpiece for those in power in order to remain close to power. They will not serve the public by being more agreeable than confrontational and more features-oriented than hard news-oriented. In a model where the news media is a high-stakes, revenue-trawling business, where news divisions are merged with entertainment divisions, and where just a few corporations have control over the content, the public good is often traded. Higher ratings, bigger audience shares, increased subscriptions, and traffic on websites often all take precedence over the quality of the reporting.

Some at the major broadcast and cable networks and at major newspapers and other higher-profile publications command exorbitant salaries. Today they are expected to do more for those salaries, such as file stories for radio and the web and to be more flexible in helping to promote programming, both news related and softer, entertainment programming. Many have become celebrities, elites themselves, who socialize with those they cover, compromising integrity, and perhaps adding to any perceived appearance of favoritism. Washington, particularly, often has become an incestuous collection of individuals in power, who seem to want to advance each other's agendas.

At the same time newsrooms across the country employ rank-and-file news gatherers, many of whom are paid little and have limited experience. For young people coming to the news business, this has always been true to an extent. What is different today is that they are not working their way up to larger organizations from smaller broadcast or cable stations and from small newspapers in tiny towns. They often come immediately to larger organizations and are placed in challenging, responsible positions before they are seasoned and ready. They are reticent to challenge editors and producers, and are being employed in increasing numbers to defray costs. They lack a depth of knowledge about the stories they write, where providing context to those stories is essential. They also often lack basic foundational knowledge from the disciplines of history, economics, politics, government, and finance, to name a few areas that would inform storytelling. This has also hurt journalism.

Overall, today's journalists are insufficiently prepared to look at national and world events in historical context so that the news is smart and enriched by the past. Also, their persistent dependence on a computer and the Internet for research and information cannot replace experience in the field, meeting people face to face, interviewing primary sources, traveling to where the news is unfolding, seeing with their own eyes, and evaluating, firsthand, an event by being there. The usage and dependence on young people, some fresh out of college, is a financial decision, but a shortsighted one.

In the larger picture, newspaper and magazine publishers and broadcast and cable owners and operators should have encouraged and expected independence of thought and reporting from those who were in the trenches working and investigating the Iraq war story. They should have invested in better-experienced reporters, keeping them on the story, in the field for as long as necessary. This was not the case. Also, there was hesitancy and, in some cases, outright refusal to question and challenge information when they understood it was suspect. This was because it would have an impact on business and would also affect the relationship between media owners and, in this particular case, those in the Bush administration—those who cover the news versus those who make it. Reporters could have been denied access to events and the newsmakers themselves.

The news media and those who govern should not be regarded as partners, nor are they necessarily adversaries. There must be a mutual understanding that while their ultimate goal might be the same—serving the public and advancing the public good—their roles to that end are quite different.

What has happened to the ideal notion of a news media whose only mission is to serve the public? Has that been lost in the motivation of profit and ad revenue? Can we expect that the media be beholden only to the people? Can the news media operate separately from the entertainment divisions of big media conglomerates? Corporations hope that the news media generate profits, but should they be expected to?

Many in journalism and journalism education have advocated more nonprofit models, publicly supported journalism, to avoid the challenges and pressure the press faced during the events preceding the Iraq war after 9/11. Some across the country are currently experimenting with "community-based" models of news reporting and distribution. It has had both its challenges and detractors. Whatever the results, there is no question that decisions about reporting the news to the public should not be as heavily guided by economic factors.

Finally, there was the fear factor and the American public. As a public, how can we avoid feeling afraid? It is unclear that any president can assuage fear in the people. In the case of 9/11 the feelings of fear and vulnerability affected us as they did when Pearl Harbor was bombed in 1941. Our enemies were real in 2001 as they were in 1941, but in 2001 Americans had little to no knowledge about who the enemy was.

President Bush issued some conflicting messages. Attempting to calm, he encouraged Americans to go about their business and to watch out for one another. Later stoking fear, he spoke of the "Axis of Evil" and the potential for "mushroom shaped clouds." Years have gone by without another attack, which perhaps has lulled Americans into complacency. In fact, there are forces, which continue to threaten and recently have come close to killing and destroying again on American soil.

On December 22, 2001, Richard Reid, a British citizen, attempted to detonate an explosive implanted in his shoe aboard American Airlines flight 63. Later known as the "Shoe Bomber," his efforts were thwarted. On December 25, 2009, Umar Farouk Abdulmutallab, a Nigerian, hid explosives in his underwear aboard Northwest flight 253. Later known as the "Underwear Bomber," his efforts were thwarted. And on May 1, 2010, in Time Squares, ordinary citizens reported to police a suspicious SUV parked in the bustling area, thwarting an attempt by Pakistani Faisal Shahzad to remotely detonate a crude bomb that was inside.

Fear may not be something a leader can do anything about. While the shock of 9/11 has worn away with the years, there is legitimate reason to be uncertain of our security. Many who work in think tanks and in intelligence circles have reminded us that a terrorist attack could come again and at any time—that it is not a question of if another attack will come in the United States, but a question of when another attack will come. Our enemies are actively conspiring against this country. Because of this, the American public has no other choice but to trust the honesty and integrity of their leaders and to trust the information they receive about events from a news media they can rely on for fair, balanced, and accurate coverage and news coverage independent of any other motivation than to serve the public interest.

A singular event on September 11, 2001, changed America. Its connection to the Iraq war was the problem, becoming a motivating factor in the decisions to follow by a president of the United States, the United States Congress, and the American news media. There is no question that people in those circles did not know for certain that another attack would not happen again while they led the country, while they deliberated about the country, while they covered the news for the American public. Fear did affect decisions when clearer heads should have been summoned and ultimately prevailed.

In sum, a confluence of factors came together to create the perfect storm, which paved the road toward the invasion of the ill-fated Iraq war of 2003. Those factors created a foreign policy window of opportunity for what would be the catastrophe to follow. Any one of those factors, operating optimally and as they were designed to do, could have helped prevent or slow such an event as it was unfolding. All involved were culpable, chief among those, the president of the United States and his administration, the Congress, and the news media, although admittedly the degree of culpability is determined by position and station. Most of the responsibility for the Iraq war remains with President Bush. But not all.

History has a way of repeating itself. Often we fail to learn from the past so that we can apply those experiences to future problems we will inevitably face. This was the case in the invasion of Iraq. We had the ability, with measured thought and action, to prevent the war by, in part, evaluating decisions that were made during other crises in history and heeding the lessons they provided. The president overreached, the Congress failed to adequately temper the executive branch, and the press did not do a very good job holding either branch to account.

The answers to our questions about why the Iraq war happened or how it happened will not be found looking outward, for something or someone else to blame. Collectively, our news media, our government, we the people, we were the masters of our fate. As Shakespeare's Julius Caesar said to Brutus and as we must acknowledge today, "The fault was not in our stars. It was in ourselves."[84]

NOTES

1. Official transcript, *60 Minutes*, May 12, 2011.

2. Official White House transcript, May 19, 2011.

3. Security Council Department of Public information press release, March 17, 2011.

4. Official White House transcript, March 28, 2011.

5. Official White House transcript, May 19, 2011.

6. Official transcript, *The Daily Show*, June 1, 2011.

7. Grossman, Lev. "Iran Protests: Twitter, the medium of the Movement." *Time*, June 17, 2009.

8. Glanz, James, and John Markoff. "U.S. Underwrites Internet Detour around Censors." *New York Times*, June 12, 2011.

9. Cooper, Helene, and Mark Mazzetti. "Prizing Status Quo, Mubarek Resists Pressure to Resign." *New York Times*, February 6, 2011.

10. Dowd, Maureen. "Bye, Bye Mubarek." *New York Times*, February 1, 2011.

11. Haass, Richard, speech before the Zocolo Public Square Series, May 19, 2009.

12. Rumsfeld, Donald. *Known and Unknown* (New York: Sentinel, 2011), 449.

13. Ibid.

14. Gore, Al, speech, "Iraq and the War on Terrorism," The Commonwealth Club, San Francisco, CA, September 23, 2002.

15. Pidd, Helen, and Martin Chulov. "Curveball Admissions Vindicate Suspicions of C.I.A.'s Former Europe Chief." *The Guardian*, February 15, 2011.

16. Ross, Carne. "Curveball and the Manufacture of a Lie." *The Guardian*, February 15, 2011.

17. Pilkington, Ed, Helen Pidd, and Martin Chulov. "Colin Powell Demands Answers over Curveball's WMD Lies." *The Guardian*, February 16, 2011.

18. Ibid.

19. Bush, George W. *Decision Points* (New York: Crown Publishers, 2010), 251.

20. Powell, Colin. *My American Journey* (New York: Ballantine, 1995, 2003), 309.

21. Rumsfeld, Donald. *Known and Unknown* (New York: Sentinel, 2011), 425.

22. Dowd, Maureen. "Simply the Worst." *New York Times*, February 12, 2011 and rumsfeld.com.

23. Diamond, John, Judy Keen, and the Associated Press. "Final Report: Iraq Had No WMDs." *USA Today*, October 7, 2004.

24. Bush, George W. *Decision Points* (New York: Crown Publishers, 2010), 270.

25. Quoted in Paul Pillar, "Intelligence, Policy and the War in Iraq." *Foreign Affairs* (March/April 2006): 17–18.

26. WMUR-TV Republican debate, December 2, 1999.

27. Nyhan, David. "A Bush Slip-Up at the End." *Boston Globe*, December 3, 1999.

28. Official PBS *NewsHour* transcript, February 16, 2000.

29. Official transcript, Commission on Presidential Debates, October 11, 2000.

30. Baker, Russ. *Family of Secrets* (New York: Bloomsbury Press, 2009), 421.

31. Ibid.

32. Ibid., 422.

33. Ibid.

34. Ibid., 423.

35. Unger, Craig. *The Fall of the House of Bush: The Untold Story of How a Band of True Believers Seized the Executive Branch, Started the Iraq War and Still Imperils America's Future* (New York: Scribner, 2007), 169.

36. Baker, Russ. *Family of Secrets* (New York: Bloomsbury Press, 2009), 423.

37. Official Transcript, CBS *60 Minutes*, January 11, 2004.

38. Bush, George W. *Decision Points* (New York: Crown Publishers, 2010), 228–29.

39. Ibid.

40. Official White House transcript, May 1, 2003.

41. Ibid.

42. BBC News, December 15, 2003.

43. Official White House Transcript, August 31, 2010.

44. Bush, George W. *Decision Points* (New York: Crown Publishers, 2010), 270.

45. Gearan, Anne. "Robert Gates: History Will Judge If Iraq War Was Worth It." *Huffington Post*, September 1, 2010.

46. Myers, Steven Lee, and Duraid Adnan. "Attack Shows Lasting Threat to U.S. in Iraq." *New York Times*, September 5, 2010.

47. Bush, George W. *Decision Points* (New York: Crown Publishers, 2010), 236.

48. Carpenter, Ted Galen, and Malou Innocent. "The Iraq War and Iranian Power." *Survival Global Politics and Strategy* 49, no. 4 (Winter 2007–2008): 67–82.

49. Witt, John-Paul. "Israel Threatened by Nuclear Iran." *The Observer*, February 9, 2007.

50. Bush, George W. *Decision Points* (New York: Crown Publishers, 2010), 247–48.

51. Boyle, Francis A. "International Crisis and Neutrality: U.S. Foreign Policy Toward the Iraq-Iran War." *Global Research*, February 1986.

52. Baker, Russ. *Family of Secrets* (New York: Bloomsbury Press, 2009), 429.

53. Ibid.

54. Ibid.

55. Bush, George W. *Decision Points* (New York: Crown Publishers, 2010), 262.

56. Ibid., 261.

57. Bush, George W. *Decision Points* (New York: Crown Publishers, 2010), 268.

58. Ibid.

59. Ibid., 262.

60. Tenet, George. *At the Center of the Storm, My Years at the CIA* (New York: HarperCollins Publishers, 2007), 480–81.

61. Bush, George W. *Decision Points* (New York: Crown Publishers, 2010), 174.

62. Ibid., pg. 181.

63. Dowd, Maureen. "Going Mad in Herds." *New York Times*, August 23, 2010.

64. Official transcript, Department of Defense, February 25, 2011.

65. Ibid.

66. Ibid.

67. CNN/Opinion Research Corp. Survey, May 1, 2008.

68. Ibid.

69. Siena Research Institute, America's Presidents: Greatest and Worst, 5th Presidential Expert Poll 1982–2010, July 1, 2010.

70. Official transcript, Kennedy speech to The Center for American Progress, Washington, DC, January 14, 2004.

71. Kennedy, Edward M. *True Compass* (New York: Twelve, Hachette Book Group, 2009), 496.

72. Ibid., 495–96.

73. Ibid., 494–95.

74. Byrd, Robert C. *Losing America* (New York: W. W. Norton & Company, Inc., 2005), 167.

75. Ibid., 168.

76. Jones, Jeffrey M. "Congress' Job Approval Rating the Worst in Gallup History." Gallup, December 15, 2010.

77. Rasmussen Reports, "Congressional Performance, Voters Give This Congress a Failing Grade," October 27, 2010.

78. Campbell, W. Joseph. "Debunking the Bay of Pigs Suppression Myth." University of California Press Blog, June 9, 2010.

79. Ibid.

80. From the official website of Professor W. Joseph Campbell and from his book, *Yellow Journalism: Punctuating the Myths, Defining the Legacies* (Westport, CT: Praeger Publishers, 2003), 119–21.

81. Ibid.

82. The Pew Research Center for the People & the Press, "Press Accuracy Rating Hits Two Decade Low," September 13, 2009.

83. Ibid.

84. Shakespeare, William. "The Tragedy of Julius Caesar," circa 1599.

Epilogue

So, where are we now? Iraq? The executive and legislative branches of government? The news media? And what of those five people most responsible for launching the Iraq war?

Iraq: The Iraq war of 2003 hurt us all and hurt the world. To say that there have been serious repercussions, which have stubbornly persisted since the war began and officially ended in 2011, is an understatement. Take into account the following: The heartbreak in loss of life on both sides. The continuance of roadside and random suicide bombs. Since the war officially ended, hardship remains for Iraqis who only want a peaceful, stable life and a sense of well-being. A government is in place, but remains precarious. There have been billions of dollars spent and wasted. And there is anger toward Americans, and the country's reputation is tainted.

Disorder persists in the already disorderly Middle East, even after the demise of Osama bin Laden. No problem anywhere in the region on its way to really being solved with any permanence. Save for Afghanistan, the greater Middle East region was almost destined to ignite all on its own, without the heavy hand of American military intervention. And it did. The "Arab Spring" continues and has been most pronounced in Egypt and in Syria. Meanwhile, the Palestinians still hope for their own country and continue to spar with Israel. All political actors have a watchful and suspicious eye toward Iran as a wild card.

On one hand, the people of Tunisia, Egypt, Libya, Syria, in the West Bank and Gaza, for the most part have the will to move toward, to fight and die for a western-style democracy. Then there are those from the perch of entrenched power, who want to stop them. But the revolution is happening just the same. And it is happening from within each country, by and because of the people who live there. *That* is a legitimate revolution, unlike the one imposed upon Iraq from the outside by the United States.

The executive and legislative branches of government and the news media: What trust do the American people have in these institutions since the Iraq war? Beginning with the executive branch, the White House, there is a reasonable chance, even with more distance between George W. Bush and the war he instigated, that he would continue to be ranked by historians among the worst presidents in United States history. That has been where he rates since he left office.

Barack Obama brought a sense of optimism and hope back to the White House when he was first elected president in 2008. In 2012, he was re-elected. There has been some discomfort about his foreign policy in the Middle East because of his use of drones to eliminate al Qaeda in various parts of the region, threats to militarily intervene in Syria, and his relative inaction to lead and broker a peace agreement between the Palestinians and Israel. No matter. After the president gave the order to storm a compound in Pakistan, killing Osama bin Laden in May 2011, his approval rating went up to above 50 percent. It waxed and waned a bit during the campaign for the 2012 election, but rose again to the highest point in his tenure yet, following his re-election, according to an Associated Press-GfK poll taken in December 2012.

Overall, according to a Gallup poll in September 2012, trust in the executive branch fell to just above 40 percent during the last years of the Bush administration, but steadily rose after Obama took office in 2009. In December 2012 trust in the executive branch was at 56 percent.

The American people have struggled the most with Congress on trust. That institution remains the least trustworthy of the three branches of our government. In the last ten years, according to the same September 2012 Gallup poll, Congress plummeted from 67 percent in 2002 to 34 percent this year, but that was up three points from its lowest level in 2011.

The news media fared no better. In fact, Gallup, in the same September 2012 round of polling, recorded the highest level of distrust by Americans in the news media ever. Sixty percent of those polled said "they have little or no trust in the mass media to report the news fully, accurately, and fairly. Distrust is up from the past few years, when Americans were already more negative about the media than they had been in years prior to 2004." This, of course, was during the time when the United States had launched the Iraq war.

And the five people responsible for the Iraq war: George W. Bush, Richard Cheney, Donald Rumsfeld, Colin Powell, and Condoleezza Rice. All have written books since leaving public office. All have commanded hundreds of thousands of dollars in speaking fees. All, except President Bush, have appeared from time to time on television and radio as guests and as political pundits.

Secretary Rice is back at Stanford University in Palo Alto, California, but this time as a professor in the graduate school of business. (She was provost at Stanford.) She continues to play the piano and became the first of two female golfers to be admitted to the Augusta (Georgia) National Golf Club. She spoke at the 2012 Republican National Convention in Tampa, Florida.

Vice President Cheney underwent a heart transplant early in 2012 after years of heart disease, including five heart attacks. In one of his first interviews with ABC News after the transplant, he said he hadn't felt that good in years and he is not bothered that he may be remembered as the most unpopular vice president in American history. He remains comfortable and confident about the decisions made regarding Iraq and looks back with no regret.

President Bush has kept a low profile since leaving office. He has not criticized President Obama. He stayed far away from politics and the election of 2012 and did not endorse anyone for president. In December 2012 he emerged to speak to the Federal Reserve Bank of Dallas and addressed the issue of immigration reform. He said he "regretted" not pushing harder for that during his tenure. The George W. Bush Presidential Library and Museum on the campus of Southern Methodist University in Dallas is scheduled to open sometime in 2013.

Many in politics, historians, academics, peace activists, and spiritual leaders have called for criminal charges against those who committed us to war in Iraq—crimes against humanity at the Hague. There is no sign, near or far, of any such action. With the march of time outlooks and attitudes may change. But for now, history will judge. President George W. Bush agreed. For his 2004 book *Plan of Attack, Washington Post* reporter, Bob Woodward, asked the president about history and how "his war" would be judged.

How did he reply? "History. We don't know. We'll all be dead."

Bibliography

BOOKS

Auletta, Ken. *Fortress Bush*. New York: Penguin, Inc., 2003.

Bagdikian, Ben. *The New Media Monopoly*. Boston: Beacon Press, 2004.

Baker, Ross K. *House and Senate*. New York: W. W. Norton & Company, Ltd., 2001.

Baker, Russ. *Family of Secrets*. New York: Bloomsbury Press, 2009.

Bamford, James. *A Pretext for War*. New York: Doubleday, 2004.

Bennett, Lance W. *News: The Politics of Illusion*. New York: Longman, 1988.

Boehlert, Eric. *Lapdogs: How the Press Rolled Over for Bush*. New York: Free Press, 2006.

Braestrup, Peter. *The Big Story: How the American Press Covered and Interpreted the Crisis of Tet in Vietnam and Washington*. New Haven: Yale University Press, 1983.

Bush, George W. *Decision Points*. New York: Crown Publishers, 2010.

Byrd, Robert C. *Losing America: Confronting a Reckless and Arrogant Presidency*. New York: W. W. Norton & Company, 2005.

Campbell, Joseph W. *Yellow Journalism: Punctuating the Myths, Defining the Legacies*. Westport, CT: Praeger Publishers, 2003.

Chomsky, Noam. *Understanding Power*. New York: W. W. Norton & Company, Inc., 2002.

Clarke, Richard A. *Against All Enemies*. New York: Free Press, 2004.

Cohen, Bernard Cecil. *The Press and Foreign Policy*. Princeton: Princeton University Press, 1963.

Cronkite, Walter. *A Reporter's Life*. New York: Alfred A. Knopf, 1996.

Dadge, David. *The War in Iraq and Why the Media Failed Us*. Westport, CT: Praeger, 2006.

Eisner, Peter, and Knut Royce. *The Italian Letter*. New York: Rodale, 2007.

Emery, Michael, Edwin Emery, and Nancy L. Roberts. *The Press and America*. Boston: Allyn and Bacon, 2000.

Fellow, Anthony R. *American Media History*. Belmont, CA: Wadsworth Group, 2005.

Fenton, Tom. *Junk News: The Failure of the News Media in the 21st Century*. Golden, CO: Fulcrum Publishing, 2009.

Final Report of the National Commission on Terrorist Attacks upon the United States. *The 9/11 Commission Report*. New York: W. W. Norton & Company, 2004.

Gore, Al. *The Assault on Reason*. New York: Penguin Group, 2007.

Graubard, Stephen. *Command of Office*. New York: Basic Books, 2004.

Greenstein, Fred I. *The Presidential Difference*. Princeton: Princeton University Press, 2001.

Hallin, Daniel C. *The "Uncensored War": The Media and Vietnam*. New York: Oxford University Press, 1986.

Hamilton, Lee. *Strengthening Congress*. Bloomington: Indiana University Press, 2009.

Hersh, Seymour M. *Chain of Command*. New York: HarperCollins Publishers, 2004.

Isikoff, Michael, and David Corn. *Hubris*. New York: Three Rivers Press, 2006.

Ivie, Robert L. "Cold War Motives and the Rhetorical Metaphor: A Framework of Criticism," in *Cold War Rhetoric: Strategy, Metaphor and Ideology*, by Martin J. Medhurst, Robert L. Ivie, Philip Wander, and Robert L. Scott. New York: Greenwood Press, 1990.

Jefferson, Thomas. *The Writings of Thomas Jefferson.* Washington, DC: Thomas Jefferson Memorial Association, 1903.

Jenkins, Henry. *Convergence Culture.* New York: New York University Press, 2006.

Kingdon, John. *Agendas, Alternatives, and Public Policies.* New York: HarperCollins, 1995.

Kuypers, Jim A. *Bush's War.* Lanham, MD: Rowman & Littlefield Publishers, Inc., 2006.

Lippmann, Walter. *Public Opinion.* New York: Macmillan, 1949.

Mann, Thomas E., and Norman J. Ornstein. *The Broken Branch.* New York: Oxford University Press, Inc., 2006.

McChesney, Robert W. *Rich Media, Poor Democracy: Communication in Dubious Times.* New York: New Press, 2003.

McClellan, Scott. *What Happened.* New York: Public Affairs, 2008.

O'Neill, Paul. *The Price of Loyalty: George W. Bush, The White House and the Education of Paul O'Neill.* Waterville, ME: Thorndike Press, 2004.

Pitt, William Rivers, with Scott Ritter. *War on Iraq: What Team Bush Doesn't Want You to Know.* New York: Context Books, 2002.

Plato. *The Allegory of the Cave, Book VII, The Republic, 360 BC* (Taken from the Benjamin Jowett translation). United Kingdom: Vintage Books, 1991.

Powell, Colin. *My American Journey.* New York: Ballantine, 1995, 2003.

Reeves, Richard. *What the People Know: Freedom and the Press.* Cambridge, MA: Harvard University Press, 1998.

Rich, Frank. *The Greatest Story Ever Sold.* New York: The Penguin Press, 2006.

Ricks, Thomas E. *Fiasco.* New York: The Penguin Press, 2006.

Risen, James. *State of War.* New York: Free Press, 2006.

Rumsfeld, Donald. *Known and Unknown.* New York: Sentinel, 2011.

Russell, Bertrand. *Unpopular Essays.* New York: Routledge, 2009.

Schattschneider, E. E. *The Semi-Sovereign People: A Realist's View of Democracy in America.* New York: Wadsworth, Thompson Learning, 1975.

Schlesinger, Arthur M. *War and the American Presidency.* New York: W. W. Norton & Company, 2004.

Shakespeare, William. *The Complete Works of William Shakespeare.* United Kingdom: Wordsworth Editions Limited, 1996.

Suskind, Ron. *The One Percent Doctrine.* New York: Simon & Schuster, 2006.

Tenet, George. *At the Center of the Storm, My Years at the CIA.* New York: HarperCollins Publishers, 2007.

Unger, Craig. *The Fall of the House of Bush: The Untold Story of How a Band of True Believers Seized the Executive Branch, Started the Iraq War and Still Imperils America's Future.* New York: Scribner, 2007.

Wilson, James. *The Founders Constitution.* Chicago: The University of Chicago Press, 1987.

Woodward, Bob. *Bush at War.* New York: Simon & Schuster, 2002.

———. *Plan of Attack.* New York: Simon & Schuster, 2004.

———. *State of Denial.* New York: Simon & Schuster, 2006.

JOURNALS

Carpenter, Ted Galen, and Malou Innocent. "The Iraq War and Iranian Power." *Survival Global Politics and Strategy* 49, no. 4 (Winter 2007–2008): 67–82.

Chomsky, Noam. "Propaganda System: Orwell's and Ours." *Propaganda Review*, no. 1 (1987–1988): 14-18.

Dinh, Viet D. "America after 9/11: Freedom Preserved or Freedom Lost: Hearing before the S. Comm. on the Judiciary, 108th Cong., November 18, 2003." *Georgetown Law, The Scholarly Commons,* CIS-No.: 2004-S521-47, http://scholarship.law.georgetown.edu/cgi/viewcontent.cgi?article=1055&context=cong.

Fisher, Louis. "Deciding on War against Iraq: Institutional Failures." *Political Science Quarterly* 118 (2003): 389–90.

Fluker, Krys. "Columnists Fired for Criticism." *Masthead* 53, no. 4 (Winter 2001).

Getler, Michael. "The Pentagon and the Press Again." Organization of News Ombudsmen, September 23, 2001, http://newsombudsmen.org/columns/the-pentagon-and-the-press-again.

Jacobson, Gary C. "The Bush Presidency and the American Electorate." *Presidential Studies Quarterly* 33, no. 4 (2003): 701–7.

Ornstein, Norman J., and Thomas E. Mann. "When Congress Checks Out." *Foreign Affairs* (November/December 2006): 2.

Stead, W. T. "Thomas Carlyle: The Hero as Man of Letters. Johnson, Rousseau, Burns, Lecture V, May 19, 1840." *The Contemporary Review* 50 (November 1886): 663–79.

MAGAZINES

Alterman, Eric. "Bush Lies, Media Swallows." *The Nation*, November 2002, http://www.thenation.com/article/bush-lies-media-swallows.

Blumenthal, Sydney. "Journalism and Its Discontents." *Salon*, October 25, 2007, http://www.salon.com/2007/10/25/walter_lippmann/.

Boehlert, Eric. "Lapdogs." *Salon*, May 6, 2006, http://www.salon.com/2006/05/04/lapdogs/.

Dizard, John. "How Ahmed Chalabi Conned the Neocons." *Salon*, May 4, 2004, http://www.salon.com/2004/05/04/chalabi_4/.

Dunkin, Andrea. "Journalism after 9/11." *The Newark Metro*, September 2006, http://www.newarkmetro.rutgers.edu/essays/display.php?id=211.

Grieve, Tim. "Climate of Intimidation." *Salon*, March 24, 2003, http://sci.rutgers.edu/forum/archive/index.php/t-32027.html.

Grossman, Lev. "Iran Protests: Twitter, the Medium of the Movement." *Time*, June 17, 2009, http://www.time.com/time/world/article/0,8599,1905125,00.html.

Hersh, Seymour M. "Who Lied to Whom?" *The New Yorker*, March 31, 2003, http://www.newyorker.com/archive/2003/03/31/030331fa_fact1.

Jacoby, Mary. "The Cowardly Broadcasting System." *Salon*, September 29, 2004, http://www.unz.org/Pub/Salon-2004sep-00320.

Jurkowitz, Mark. "The Big Chill." *Boston Globe* (Sunday Magazine), January 27, 2002, pg. 10.

Kinsley, Michael. "Filter Tips." *Slate*, October 16, 2003, http://www.slate.com/articles/news_and_politics/readme/2003/10/filter_tips.html.

Klein, Edward. "We're Not Destroying Rights, We're Protecting." *Parade Magazine*, May 19, 2002, pg. 5.

Lindsay, Daryl. "My Only Regret." *Salon*, April 28, 2000, http://www.unz.org/Pub/Salon-2000apr-00449.

Mahler, Jonathan. "After the Imperial Presidency." *New York Times Magazine*, November 9, 2008, pgs. 44–47.

Moore, James C. "Not Fit to Print." *Salon*, May 27, 2004, http://www.salon.com/2004/05/27/times_10/.

Murphy, Cullen, and Todd S. Purdum. "Uncovering the Darkest Secrets of the Bush White House (An Oral History)." *Vanity Fair*, February 2009, pg. 100.

Ricchiardi, Sherry. "Second Time Around." *American Journalism Review*, February/March 2008, http://www.ajr.org/Article.asp?id=4459.

Shafer, Jack. "Dealing with Defective Defectors." *Slate*, April 13, 2004, http://www.slate.com/articles/news_and_politics/press_box/2004/04/dealing_with_defec-tive_defectors.html.

———. "The Master of Debunk." *Slate Magazine*, May 21, 2010, http://www.slate.com/articles/news_and_politics/press_box/2010/05/the_master_of_debunk.html

———. "The *Times* Scoop That Melted." *Slate*, July 25 2003, http://www.slate.com/articles/news_and_politics/press_box/2003/07/the_times_scoops_that_melted.html.

Stewart, Thomas A. "The Cunning Plot of Leadership." *Fortune*, September 1998. http://money.cnn.com/magazines/fortune/fortune_archive/1998/09/07/247869/index.htm.

Tapper, Jake. "White House Whitewashers." *Salon*, September 27, 2001, http://www.salon.com/2001/09/27/spin_5/.

Taylor, Stuart, Jr., and Evan Thomas. "Obama's Cheney Dilemma." *Newsweek*, January 19, 2009, pg. 26.

NEWSPAPERS

Baird, Brian. "We Need to Read the Bills." *Washington Post*, November 27, 2004, A31.

Cooper, Helene, and Mark Mazzetti. "Prizing Status Quo, Mubarek Resists Pressure to Resign." *New York Times*, February 6, 2011, http://www.nytimes.com/2011/02/07/world/middleeast/07mubarak.html?pagewanted=all.

Cotts, Cynthia. "Smoke Signals." *Village Voice*, November 19, 2002, http://www.villagevoice.com/2002-11-19/news/smoke-signals/.

Dewar, Helen, and Juliet Eilperin. "Iraq Resolution Passes Test, Gains Support." *Washington Post*, October 10, 2002, A16.

Diamond, John, Judy Keen, and the Associated Press, "Final Report: Iraq Had No WMDs." *USA Today*, October 7, 2004, http://usatoday30.usatoday.com/news/world/iraq/2004-10-06-wmd_x.htm.

Dowd, Maureen. "Bye, Bye Mubarek." *New York Times*, February 1, 2011, http://www.nytimes.com/2011/02/02/opinion/02dowd.html.

———. "Going Mad in Herds." *New York Times*, August 23, 2010, http://www.nytimes.com/2010/08/22/opinion/22dowd.html.

———. "Liberties: We Love the Liberties They Hate." *New York Times*, September 30, 2001, http://www.nytimes.com/2001/09/30/opinion/liberties-we-love-the-liberties-they-hate.html.

———. "Simply the Worst." *New York Times*, February 12, 2011, http://www.nytimes.com/2011/02/13/opinion/13dowd.html.

———. "Woman of Mass Destruction." *New York Times*, October 22, 2005, http://archive.truthout.org/article/maureen-dowd-woman-mass-destruction.

Drehle, David Von, and R. Jeffrey Smith. "US Strikes Iraq for Plot to Kill Bush." *Washington Post*, June 27, 1993, A01.

Eisner, Peter. "How Bogus Letter Became a Case for War." *The Washington Post*, April 3, 2007, http://www.washingtonpost.com/wp-dyn/content/article/2007/04/02/AR2007040201777.html.

Fournier, Ron. "White House Lawyers Give Bush OK on Iraq." *Washington Times*, August 26, 2002.

Gearan, Anne. "Robert Gates: History Will Judge If Iraq War Was Worth It." *Huffington Post*, September 1, 2010, http://www.huffingtonpost.com/2010/09/01/robert-gates-history-will_n_701863.html.

Glanz, James, and John Markoff. "U.S. Underwrites Internet Detour around Censors." *New York Times*, June 12, 2011, http://www.nytimes.com/2011/06/12/world/12internet.html?pagewanted=all&_r=0.

Goldenberg, Suzanne, Nick Paton Walsh, and Ewan MacAskill. "Iraq Weapons Inspectors Find Empty Chemical Warheads." *The Guardian*, January 17, 2003, http://www.guardian.co.uk/world/2003/jan/17/iraq.ewenmacaskill.

Greenhouse, Linda. "Ideas & Trends: Executive Decisions; A Penchant for Secrecy." *New York Times (Week in Review)*, May 5, 2002, 17.

Hanley, Charles J. "Piecing Together the Story of the Weapons That Weren't." *USA Today*, September 2, 2005, http://usatoday30.usatoday.com/news/world/iraq/2005-09-02-WMD-indepth_x.htm.

Hentoff, Nat. "Terrorizing the Bill of Rights." *Village Voice*, November 9, 2001, http://www.villagevoice.com/2001-11-13/news/terrorizing-the-bill-of-rights/.

Huffington, Arianna. "Chris Matthews and the Power of Repetition." *Huffington Post*, November 2, 2005, http://www.huffingtonpost.com/arianna-huffington/chris-matthews-and-the-po_b_10039.html.

Hulse, Carl, and Sheryl Gay Stolberg. "State of the Union: Opposition Response; Democrats Say the Nation Heads in 'Wrong Direction.'" *New York Times*, January 29, 2003, http://www.nytimes.com/2003/01/29/us/state-union-opposition-response-democrats-say-nation-heads-wrong-direction.html.

Jacobs, Andrew. "My Weekend at Embedded Boot Camp." *New York Times*, March 2, 2003, http://www.nytimes.com/2003/03/02/magazine/02PROCESS.html.

Johnson, Peter. "Bush Has Media Walking a Fine Line." *USA Today*, March 10, 2003, http://usatoday30.usatoday.com/life/television/news/2003-03-09-media-mix_x.htm.

Karl, Jonathan. "Kennedy to Seek New Measure on War with Iraq." *CNN*, January 28, 2003, http://www.cnn.com/2003/ALLPOLITICS/01/28/sprj.irq.war.approval/index.html.

Keen, Judy. "Strain of Iraq Showing on Bush, Those Who Know Him Say." *USA Today*, April 2, 2003, http://usatoday30.usatoday.com/news/washington/2003-04-01-bush-cover_x.htm.

Kennedy, Edward M. "A Dishonest War." *Washington Post*, January 18, 2004, B04.

King, John. "White House: We've Made History." *CNN*, November 6, 2002, http://articles.cnn.com/2002-11-06/politics/elec02.bush_1_gop-candidates-white-house-house-spokesman-ari-fleischer?_s=PM:ALLPOLITICS.

Kornblut, Anne E., and Bryan Bender. "Cheney Link of Iraq, 9/11 Challenged." *Boston Globe*, September 16, 2003, http://www.boston.com/news/nation/articles/2003/09/16/cheney_link_of_iraq_911_challenged/.

Lancaster, John. "Anti-Terrorism Bill Hits Snag on the Hill: Dispute between Senate Democrats, White House Threatens Committee Approval." *Washington Post*, October 3, 2001.

Leiby, Richard. "Fighting Words." *Washington Post*, October 21, 2002, C01.

Lewis, Neil A. "A Nation Challenged: The Resolution; Measure Backing Bush's Use of Force Is as Broad as a Declaration of War, Experts Say." *New York Times*, September 18, 2001.

Myers, Steven Lee, and Duraid Adnan. "Attack Shows Lasting Threat to U.S. in Iraq." *New York Times*, September 5, 2010, http://www.nytimes.com/2010/09/06/world/middleeast/06iraq.html.

Nichols, Bill. "Barbs Fly as No. 2's Try to Inflict Dmage." *USA Today*, October 5, 2004, http://usatoday30.usatoday.com/news/politicselections/nation/president/2004-10-05-vp-debate-inside_x.htm.

Norton-Taylor, Richard. "Iraq War Inquiry: Britain Heard US Drumbeat for Invasion before 9/11." *The Guardian*, November 24, 2009, http://www.guardian.co.uk/uk/2009/nov/24/iraq-war-chilcot-inquiry.

Nyhan, David. "A Bush Slip-Up at the End." *Boston Globe*, December 3, 1999, A31.

O'Meara, Kelly Patricia. "Police State." *Insight*, November 9, 2001, http://www.freerepublic.com/focus/fr/569308/posts.

Pidd, Helen, and Martin Chulov. "Curveball Admissions Vindicate Suspicions of C.I.A.'s Former Europe Chief." *The Guardian*, February 15, 2011, http://www.guardian.co.uk/world/2011/feb/15/curveball-cia-europe-chief-vindicate.

Pilkington, Ed, Helen Pidd, and Martin Chulov. "Colin Powell Demands Answers over Curveball's WMD Lies." *The Guardian*, February 16, 2011, http://www.guardian.co.uk/world/2011/feb/16/colin-powell-cia-curveball.

Pincus, Walter, and Dana Milbank. "Al Qaeda-Hussein Link Is Dismissed." *Washington Post*, June 17, 2004, A1.

Rayner, Jay. "How Much Can We Believe in the News Campaign?" *The Observer*, October   14,   2001,   http://www.guardian.co.uk/media/2001/oct/14/ warinafghanistan2001.terrorism.

Rosenberg, Howard. "A New Kind of War of Words." *Los Angeles Times*, September 26, 2001, http://articles.latimes.com/2001/sep/26/entertainment/ca-49854.

Ross, Carne. "Curveball and the Manufacture of a Lie." *The Guardian*, February 15, 2011,   http://www.guardian.co.uk/commentisfree/2011/feb/15/curveball-wmd-carne-ross.

Steinhauser, Paul. "Poll: Bush's Popularity Hits a New Low." *CNN*, March 19, 2008, http://articles.cnn.com/2008-03-19/politics/bush.poll_1_iraq-war-approval-number-approval-rating?_s=PM:POLITICS.

Stelter, Brian."Was Press a War 'Enabler'?" *New York Times*, May 30, 2008, http://www. nytimes.com/2008/05/30/washington/30press.html?_r=0.

———. "When the President Travels, It's Cheaper for Reporters to Stay Home." *New York Times*, May 23, 2010, http://www.nytimes.com/2010/05/24/business/media/ 24press.html?pagewanted=all&_r=0.

Thomas, Evan, and Mark Hosenball. "The Rise and Fall of Chalabi: Bush's Mr. Wrong." *Newsweek*, May 31, 2004, http://www.playtime.rlbunn.com/Poli-tics_and_Policy/Content_Text/Dubya/HlpMeUnd/The%20Rise%20and%20Fall%20-of%20Chalabi_%20Bush's%20Mr.%20Wrong%20-%20Newsweek_%20Wo...pdf.

Wallis, David. "The Way We Live Now." *New York Times*, April 14, 2002, http://www.nytimes.com/2002/04/14/magazine/the-way-we-live-now-4-14-02-ques-tions-for-phil-donahue-from-left-field.html.

Weinstein, Henry, Daren Briscoe, and Mitchell Landsberg. "Civil Liberties Take Back Seat to Safety." *Los Angeles Times*, March 10, 2002, http://articles.latimes.com/2002/ mar/10/news/mn-32096/3.

Wilson, Joseph. "What I Didn't Find in Africa." *New York Times*, July 3, 2003,http:// www.nytimes.com/2003/07/06/opinion/what-i-didn-t-find-in-africa.html?pagewan-ted=all&src=pm.

Witt, John-Paul. "Israel Threatened by Nuclear Iran." *The Observer*, February 9, 2007,http://www.ndsmcobserver.com/2.2754/israel-threatened-by-nuclear-iran-in-bar-says-1.262775#.UNx0sonjkt0.

Yoo, John. "Behind the Torture Memos." *UC Berkeley News*, January 4, 2005, http:// www.berkeley.edu/news/media/releases/2005/01/05_johnyoo.shtml.

SPECIAL REFERENCES

Boyle, Francis. "U.S. Policy Toward the Iran-Iraq War," in *Neutrality: Changing Con-cepts and Practices*, from the Institute for Comparative Study of Public Policy at the University of New Orleans, 59.

Committee on Government Reform, Minority Staff, Special Investigations Division, United States House of Representatives. "Iraq on the Record, The Bush Administra-tion's Public Statements on Iraq," prepared for Rep. Henry Waxman, March 16, 2004.

Fenno, Richard F., Jr. *The United States Senate: A Bicameral Perspective*, American Enter-prise Institute for Public Policy Research, 1982, 5.

Gore, Al. Speech, Commonwealth Club of San Francisco, "Iraq and the War on Terror-ism,"   September   23,   2002,   http://www.gwu.edu/~action/2004/gore/ gore092302sp.html.

Katzman, Kenneth. *Foreign Terrorist Organizations*, CRS Report for Congress, February 5, 2004, 8.

Kaysen, Carl, Steven E. Miller, Martin B. Malin, William D. Nordhaus, and John D. Steinbruner. *War with Iraq: Costs, Consequences, and Alternatives*, American Academy of Arts and Sciences, Committee on International Security Studies, 2002, pg. 7.

Kerry, John F. "Tora Bora Revisited: How We Failed to Get bin Laden and Why It Matters Today," Report to the Senate Committee on Foreign Relations, November 30, 2009, pg. 1.
Letter to Edward Carrington (16 Jan 1787). *The Writings of Thomas Jefferson* (19 Vols. 1905), edited by Andrew A. Lipscomb and Albert Ellery Bergh, ed. 6:57.
Letter to John Tyler, 1804. University of Virginia, Thomas Jefferson on Politics and Government, ME 11:33.
Lewis, Patricia. "Why We Got It Wrong: Attempting to Unravel the Truth of Bioweapons in Iraq." *UNU Iraq*, Vol. 2, Chap. 8, 12.
Siena Research Institute. America's Presidents: Greatest and Worst, 5th Presidential Expert Poll 1982-2010, July 1, 2010, http://www.siena.edu/pages/179.asp?item=2566.
Westphal, Stephen D. "Counterterrorism: Policy of Preemptive Action" (USAWC Strategy Research Project), April 4, 2003.

WEBSITES

ABC News

This Week. "Interview with Karl Rove," March 21, 2010, http://abcnews.go.com/This-Week/week-transcript-karl-rove-david-plouffe/story?id=10137059&page=9#.UNR1-M5Pjkt0.
World News. "Interview with President Barack Obama, "January 25, 2010, http://abcnews.go.com/WN/Obama/abc-world-news-diane-sawyer-diane-sawyer-interviews/story?id=9659064#.UNR1yJPjkt0.

American Civil Liberties Union (ACLU)

BBC News. "Profile: Ahmed Chalabi," October 3, 2002, http://news.bbc.co.uk/2/hi/not_in_website/syndication/monitoring/media_reports/2291649.stm.
"Insatiable Appetite: The Government's Demand for New & Unnecessary Powers after September 11," April 2002, http://www.aclu.org/files/FilesPDFs/insatiable%20appetite%20final.pdf.
"Testimony of ACLU President Nadine Strossen on National Security and the Constitution," January 24, 2002, http://www.aclu.org/national-security/testimony-aclu-president-nadine-strossen-national-security-and-constitution.

CBS News

60 Minutes. "Paul O'Neill Speaks Out," January 11, 2004, http://www.cbsnews.com/video/watch/?id=592691n.
"Ahmed Chalabi, March 3, 2004, http://www.cbsnews.com/video/watch/?id=887978n.
Center for American Progress Action Fund. "America, Iraq and Presidential Leadership, Sen. Edward M. Kennedy," January 14, 2004, http://www.americanprogressaction.org/events/2004/01/14/16221/america-iraq-and-presidential-leadership-by-sen-edward-m-kennedy/.
Center for Public Integrity. "False Pretenses (by Charles Lewis and Michael Reading Smith)," January 23, 2008,http://www.publicintegrity.org/2008/01/23/5641/false-pretenses.
Constitution Society. "Abraham Lincoln's Address before the Young Men's Lyceum of Springfield, Illinois," January 27, 1838, http://constitution.org/lincoln/lyceum.htm.
Face the Nation. "Interview of Colin Powell by Bob Schieffer and Gloria Borger, February 3, 2002, Transcript through U.S. Department of State, http://2001-2009.state.gov/secretary/former/powell/remarks/2002/7781.htm.
"FBI: Niger Documents Fraudulent," November 5, 2005.

"It Was a Gutsy Call," May 12, 2011, http://www.cbsnews.com/video/watch/?id=7366134n.

CNN

"Bush, 'Leave Iraq in 48 Hours,'" March 17, 2003, http://www.cnn.com/2003/WORLD/meast/03/17/sprj.irq.bush.transcript/.
"Cheney Blasts Media on al Qaeda-Iraq link," June 18, 2004, http://www.cnn.com/2004/ALLPOLITICS/06/18/cheney.iraq.al.qaeda/.
Commission on Presidential Debates, "October 11, 2000 Debate Transcript," http://www.debates.org/index.php?page=october-11-2000-debate-transcript.
"Interview with Condoleezza Rice," May 19, 2002, http://edition.cnn.com/TRANSCRIPTS/0205/19/le.00.html.
"Interview with Condoleezza Rice," September 8, 2002, http://edition.cnn.com/TRANSCRIPTS/0209/08/le.00.html.
Late Edition, "Interview with Dick Cheney," March 24, 2002, http://edition.cnn.com/TRANSCRIPTS/0203/24/le.00.html.
"President Bush's Address to the United Nations," September 12, 2002, http://articles.cnn.com/2002-09-12/us/bush.transcript_1_generations-of-deceitful-dictators-commitment-peace-and-security?_s=PM:US.
"Rice: Bush Won't Back Down on Iraq," February 17, 2003, http://www.cnn.com/2003/US/02/16/sprj.irq.us.un/.
"Transcript of weapon inspector's U.N. presentation," February 14, 2003, http://www.cnn.com/2003/US/02/14/sprj.irq.un.transcript.elba/index.html.

Common Dreams

C-SPAN Video Library, "WMUR Republican Debate, December 2, 1999, http://www.c-spanvideo.org/program/153955-1.
"The Day Ashcroft Censored Freedom of Information," January 7, 2002, http://www.commondreams.org/views02/0108-04.htm.
Digital History, "Walter Cronkite's 'We Are Mired in a Stalmate' Broadcast," February 27, 1968, http://www.digitalhistory.uh.edu/learning_history/vietnam/cronkite.cfm.
"Media Fear Censorship as Bush Requests Caution," October 11, 2001, http://www.commondreams.org/headlines.shtml?/headlines01/1011-02.htm.
"The Sixty Minutes Story That Didn't Run," September 23, 2004, http://www.commondreams.org/headlines04/0923-02.htm.
"With Powers Like These, Can Repression Be Far Behind," October 30, 2001, http://www.commondreams.org/views01/1030-10.htm.

FOX News

Human Rights Interactive Network. "Ashcroft Presents Anti-Terrorism Plan to Congress," September 20, 2001, http://www.guidetoaction.org/magazine/ashcroft.html.
"Interview with Condoleezza Rice," October 15, 2006, http://www.foxnews.com/story/0,2933,220948,00.html.
"Iraq Bans Weapons of Mass Destruction" (Associated Press), February 14, 2003, http://www.foxnews.com/story/0,2933,78592,00.html.
Libel Defense Resource Center. "In the Trenches: War Reporting and the First Amendment," November 13, 2002, http://www.medialaw.org/images/stories/files/events/annualdinner/2002DinnerTranscript.pdf.
Media Education Foundation. "War Made Easy: How Presidents and Pundits Keep Spinning Us to Death," November 1, 2007, http://www.mediaed.org/assets/products/125/transcript_125.pdf.

Media Matters. "Some journalists caught expressing political views not as lucky as *Boston Globe*'s Hiawatha Bray," March 4, 2005, http://mediamatters.org/research/2005/03/04/some-journalists-caught-expressing-political-vi/132845.

Move On and the Center for American Progress. "Uncovered: The War on Iraq," 2004, http://acmecoalition.org/files/ACME_uncovered_transcript.pdf.

New York Times. "Pentagon Papers," June 30, 1971, http://topics.nytimes.com/top/reference/timestopics/subjects/p/pentagon_papers/index.html.

NBC

Hardball (with Chris Matthews). "CIA Leak Story," October 10, 2005.

"Interview with former Secretary of State, Colin Powell," June 10, 2007, http://www.msnbc.msn.com/id/19092206/ns/meet_the_press/t/meet-press-transcript-june/#.UNNXjJPjkt0.

"Interview with Vice President Dick Cheney," September 8, 2002, https://www.mtholyoke.edu/acad/intrel/bush/meet.htm.

"Interview with Vice President Dick Cheney," March 16, 2003, https://www.mtholyoke.edu/acad/intrel/bush/cheneymeetthepress.htm.

"Interview with Vice President Dick Cheney," September 10, 2006, http://www.msnbc.msn.com/id/14720480/ns/meet_the_press/t/transcript-sept/.

Meet the Press. "Tim Russert Interviews Secretary Colin Powell" (Transcript from State Department), February 17, 2002, http://2001-2009.state.gov/secretary/former/powell/remarks/2002/8071.htm.

On the Media. "Former *New York Times* Staffer Judith Miller: Transcript," November 11, 2005, http://www.onthemedia.org/2005/nov/11/former-new-york-times-staffer-judith-miller/transcript/.

"Tim Russert Interviews Andrew Card, Chris Dodd and Mitch McConnnell," http://cafe.daum.net/transcript/HbZT/819?docid=GdlAHbZT81920030217143901.

"Tim Russert Interviews Vice President Dick Cheney," May 19, 2002, http://kucinich.house.gov/uploadedfiles/arti1d.pdf.

PBS

The American Presidency Project, Dwight D. Eisenhower. "354-Address in Pittsburgh at a Dinner Sponsored by the Allegheny County Republican Executive Committee, November 4, 1960, http://www.presidency.ucsb.edu/ws/?pid=12011.

Bill Moyers Journal. "Buying the War," April 27, 2001, http://www.pbs.org/moyers/journal/btw/transcript1.html.

"Bill Summary & Status, 107th Congress (2001–2002) S.1510, October 11, 2001, http://thomas.loc.gov/cgi-bin/bdquery/z?d107:S1510.

"Bill Text, 107th (2001-2002) S.J.RES.46.PCS," October 3, 2002, http://thomas.loc.gov/cgi-bin/query/z?c107:S.J.RES.46.PCS.

"Chasing Saddam's Weapons," January 22, 2004, http://www.pbs.org/wgbh/pages/frontline/shows/wmd/etc/script.html.

The Daily Show with Jon Stewart. "Interview with Bill Moyers," June, 1, 2011, http://www.thedailyshow.com/watch/wed-june-1-2011/bill-moyers-pt--1.

Frontline, "Bush's War," March 24, 2008, and March 28, 2008, http://www.pbs.org/wgbh/pages/frontline/bushswar/etc/tapes.html.

"Interviews with Harry Reid, Richard Shelby and Duncan Hunter," http://www.pbs.org/newshour/bb/middle_east/july-dec02/iraqconsent_9-4.html.

The Library of Congress Congressional Record. "Congressional Record 107 Congress (2001–2002)," September 14, 2001, http://thomas.loc.gov/cgi-bin/query/D?r107:25:./temp/~r107l8BkeK.

"Military Campaigns in Afghanistan," October 9, 2001, http://www.pbs.org/newshour/bb/military/july-dec01/campaign_10-9.html.

The Museum of Broadcast Communication. "Vietnam on Television, http://www. museum.tv/eotvsection.php?entrycode=vietnamonte.

NewsHour. "Interview with George W. Bush," February 16, 2000, http://www.pbs.org/ newshour/bb/politics/jan-june00/bush_02-16.html.

Newsmakers. "Jim Lehrer Interviews Secretary of Defense Donald Rumsfeld" (Transcript from Free Republic.com), February 4, 2002, http://www.freerepublic.com/ focus/fr/622174/posts.

The Rumsfeld Papers. http://rumsfeld.com/.

Society of Professional Journalists. http://www.spj.org.

Washington Post. "Gore Assails Bush Iraq Policy," September 23, 2002, http://www. washingtonpost.com/wp-srv/politics/transcripts/gore_text092302.html.

The (W. Bush) White House

"Remarks by the President in Commencement Address Yale University, New Haven Connecticut," May 21, 2001; "Remarks by the President after Two Planes Crash into World Trade Center, Statement by the President in Address to the Nation," September 11, 2001; "President Bush Salutes Heroes in New York, President's Remarks at National Day of Prayer and Remembrance, (Message) to the Congress of the United States" September 14, 2001; "Presidential Address to the Nation," October 7, 2001; "President Unveils 'Most Wanted' Terrorists," October 10, 2001; "President Signs Anti-Terrorism Bill," October 26, 2001; "President Bush Speaks to the United Nations," November 10, 2001; "President: We're Fighting to Win—And We Will Win," December 7, 2001; "President Proclaims Human Rights Day & Bill of Rights Week," December 9, 2001; "President Blocks More Assets in Financial War on Terrorism," December 20, 2001; "President Delivers State of the Union Address," January 29, 2002; "President Delivers Graduation Speech at West Point," June 1, 2002; "President Delivers 'State of the Union,'" January 28, 2003; "Secretary of State Addresses UN Security Council," February 5, 2003; "President Bush Discusses Iraq in National Press Conference," March 6, 2003; "President Bush Addresses Nation," March 19, 2003; "Ask the White House," April 16, 2003; "President Announces Major Combat Operations in Iraq Have Ended," May 1, 2003; "Press Conference by the President," August 26, 2006, www.georgewbush-whitehouse.archives.gov.

The (Obama) White House

"Osama bin Laden Dead," May 2, 2011, http://www.whitehouse.gov/blog/2011/05/02/ osama-bin-laden-dead.

"Remarks by the President in Address to the Nation on the End of Combat Operations in Iraq," August 31, 2010, http://www.whitehouse.gov/the-press-office/2010/08/31/ remarks-president-address-nati- on-end-combat-operations-iraq.

"Remarks by the President in Address to the Nation on Libya, March 28, 2011, http:// www.whitehouse.gov/the-press-office/2011/03/28/remarks-president-address- nation-libya.

"Remarks by the President on the Middle East and North Africa," May 19, 2011, http:// www.whitehouse.gov/the-press-office/2011/05/19/remarks-president-middle-east- and-north-africa.

United Nations Security Council

"Oral Introduction of the 12th Quarterly Report of UNMOVIC, Executive Chairman, Dr. Hans Blix," March 7, 2003, http://www.un.org/Depts/unmovic/SC7asdelivered. htm.

"Statement by Hans Blix to the U.N. Security Council" (Transcript from Global Policy Forum) February 14, 2003, http://www.un.org/Depts/unmovic/blix14Febasdel.htm.
"Statement by Mohamad Elbaradei to the U.N. Security Council" (Transcript from the Global Policy Forum), February 14, 2003, http://www.globalpolicy.org/images/pdfs/0214elbaradei.pdf.
University of California Press Blog. W. Joseph Campbell, "Debunking the Bay of Pigs Suppression Myth," http://www.ucpress.edu/blog/8761/debunking-the-bay-of-pigs-suppression-myth/.

U.S. Department of Defense

"Secretary Rumsfeld Interview with NBC *Meet the Press*," December 2, 2001, http://www.defense.gov/transcripts/transcript.aspx?transcriptid=2585.
"Speech, United States Military Academy (West Point, NY) As Delivered by Secretary of Defense, Robert M. Gates," February 25, 2011, http://www.defense.gov/speeches/speech.aspx?speechid=1539.

U.S. Department of Justice

"Attorney General John Ashcroft, Testimony before the House Committee of the Judiciary," September 24, 2001, http://www.justice.gov/archive/ag/testimony/2001/agcrisisremarks9_24.htm.

U.S. Department of State

"Interview on NBC's *Meet the Press* with Tim Russert," December 16, 2001, http://2001-2009.state.gov/secretary/former/powell/remarks/2001/dec/6865.htm.
"Remarks by Secretary of State, Colin Powell, following the Meeting of the North Atlantic Council at the level of Foreign Ministers," December 6, 2001, http://www.nato.int/docu/speech/2001/s011206g.htm.
"Richard Haass Speech at the Zocolo Public Square Series," May 19, 2009, http://www.youtube.com/watch?v=mo4M5B0XxV4.
U.S. Supreme Court Justice Louis Brandeis before the U.S. Commission on Industrial Relations Created by the Act of August 23, 1912, http://archive.org/stream/industrialrelati01unitrich/industrialrelati01unitrich_djvu.txt.
You Tube, "Tony Benn Interviews Saddam Hussein," February 4, 2003, http://www.youtube.com/watch?v=fxHtQ1__qUc&playnext=1&list=PL9CBE4B1B9BC9366E&feature=results_main.

Index

About the Author

Mary Cardaras is an assistant professor at California State University, East Bay, in the Department of Communication where she teaches journalism. She has been teaching journalism since 1991 at various institutions, including the former Massachusetts Communications College, Northeastern University in Boston, LaSalle University in Philadelphia, Syracuse University's London campus, and the American International University in Richmond, UK. Dr. Cardaras freelanced for CNN Boston, and has worked for CNN Atlanta, CNN and World Television News in London, and for numerous other news departments across the country in five other major markets spanning more than twenty-five years in journalism. She also has conducted media training workshops for students and professionals in the Arab world and in Vietnam. Dr. Cardaras is the recipient of two regional Emmy awards for excellence in spot news producing and feature producing and has been nominated numerous times during her career in journalism. She serves on the board of the Global Press Institute in San Francisco and is a member of the Radio and Television News Directors Association (RTNDA), the Association for Education in Journalism and Communication (AEJMC), the Arab-U.S. Association for Communication Educators (AUCACE), and the National Lesbian and Gay Journalist Association (NLGJA). Dr. Cardaras continues to collaborate with the Center for International Media Education (CIME) at Georgia State University and is producing the first annual Global Press Institute World Summit scheduled for 2014. Dr. Cardaras is married, has two sons, and lives in Sonoma, California.